THE LONG ROAD
FROM TAIF TO JEDDAH
RESOLUTION OF A SAUDI-YEMENI
BOUNDARY DISPUTE

THE LONG ROAD FROM TAIF TO JEDDAH
RESOLUTION OF A SAUDI-YEMENI BOUNDARY DISPUTE

Askar H. Al-Enazy

THE EMIRATES CENTER FOR STRATEGIC
STUDIES AND RESEARCH

THE EMIRATES CENTER FOR STRATEGIC STUDIES AND RESEARCH

The Emirates Center for Strategic Studies and Research (ECSSR) is an independent research institution dedicated to the promotion of professional studies and educational excellence in the UAE, the Gulf and the Arab world. Since its establishment in Abu Dhabi in 1994, the ECSSR has served as a focal point for scholarship on political, economic and social matters. Indeed, the ECSSR is at the forefront of analysis and commentary on Arab affairs.

The Center seeks to provide a forum for the scholarly exchange of ideas by hosting conferences and symposia, organizing workshops, sponsoring a lecture series and publishing original and translated books and research papers. The ECSSR also has an active fellowship and grant program for the writing of scholarly books and for the translation into Arabic of work relevant to the Center's mission. Moreover, the ECSSR has a large library including rare and specialized holdings, and a state-of-the-art technology center, which has developed an award-winning website that is a unique and comprehensive source of information on the Gulf.

Through these and other activities, the ECSSR aspires to engage in mutually beneficial professional endeavors with comparable institutions worldwide, and to contribute to the general educational and academic development of the UAE.

The views expressed in this book do not necessarily reflect those of the ECSSR.

First published in 2005 by
The Emirates Center for Strategic Studies and Research
P.O. Box 4567, Abu Dhabi, United Arab Emirates

E-mail: pubdis@ecssr.ac.ae
pubdis@ecssr.com

Website: http://www.ecssr.ac.ae
http://www.ecssr.com

Copyright© The Emirates Center for Strategic Studies and Research, 2005
Distributed by The Emirates Center for Strategic Studies and Research

All rights reserved. Except for brief quotations in a review, this book, or any part thereof, may not be reproduced in any form without permission in writing from the publisher.

ISBN 9948-00-721-2 paperback edition

Contents

Abbreviations and Acronyms		ix
Glossary of Legal Terms		xi
Foreword		xv
Preface		xvii
	Introduction	1
1	The Legal History of the Boundary Dispute	7
2	The Development of the Saudi-Yemeni Boundary Dispute since 1990	25
3	The International Boundary Treaty of Jeddah on June 12, 2000	43
4	Yemeni Arguments regarding the Treaty of Taif	51
5	Saudi Arabian Arguments regarding the Taif Treaty	83
6	Yemeni Views on the Treaty of Jeddah	107
7	Controversial Provisions under Municipal and International Law	121
8	Conclusions and Prospects	141
	Appendices	153
	Notes	189
	Bibliography	255
	About the Author	267
	Index	269

ABBREVIATIONS AND ACRONYMS

AFP	Agence France-Presse
AJIL	American Journal of International Law
EJIL	European Journal of International Law
ICJ	International Court of Justice
ILM	International Legal Materials
MEJ	Middle East Journal
MENA	Middle East News Agency
NIC	National Information Center
PCA	Permanent Court of Arbitration
PCIJ	Permanent Court of International Justice
CPSID	Convention for the Pacific Settlement of International Disputes
SABA	Yemen News Agency
SPA	Saudi Press Agency
VCS	Vienna Convention on the Succession of States in Respect of Treaties (1978)
VCT	Vienna Convention on the Law of Treaties (1969)
SYCC	Saudi-Yemeni Coordination Council

Glossary of Legal Terms

Ab initio: "From the very beginning," for example, a treaty found to be legally void from the moment of signature.

Acquiescence: Tacit agreement or acceptance of something about which one has reservations.

Adjucation: A method of dispute resolution by peaceful means, in which the disputing parties agree to submit their dispute to the International Court of Justice and undertake to abide by its decision.

Animus possidendi: A state's intention to own territory, based on conceptual notions like ancient title, without being in *precario possessionis* or *corpus possessionis*.

Arbitration: A method of alternative dispute resolution by peaceful means, in which the disputing parties agree to submit their dispute to an *ad hoc* court of arbitrator(s) and undertake to abide by its decision.

Casus belli: An event or incident that allegedly justifies the declaration of war.

Corpus possessionis: A situation where a claimant party exercises actual *de facto* possession of disputed territory.

De facto boundary: The territorial boundary between states that exist in fact, but not in law, i.e., not created by treaty.

De jure boundary: A territorial boundary sanctioned by legal arrangement, i.e. a treaty, although not necessarily corresponding to the *de facto* boundary.

Glossary of Legal Terms

Dispositive treaty: A treaty establishing rights and obligations, mostly regarding territory-related issues like peace, boundaries and servitude.

Effectivités: The legal presumption of acquiring a sovereign title to territory by effective occupation or prescription.

Effet utile: The rule that a treaty should be interpreted contextually rather than textually, so as to give practical effect to its provisions, not a literal and absurd one.

Estoppel: Refers to the legal principle of holding a state to an action or a statement it has previously made, and precluding it from denying it even when it may not correspond with its real intention.

Fait accompli: An accomplished fact that is presumably irreversible, such as a state's occupation of a particular territory.

Intertemporal law: The principle that the validity of a state's action is determined by the accepted rule of international law at the time the action was taken and not by a legal principle adopted later, and that rights regarded as lawful in the past will continue to remain valid in future.

Jus ad bellum: The right of a state or states to initiate war.

Jus cogens doctrine: The peremptory norm of general international law that international law is universally accepted and recognized by the community of nations as a norm that admits no derogation and cannot be overridden by treaties, for example on issues like the prohibition of genocide, piracy and the slave trade.

Jus in bello: The law regulating the prosecution of war between belligerent states.

Lex posterior derogat priori: The legal notion that more recent law prevails over an inconsistent earlier law. For example, when existing customary sources of law and new treaties cannot be reconciled, the latter would prevail.

Modus vivendi: A provisional settlement of a dispute between contending parties.

Pacta sunt servanda: *A priori* principle that a treaty, convention or contract must be observed by the parties who become bound by its provisions.

Plebiscite: An expression of the people's will on a political issue by direct ballot.

Precario possessionis: Refers to a situation of precarious possession, for example, where a state maintains a precarious hold on disputed territory.

Priori: A principle presupposed by or reasoning deduced from self-evident theoretical propositions, such as *pacta sunt servanda* (i.e. an agreement must be honored by the parties to it).

Prescription: The legal process whereby a state acquires a title to territory because of uninterrupted occupation for a period of time.

Proprio motu: Refers to a contract expiring of its own accord, for example, the legal force of a treaty terminates *proprio motu* through the operation of its fixed duration clause.

Rebus sic stantibus: The doctrine that a treaty's obligations only remain valid as long as the fundamental conditions that existed at the time of its conclusion remain, and that any subsequent fundamental change of circumstances may constitute a legal ground for one party to seek renunciation or modification of the existing treaty.

Res nullius: The principle referring to territory that has no owner or has no owner anymore, and is thus considered to be legally available for acquisition by occupation.

Res judicata: A general principle that a matter conclusively judged on its merits by a competent judicial court or arbitral body cannot be legally raised again.

Status quo ante natura: The return to a previous state of affairs or situation existing between states, i.e., a renewal of a state of war.

Stricto sensu: In the strict sense of the word, i.e., the Kellogg-Briand Pact is restricted to war *stricto sensu*.

Treaty: Mostly refers to an international agreement in written form concluded between two or more states and governed by international law, embodied in one or more instruments, irrespective of its particular name, i.e., a treaty, convention, protocol, charter, agreed minutes, memorandum, declaration or exchange notes.

Uti possidetis principle: The customary legal principle that a state may retain possession of territory acquired by force, for example, during the Second World War, and/or that colonial territorial boundaries continue to remain valid in the post-colonial era. Such territories are not *res nullius* or *terra nullius* and cannot be subject to lawful occupation by other states.

Foreword

Competing territorial and boundary claims have historically led to grave disputes between rulers and countries. The boundary dispute between Saudi Arabia and Yemen has been no exception. The disputed area, covering both land and sea, extends to more than 1,200 square kilometers of strategically and economically important territory between the two largest states in the Arabian Peninsula, and the issue has periodically threatened regional stability during the past seventy years.

This book is perhaps the first systematic study of the legal dimensions of this dispute. It provides an overview of various aspects of the dispute and legal attempts to resolve them. Special attention is given to the Treaty of Taif in 1934, a crucial boundary treaty between Saudi Arabia and Yemen. The book analyzes related developments, such as the 1953 renewal agreement, the 1973 joint communiqué and the 1995 Memorandum of Understanding, which constituted Yemen's first express confirmation that the Taif Treaty was valid and binding on both parties. It also discusses the 1997 informal Como Agreement, which formed the legal framework of the boundary dispute and was later incorporated in the 2000 Treaty of Jeddah.

The Treaty of Jeddah established a maritime and land boundary. The Taif Treaty, which was incorporated into the Treaty of Jeddah, contains certain contentious territorial and non-territorial clauses. The book assesses actual and hypothetical Yemeni and Saudi arguments about whether the Taif Treaty is void or voidable. The Treaty's status may even undermine the validity of the Treaty of Jeddah. In addition, the book outlines the potential conflict between the two treaties and the potential conflict between the Treaty of Jeddah and Yemeni municipal law, also with reference to the principles of international law.

The agreements and treaties since the 1990s also reflect a broader urgency among Gulf states in recent years to see the Arabian political map finalized. Linear international boundaries have become an increasingly accepted feature of the Arabian Gulf region's political landscape, but some disputes remain. In this context, this book provides both an important legal analysis of the Saudi-Yemeni boundary dispute and a valuable case study of dispute resolution.

A word of thanks is extended to ECSSR editor Heinrich Matthee for coordinating the publication of the book.

Jamal S. Al-Suwaidi, Ph.D.
Director General
ECSSR

Preface

This book is the outcome of several years of research on boundary treaties, partly undertaken for my doctoral dissertation in law at the Moscow State Institute of International Relations (MGIMO). It deals with one of the world's longest and most complex border disputes in terms of duration, spanning the last 75 years of the twentieth century. As far as I know, the book constitutes the first study that deals systematically with the legal aspects of the Saudi-Yemeni territorial border dispute and the status of the 1934 and 2000 treaties aimed at resolving it. I hope that students and specialists of the subject will find the contribution helpful regarding the legal as well as the political aspects of the boundary dispute resolution. I wish to thank Professor W. Michael Reisman of Yale Law School and Professor Uri M. Kolosov, my advisor at MGIMO, for their invaluable advice and perceptive comments on earlier drafts of the manuscript. Copyrighted materials are reproduced in this book with permission or are otherwise acknowledged. While I am very grateful for the assistance I have received, I am solely responsible for all opinions and conclusions expressed in this study.

Askar H. Al-Enazy
Riyadh, Saudi Arabia
20 November 2004

INTRODUCTION

After nearly 70 years of a bitter and almost uninterrupted territorial dispute, which frequently escalated into armed confrontations, one of the world's most persistent boundary disputes was apparently settled. On June 12, 2000, official representatives of the governments of the Republic of Yemen and the Kingdom of Saudi Arabia, the two largest states in the Arabian Peninsula, met in the Saudi Red Sea port of Jeddah and signed the "International Boundary Treaty," which was described as "final and permanent."

This book commences with an outline of the legal history leading to the signing of the treaty, which is now known as the Treaty of Jeddah. It discusses the main provisions and the boundary settlement, and then analyzes the legal issues related to the new treaty. These issues primarily arise because the treaty incorporates the controversial and apparently conflicting provisions of the Treaty of Taif without any modification. The two state parties have long contested the legal status of the Treaty of Taif.

This study evaluates the potential legal effect of these issues on the status of the new treaty, which could compound and perpetuate the very conflict it was originally supposed to resolve. The study concludes that the Treaty of Jeddah has been irreparably undermined by the basic legal defects of the Taif Treaty. The potential legal dispute that might arise from an interpretation or application of the Treaty of Jeddah's provisions could have been avoided if the new treaty had expressly abrogated the whole contentious Treaty of Taif, perhaps after adopting provisions of the

Taif Treaty on which there was mutual agreement, reformulated into clear and unambiguous language.

This study is significant in three respects. First, it deals with one of the world's most complex and most enduring boundary disputes, which spans the greater part of the twentieth century. The dispute covers a vast region of more than 1,200 kilometers of strategically and economically important sea and land territory, straddling the border area between the two largest states in the Arabian Peninsula. The conclusion of the Treaty of Jeddah was supposedly aimed at achieving what the Treaty of Taif could not achieve, namely, resolving a perennial boundary dispute that has perpetually threatened regional peace and stability during the past 70 years.

Second, as far as this writer is aware, the study constitutes the first systematic study that deals exclusively with the legal aspects of the Saudi-Yemeni boundary dispute and the status of the 1934 and 2000 treaties aimed at resolving it. The current literature on the subject contains no published academic work[1] dealing directly with the legal aspects of the Saudi-Yemeni border conflict, such as the status of the dispute or the 1934 and 2000 complementary treaties in the light of the prevailing principles of international law.[2]

Third, and most important, the Treaty of Jeddah is rare, almost unique in the annals of modern treaties. It is a multiple treaty, consisting of separate but linked bilateral international agreements concluded between Saudi Arabia and Yemen at various times and places, that is, the 1934 Treaty of Taif and the 1995 MOU. By wholly incorporating these agreements, principally the Treaty of Taif, the Treaty of Jeddah, despite its official name, became a multipurpose agreement covering all aspects of bilateral Saudi-Yemeni relations. It became a peace treaty providing for the permanent cessation of armed hostility between the two countries, a boundary treaty involving territorial cession and establishing a final maritime and land boundary, and a general agreement regulating political, military, economic and social interactions between Yemen and Saudi Arabia.

Nevertheless, it contains a fixed duration clause expressly limiting its legal force to 20 years. This apparently contradictory clause is only one of several such provisions in the Treaty of Jeddah that could seriously impede its operation. The inherent legal weakness of the new treaty emanates primarily, but not exclusively, from the fact that it incorporates the complete and contentious Treaty of Taif without any change. This is the case even though the dispute over the status of the Taif Treaty under international law has rendered it without legal effect.

Structurally, the book is composed of an introduction giving the background to the dispute, seven main chapters, a conclusion and five appendices containing a number of important documents related to the boundary dispute. These include a comprehensive listing of sources related to the Saudi-Yemeni dispute, the full text of the Treaty of Taif, the 1995 Memorandum of Understanding and the Treaty of Jeddah.

The first chapter provides a brief description of the area in dispute and outlines its legal history from the 1926 Mecca agreement until the unification of North and South Yemen into one state in 1990. The chapter deals with various aspects of the disputes and legal attempts to resolve them. Special attention is given to the controversial 1934 Treaty of Taif, since it was incorporated into the new Treaty of Jeddah. The Treaty of Taif dealt with the most important boundary settlement between the two countries and contained certain contentious territorial and non-territorial clauses that could potentially threaten the successful implementation of the new treaty.

The chapter also deals with other boundary-related issues, such as the 1953 renewal agreement and the 1973 joint communiqué between Saudi Arabia and North Yemen. In addition, it explains the so-called Hamza and Riyadh lines, the cause of the Saudi boundary dispute with the former British Protectorate of Aden and its successor state of South Yemen.

Chapter Two discusses the legal and diplomatic developments in the boundary dispute from 1990 until the conclusion of the Treaty of Jeddah. The chapter deals with the Saudi revocation in 1990 of the so-called special privileges, which constituted a material breach of the Treaty of Taif according to Yemen. It also discusses the 1992 Geneva talks, encouraged by U.S. diplomacy, which marked the first formal Saudi–Yemeni negotiations on the boundary issue since the 1973 joint communiqué. The chapter covers the 1995 MOU, which constituted Yemen's first express confirmation that the 1934 treaty was valid and binding on both parties, and the 1997 informal Como agreement, which constituted the final territorial settlement of the boundary dispute and was later incorporated into the Treaty of Jeddah.

Chapter Three deals with the salient features of the provisions in the Treaty of Jeddah. Although the treaty established a maritime and land boundary described as final and permanent, it also incorporated the Treaty of Taif, including all its attachments, without any modification. This is the fundamental legal weakness in the new treaty, which could threaten its operation.

Chapters Four and Five analyze the legal status of the Treaty of Taif in terms of conventional and customary law. They discuss actual and hypothetical Yemeni and Saudi arguments over whether the treaty can be declared void or voidable under international law. This issue is of direct relevance to the legal status of the Treaty of Jeddah, which incorporates the whole Treaty of Taif. A dispute could affect the validity of the territorial settlement created under the new treaty.

Chapter Six explains those legal aspects of the Treaty of Jeddah that form the basis of Yemen's new support of and emphasis on the position of the Treaty of Taif in the new legal framework. The non-territorial provisions pertaining to the so-called "special privileges" must be "restored" within the terms of the new treaty now incorporating them.

Chapter Seven covers certain controversial and ambiguous territorial and non-territorial clauses. It discusses the potential conflict between the Treaty of Jeddah and the Treaty of Taif regarding the interpretation and application of provisions for the adjustment of the 1934 boundary. In addition, it analyzes the status of the fixed duration clause in the new legal environment and discusses whether it is wholly or partly applicable to the Treaty of Jeddah. It also discusses when the clause would come into operation or expire.

This chapter also outlines the possible conflict between certain provisions of the treaty, especially those relating to the extradition of political dissidents, freedom of belief and association, and Yemeni municipal law. There is no such conflict with Saudi municipal law. Since these provisions potentially constitute *jus cogens* in terms of the customary and conventional international law on human rights, they also provide a legal option to declare the Treaty of Jeddah, or part of it, void or voidable.

Chapter Seven also argues that the legal status of the Treaty of Jeddah can ultimately be questioned by one party or another, either under the arbitration clauses in its text or through those contained in conventional law. In conclusion, this book, while not underestimating the success of the territorial boundary settlement achieved under the auspices of the Treaty of Jeddah, nevertheless argues that the new treaty has inherited the seed of its own demise by incorporating the Treaty of Taif. Thus, it is a document without legal effect or value.

To reach its conclusions, the study depends heavily on the examination of all documentary and other primary and secondary material sources that are publicly available and pertinent to the factual and legal aspects of the Treaty of Jeddah. It also examines the relevant preceding bilateral agreements concluded since the 1926 Mecca agreement. Published official British, Saudi and Yemeni documents, as well as other materials, including academic works, provide the legal history of the new treaty. The Treaty of Jeddah is itself subjected to systematic legal analysis and assessment in light of the customary and conventional law of treaties, international judicial and arbitral precedents, and the commentaries of prominent authors.

1
The Legal History of the Boundary Dispute

The long Saudi-Yemeni boundary dispute involves three territorial segments constituting their entire common maritime and land border, an area about 1,500 kilometers long. The first land sector covers the land border area extending from the Red Sea coast, at a land terminus point located at the quay of Ra's al-Mu'waj, north of Radif-garad, to the point of intersection between Saudi Arabia, British Aden and Yemen, at or near Radm al-Amir or Al-Akhasheem, on the south-western edges of the Empty Quarter. The largest part of this sector was demarcated from the Red Sea to Jabal Al-Thar (mountain of Al-Thar) in the east under the terms of the contentious 1934 Treaty of Taif and the boundary demarcation report of the 1937 joint commission.

The second segment involves the remaining and previously undefined common land border area not covered by the Treaty of Taif. It runs from Jabal Al-Thar to the intersection of the Saudi, Yemeni and Omani borders. This sector formed the undefined southern Saudi border with the former British Protectorate of Aden, which became the People's Democratic Republic of Yemen (South Yemen) after independence in 1968 and joined the Arab Republic of Yemen (North Yemen) in May 1990 to form the present Yemen Republic.

The third segment pertains to the maritime boundary between the two countries, which was ignored by the Treaty of Taif and extended seaward from the land terminus point on the Red Sea coast as defined in Article 4 of that treaty.

The 1926 Mecca Treaty

From a legal point of view, if not also a political one, the Saudi-Yemeni territorial dispute can be traced back to the so-called Mecca Treaty. On October 21, 1926, King Ibn Saud, King of the Hejaz and Sultan of Najd and its dependencies, and Imam Hasan al-Idrisi, ruler of the Idrisi emirate in southwest Arabia, signed an agreement, the Mecca Treaty, which formally placed the emirate under Saudi protection.[3]

As a result of the treaty, Ibn Saud extended his territory to include the former Idrisi emirate, comprising the southern Red Sea coastal and highland areas of southern Tihamat and Surat Asir. On November 20, 1930, Ibn Saud "acquired full and complete sovereignty" over the same territories that hitherto had the status of a protectorate under the 1926 Mecca Treaty.[4]

Imam Yahya of Yemen refused to recognize the 1926 Mecca Treaty on the grounds that Yemen had long maintained its own claim to the entire territory of the Idrisi emirate of Asir. The Idrisi emirate was historically and legally part of the geographical *bilad al-yemen* (land of the Yemen), which also extended eastward to include the British Protectorate of Aden.[5] In addition, Yemen asserted that the Idrisi emirate had never possessed a legal personality under international law and thus lacked the jurisdiction and capacity to cede territory by means of a treaty. Consequently, the territorial cession created under the 1926 Mecca Treaty was void because it lacked legal force from the moment of its signature. The historical and legally established status of the Idrisi emirate, "having always been Yemeni," could not be changed by Saudi incorporation of the Idrisi emirate.[6]

The Saudis counter-argued that, aside from its shaky historical claim, there was no evidence of Yemen's effective control of the Idrisi territory in the period immediately before 1926 or any evidence of the Idrisi's legal allegiance to Imam Yahya.[7] Moreover, under the terms of the international law that applied at the time of the 1926 Mecca Treaty, the Idrisi emirate appeared to meet at least the minimum requirements for an independent state enjoying legal personality. The emirate had concluded international treaties with Great Britain and Italy, and the British government, for one, acknowledged that before 1926 the Idrisi emir was "an independent ruler exercising sovereignty over certain territories in South-West Arabia."[8]

Thus, the Idrisi emirate possessed the legal power under international law to cede territory to Saudi Arabia under the 1926 agreement. As a result of the agreement, it "ceased to possess the status of an international person under international law," as declared by the British government.[9] Ibn Saud became the sovereign ruler over the territory of the former Idrisi emirate, whose "sovereignty over these territories was effective in international law and did not require any express or implied recognition by any other power to render it legally complete and effective."[10] The territorial cession under the 1926 Mecca Treaty constituted the main basis for the Saudi claim to Asir,[11] and according to this claim the boundary in Article 4 of the 1934 Treaty of Taif formed the Saudi-Yemeni borders. The Saudi-Yemeni dispute over the territorial settlement created by the 1926 agreement gradually intensified, leading to mutual accusations of frontier violations between the two countries.

The 1931 'Aru Agreement

In an attempt to peacefully resolve their escalating border dispute, Saudi Arabia and Yemen signed the so-called 'Aru Agreement on December 15, 1931, in which Ibn Saud acknowledged that the disputed 'Aru mountain was Yemeni territory.[12] From the Saudi point of view, the conclusion of the 'Aru Agreement meant that a Saudi-Yemeni frontier line had been established, extending from the Red Sea coast to the inland Najran area in the east. Under the 'Aru Agreement, Saudi Arabia ceded the Jabal 'Aru and all the territory to the south of it to Yemen. This defined the boundary of the western coastal region of Asir Tihamat and, under the terms of an earlier 1927 agreement, retained the inland eastern area of Najran and all the territory to the north of it, thus creating a connecting frontier line in the eastern highland of Asir Surat.

However, the Yemeni government subsequently denied both the Saudi assertion that it had ratified the 'Aru Agreement[13] and the provisions of the alleged 1927 agreement, and asserted its claim to the Najran area while rejecting the 'Aru Agreement.[14] In 1933, the Saudi government proposed a comprehensive formal border agreement with Yemen along the lines of the 1927 and 1931 agreements. In reply, Yemen agreed to such talks on condition that Saudi Arabia recognize the Najran area as Yemeni territory.[15] In 1933, following protracted but fruitless diplomatic communications, Yemeni troops occupied Najran and the southern mountains of Al Abide and Fayfa in the central highland of Surat Asir.

In response, the Saudi king sent a letter articulating the Saudi conditions for averting the looming war. It first called for the settlement of the boundary issue "in the same legitimate manner agreed upon" in the 1927 and 1931 agreements, by defining the boundary points along their common border from the Red Sea coast to the eastern hinterland of Najran. Second, it called for the evacuation of Yemeni troops from occupied mountain areas and the elimination of all acts "violating the concluded covenants."

Finally, it called for the settlement of the dispute on the Najran valley by "the return of Najran to its previous status of neutrality" or by dividing it so that the city of Najran itself, the tribe of Yam and the area north of it would be incorporated in Saudi Arabia, and the southern section along with the tribe of Wa'ilah would become part of Yemen.[16] When the Imam ignored the Saudi letter, which amounted to an ultimatum, war broke out between the two countries.

The Taif Treaty of 1934

The Saudi-Yemeni war was short-lived, ending with the defeat of Yemen and a brief Saudi occupation of the Yemeni Red Sea port of Hodiedah.[17] Yemen accepted the Saudi demands, which were later embodied in the provisions of the Treaty of Taif, the first Saudi-Yemeni agreement to be formulated according to the modern Western notion of legal instruments. The treaty was comprehensive in its scope, regulating all aspects of Saudi-Yemeni relations. In addition to establishing peace and creating a territorial settlement, it also contained provisions pertaining to political, military, economic, social and cultural issues. Since the Treaty of Taif was later formally incorporated without modification into the Saudi-Yemeni Treaty of Jeddah in June 2000, it will be discussed in more detail below, with the emphasis on an analysis of its important and controversial articles.

On May 20, 1934, representatives of King Abdulalaziz Al-Saud of Saudi Arabia and Imam Yahya Hamidaddin of the kingdom of

Yemen signed the Treaty of Islamic Friendship and Arab Brotherhood, also called the Treaty of Taif.[18]

Soon afterwards, Imam Yahya ratified the Treaty on June 18, 1934.[19] The instruments of its ratification were exchanged on June 22, 1934, at Hodiedah, North Yemen.[20] The text of the Treaty of Taif was published on June 23, 1934, in *Um Alqura*, the official gazette of the government of Saudi Arabia.[21] It contained 23 articles, a covenant of arbitration and five attachments, in addition to the 1936 General Agreement and the demarcation report of the 1937 joint commission.[22]

The treaty formally ended the state of war existing between the two countries, established permanent peace and mutual state recognition, and created a boundary settlement. It provided for the peaceful settlement of future disputes by means of arbitration. It also stipulated the mutual withdrawal of troops, repatriation of prisoners-of-war, extradition of political dissidents, non-interference in each other's internal affairs, benevolent neutrality in the event of external aggression against a party, and the regulation of cross-border movement by their nationals.

Peace and the Cession of Territory

The first article of the Treaty of Taif officially terminated the state of war existing between the two countries and established "a state of perpetual peace, firm friendship, and permanent Islamic Arab brotherhood..."[23]

Article 2 of the Treaty of Taif stipulated that Yemen and Saudi Arabia would each abandon any right to claims on the other party's territory beyond the boundary defined in Article 4 of the treaty. It also provided that Yemen would abandon any right to claim "in the name of Yemeni unity" or any other pretext the territory that once "belonged to the Idrisi or the 'Aayidh, or in Najran, or in the Yam country" that had become part of Saudi Arabia under terms of the treaty.[24]

Thus, one of the immediate and significant legal effects of the Treaty was Yemen's formal recognition of Saudi sovereignty over the regions of Asir, Jizan and Najran, thereby renouncing all previous Yemeni claims to those areas. Article 4 established a "fixed dividing...boundary" between the territories of the two contracting parties."[25] Providing no geographical coordinates or accompanying maps, the article then proceeded to describe in lengthy and confusing detail the physical and tribal names along the common border area and linked the starting and finishing points of the line as follows:

> The boundary between the two kingdoms begins at a point half-way between *Midi* and *Al Muwassam* on the coast of the Red Sea, and extends up to the mountains of the Tihamah in an easterly direction...This line then extends from the end of the above-mentioned limits between the edges of the Saudi Arab tribes and of those of the Hamdam-bin-Zaid (tribes), and all the Yemeni tribes who are outside Yam (tribe). All the borders and the Yemeni territories up to the end of the Yemeni frontier in all directions belong to the Yemeni Kingdom; and all the borders and territories up to the end of their boundaries, in all directions, belong to the Saudi Arab Kingdom.[26]

The article provided for the formation of a joint commission, composed of an equal number of representatives from each side, to demarcate this line in a friendly manner and without prejudice according to "tribal usage and custom."[27]

In 1937, the joint Saudi-Yemeni commission for boundary demarcation completed its task of placing more than 200 markers on specific locations along the common border. The commission's subsequent report was officially approved by both countries and became an integral part of the Treaty of Taif.[28]

However, the joint commission was only partially successful in fulfilling its task. The demarcation report had indicated R'as al-Mu'waj, north of Radif-garad, as a boundary marker on the western end of the 1934 line, defining it in Article 4 as "the point half-way between Midi and Al Muwassam on the coast of the Red Sea." However, the joint commission halted its demarcation work at Jabal Al-Thar in the east, well short of the presumed eastern end of the line. It cited a tribal dispute involving the Saudi Yam tribe and the Yemeni tribe of Wa'ilah as the principal cause that prevented it from completing this part of its demarcation work, which ran east of the Jabal Al-Thar to the undefined intersection point where the frontiers of the Saudi-Yemeni-British Aden Protectorate met at Radm al-Amir.[29]

Due to tribal opposition, the commission recommended that the border area east of Jabal Al-Thar remained demarcated as before and that the dispute be resolved in accordance with "the law of God and the text of the Treaty of Taif" in the event of future tribal conflict. Meanwhile, in reversing the order stipulated in Article 4, the demarcation report declared the demarcated boundary marker on the summit of the Jabal Al-Thar as the starting point of the 1934 boundary line. This action by the joint commission would seem to support the later Yemeni claim that the Treaty of Taif did not, as claimed by Saudi Arabia, cover the border area east of the Jabal Al-Thar.

In fact, Article 4 itself is imprecise in its definition of the frontier east of Jabal Al-Thar. The wording of the relevant paragraph appears to allocate and then delimit that part of the border area as claimed by Saudi Arabia.[30] In addition, the joint commission did not use geographical coordinates or maps, and most of its boundary markers were temporary and removable, thus setting the stage for a future Saudi-Yemeni dispute over their locations and the exact course of the 1934 line.

According to Article 12, the two parties recognize that people of all areas accruing to the other party by virtue of the Treaty of Taif are subjects of that party, and each of the two parties undertakes "not to accept as its subjects" any person or persons who are subjects of the other party, "except with the consent" of the party concerned.[31]

The Modification and Extension Clause

Significantly, the Treaty of Taif included a clause providing for future amendments and limiting its duration to 20 lunar years, at the end of which it could be renewed, modified or terminated. Article 22 specified that the Treaty of Taif:

> …shall remain in force for a period of twenty lunar years. It may be renewed or modified during the six months preceding its expiration. If not so renewed or modified by that date, it shall continue to remain in force for six months after the date of the notice by one party to the other party of his desire to amend it.[32]

As discussed later, the presence of this rather unusual clause in a treaty involving territorial settlement would have important legal implications for the status of the Treaty of Taif, and by extension for the status of the Treaty of Jeddah, which incorporated the Taif Treaty.

Non-Interference and Extradition Clauses

The Treaty of Taif also included some potentially controversial provisions pertaining to non-interference and the extradition of criminals. Under Articles 7, 9, 10 and 18 both parties were required to prevent "with all material and moral means available" the use of their respective territories as a base for any actual or potential threat against each other in whatever form.[33]

Each party would also undertake "immediate measures" against any of its nationals "fomenting disturbances" by meting out deterrent punishment in a way that would "put an end to (the effect of) his actions and prevent their recurrence."[34] If such a person was a national of the targeted country, he would be "immediately arrested and…extradited without delay or excuse."[35] Furthermore, the Treaty of Taif prohibited each party from granting refuge to political dissidents and mandated their prompt and unconditional return if they tried to enter either country.[36]

Covenant of Arbitration

Article 8 of the Treaty of Taif stipulated a compulsory legal mechanism for the peaceful settlement of disputes between the two states that might arise from or outside the provisions of the treaty. It stated that each party should "refrain from resorting to force" to settle any of their differences and committed them to exert their utmost effort to settle any dispute between them by friendly representation, "whether caused by this treaty or the interpretation of all or any of its articles or resulting from any other cause." Otherwise, either party could unilaterally resort to an arbitration settlement.

The procedures and rules governing the establishment of such an arbitral body were described in the attached Covenant of Arbitration, which, according to Article 8, would have "the force and authority of this treaty and shall be considered as an integral part of it." The covenant provided for the formation of an arbitration court with equal representation by each party and presided over by a chief arbitrator chosen by mutual consent.[37] It further stipulated that the award of the arbitration body would be given by "a majority of votes" and be binding on both parties, who would be under an obligation to execute a judgement "immediately" upon its announcement.[38]

The Side Letters and Cross-Border Movements

The Treaty of Taif contains six side letters between the plenipotentiaries of Ibn Saud and Imam Yahya, signed on the same date as the treaty itself. In effect they constituted reservations of the Saudi government that were acknowledged and accepted by Yemen.[39] The Saudi side letter number 5, relevant to this study, deals with the cross-border "movement of subjects" of the two countries. The side letter, acknowledged by the Yemeni envoy in his reply,[40] states as follows:

> With reference to the signature of the Treaty of Taif between our Kingdom and that of Yemen, I hereby confirm our agreement concerning the movement of subjects of the Kingdom of Saudi Arabia and of the Kingdom of Yemen in the two countries, namely that movement at the present time shall continue as in the past, until a special agreement is drawn up between the two governments regarding the method that they agree to adopt on the regulation of such movements, whether for pilgrimage, trade or any other purpose or reason. I hope to receive your reply agreeing on this issue.[41]

[17]

The 1936 Agreement between Saudi Arabia and Yemen

Article 7 of the Treaty of Taif stipulated the conclusion of a bilateral agreement to regulate the cross-border movement of subjects and related matters. In line with this article, as well as letter number 5 mentioned above, Saudi Arabia and Yemen concluded the General Agreement for the Settlement of Frontier Questions and Movement of Subjects between the Two Countries on November 2, 1937.[42]

The agreement was a bilateral arrangement intended to regulate the age-old cross-border trade and movement of local tribesmen and villagers living in the common border area between the two countries. It undertook to facilitate the movement of persons "residing on either side of the frontier line" and the settlement of disputes between them. It required a "special permit" for such cross-border movement, which would only be issued to those individuals who had "direct business near the border and are accustomed to cross from one side to another from time immemorial in search of pasture, or who own farms or gardens on the other side, or who have been in the habit of attending markets."

The agreement apparently did not apply to subjects of either state party who lived outside the common border area and needed regular passport and travel visas. It also did not seem to apply to inhabitants of the border area, who, if they wished to venture beyond the common border area for whatever purpose, i.e., pilgrimage or trade, had to obtain "special prior permission" from the relevant local authorities on either side of the border.

In addition, Article 4 of the Treaty of Taif granted both Saudi and Yemeni subjects belonging to the Wa'ilah tribe in and around the Najran area exclusive privileges pertaining to their inter-tribal customary visitation rights and communication.[43]

[18]

The 1953 Agreement to extend the Treaty of Taif

Shortly before the expiration of its fixed duration date in accordance with the Islamic lunar calendar, Imam Ahmad of Yemen informed King Ibn Saud of Saudi Arabia that, in terms of Article 22, he wished to extend the Treaty of Taif for another twenty years. Ibn Saud concurred and the two rulers issued the following official joint statement in March 1953:

> In view of the firm ties of friendship and mutual trust existing between the Kingdom of Saudi Arabia and the Mutawakelite Yemeni government and in view of the fact that the force of the Treaty of Taif concluded (in May 1934) will shortly expire, the two Kings, King (Ibn Saud) of Saudi Arabia and King Ahmad, king of the Mutawakelite kingdom of the Yemen, have agreed to extend the said treaty for a further twenty years, starting with the termination of the period of the aforesaid treaty.[44]

The 1953 agreement was the first and only formal renewal of the Treaty of Taif concluded in terms of Article 22 of the Treaty of Taif. The text of the 1953 extension agreement appeared to imply that the legal force of the Treaty of Taif as a whole would expire upon the date indicated, if either party refused to agree to another renewal. It was this interpretation of Article 22 that successive Yemeni governments adopted as a legal basis for renouncing the Treaty of Taif in whole or in part, particularly with regard to its provisions on territorial settlement.

Saudi Renunciation of the Treaty of Taif in 1960

The monarchical government of Yemen never disguised its dissatisfaction with the Treaty of Taif's territorial settlement, which, in its view, had been imposed on Yemen by force. In the summer of

1960, Imam Ahmad, who had opposed the treaty as heir apparent, declared Yemen's intention to join the Egyptian-Syrian political union of the United Arab Republic, which was perceived as an anti-Saudi alliance. In response, Saudi Arabia reportedly decided to unilaterally abrogate the Treaty of Taif, invoking the principle of a fundamental change of circumstances.[45]

A senior official of the Yemeni foreign ministry confirmed that the Yemeni government had received the Saudi note renouncing the "whole" treaty, with the result that "Yemenis would now be free to reassert their territorial claims to a certain part of the border area."[46] However, other foreign ministry officials contradicted their colleague's assertion and indicated instead that Saudi Arabia only wanted to amend the treaty provisions relating to the "employment of Yemenis within the Kingdom of Saudi Arabia" by subjecting them to the same regulations applied to other nationals from Arab League countries.[47]

The apparently confused Yemeni comments on the Saudi move stemmed in part from the seemingly contradictory Saudi official announcements made on July 10 and 14, and again on August 9. On the latter date, a statement was issued in the name of Prince Faysal, then Saudi Crown Prince, Prime Minister and Foreign Minister, declaring that Yemeni nationals working in Saudi Arabia would henceforth be subject to the same employment regulations as other Arab League nationals.[48] Imam Ahmad of Yemen, alarmed by the Saudi action, initiated contacts with King Saud and expressed his readiness to "discuss with King Saud any outstanding matters with goodwill whenever King Saud so wished."[49] Soon afterwards, the Saudi government rescinded all previous decisions intended to terminate or otherwise modify the Treaty of Taif, and both countries agreed to return to "the status quo ante."[50]

Yemen's Implicit Renunciation of the Taif Treaty

Saudi-Yemeni relations on boundary issues remained relatively peaceful until the 1962 revolution in Yemen and the ensuing civil war between loyalists of the former monarchy, supported by Saudi Arabia, and the new republican regime, supported by Egypt.[51] Although the new revolutionary government in Yemen, upon its inception, declared its commitment to international agreements and treaties concluded under the former monarchy, it made no reference to specific bilateral agreements like the 1934 Treaty of Taif.

However, the new Yemeni government took a new line that culminated in a formal statement in 1965 at the height of the civil war. This formal statement constituted a unilateral termination of the Treaty of Taif on the ground that it was an unequal treaty imposed by force and thus null and void. In May 1965, following an extraordinary joint session of the two highest ruling bodies, the Republican Council and the Council of Ministers, the revolutionary government declared:

> …anew its determination to recover by force if necessary the Yemeni territories in the north and northwest, including the regions of Najran, Jizan and Asir, which Saudi Arabia had acquired by force of arms, in spite of the fact that they are geographically and historically part of the territory of Yemen. In this respect, the Yemeni people affirm their adherence to their infringed rights.[52]

In a later statement, a senior Yemeni official announced in Cairo that Yemen would initially resort to "all legitimate means" via the good offices of the Arab League and the UN to claim "the return to Mother Yemen (of) the regions of Najran, Jizan and Asir."[53]

However, though Yemen subsequently formally lodged a request to this effect with the Arab League and the UN, it did not pursue the matter further. Nevertheless, the two statements came to represent the general position of all subsequent Yemeni governments on the Treaty of Taif until the signing of the Treaty of Jeddah in June 2000.

The 1973 Joint Communiqué

After the end of the Yemeni civil war in 1970 and the subsequent Saudi recognition of the new republican government in North Yemen, the two countries held their first high-level bilateral talks in the Saudi capital, Riyadh, in March 1973. This also was the expiration date of the Taif Treaty's first period of extension.[54]

The Yemeni delegation refused the Saudi request to sign another formal agreement extending the Treaty of Taif indefinitely or for at least another 20 years. However, in an apparent compromise, the two sides agreed to include a paragraph in their joint communiqué issued after the bilateral talks that expressly recognized the validity of the Treaty of Taif and the boundary established under it. The relevant paragraph stated:

> ...the two sides confirm anew that they consider the boundary between their two countries as definite, final and permanent as stipulated in articles 2 and 4 of the Treaty of Taif and the relevant annexures attached.[55]

The Saudi government appeared to be satisfied with the statement, since it possibly constituted an agreement on the indefinite extension they sought. However, the Yemeni government, under strong domestic pressure, soon distanced itself from the content of the statement, declaring that it was made without authority and was, in any case, merely part of a joint press communiqué that entailed no legal obligation under international law.[56]

The Saudi Arabia-British Aden Border

Previous Saudi government talks with the British authorities in the Protectorate of Aden and, since 1968, with its successor state of South Yemen, failed to lead to a settlement of the Saudi-South Yemen boundary. Saudi-British diplomatic correspondence concerning the Saudi-Aden border commenced in 1934 and ended in a deadlock in the early 1960s, with each side refusing to compromise further on the boundaries of its respective claims.

The Saudi territorial claim, based primarily on tribal allegiance and constituting a modified form of the so-called Hamza Line of 1935,[57] was presented to the British government on October 18, 1955.[58] The British territorial claim, based on the 1914 Anglo-Ottoman Violet Line,[59] was reflected in the 1935 Riyadh Line,[60] as modified in a note presented to the Saudi government on August 4, 1955.[61] The Riyadh Line, after some minor changes, was later renamed the Independence Line and adopted by both Yemens in their territorial dispute with Saudi Arabia. The competing claims thus constituted overlapping boundaries between the two countries.[62]

The Saudi Arabia-South Yemen Border, 1968-1990

Since its independence from British colonial rule in 1968 to its political union with North Yemen in 1990, the emergent state of the People's Democratic Republic (South Yemen) held no serious border talks with Saudi Arabia. This was largely due to two reasons. First, ideological differences and lack of diplomatic recognition between the conservative Saudi monarchy and the self-declared Marxist Arab state until 1975 were further compounded by brief wars in 1969 and 1972, in which South Yemen accused Saudi Arabia of occupying Yemeni territory, including the town of Al-

Wadi'ah.[63] Second, and more important, the North and South Yemen governments reached a formal understanding that neither side would conclude separate border agreements with their neighboring countries, including Saudi Arabia,[64] until the two Yemens achieved their ultimate declared political objective of forming one unified Yemeni state.[65]

2

The Development of the Saudi-Yemeni Boundary Dispute since 1990

After the proclamation of the Yemen Republic on May 22, 1990, the new government, in a formal statement presented by the first unity cabinet to the Council of Representatives, declared that it would make the resolution of border issues between Yemen and its neighbors its top priority.[1] Of all these border issues, perennial disputes with Saudi Arabia were the most complex.[2] However, possible Saudi-Yemeni border talks were shelved soon after the Iraqi invasion of Kuwait in August 1990, and the subsequent deterioration of relations between the two countries reached a new low.

Saudi Revocation of Yemeni Privileges in 1990

In August 1990, the Saudi Arabian government issued a decision revoking the special work and residence exemptions of Yemeni nationals for the second time since August 1960. Under the new rules, Yemeni citizens would be subject to the same regulations as other foreign workers.[3] Although clearly motivated by Yemen's attitude toward the 1990 Iraqi invasion of Kuwait and its potential threat to Saudi security, the Saudi government, as in 1960, made no reference to the relevant provisions of the Treaty of Taif. It did not attempt, for example, to invoke any of the articles pertaining to third party aggression and alliance as grounds for its decision.[4] This was perhaps due to the Saudi government's assertion that granting and revoking such privileges had no legal connection to the Treaty of Taif.

However, Yemen did not share this view. After an emergency session, the Yemeni cabinet issued a public statement strongly condemning the Saudi decision that led to the "expulsion" of nearly one million "sons of Yemen" and depriving them of their "legitimate and acquired rights" under the provisions of the Treaty of Taif.[5] It declared that the Saudi government's action constituted a violation of its treaty obligations and that Yemen had the right to renounce the Treaty. Thus, the Yemeni government declared it would not only "oppose renewal" of the treaty, but would also demand its termination.[6]

In addition, as the injured party, Yemen claimed "compensation for losses suffered by Yemenis who left Saudi Arabia following the rescission of their special privileges." It also claimed compensation for the damage incurred by Saudi support for the royalist faction during the 1960s civil war.[7] However, as in its public statement on the Treaty of Taif in 1965, the Yemeni government chose not to implement its threat of sending a formal note to Saudi Arabia on the Treaty as would be customary under international law.

After serious escalation of their border conflict,[8] both Yemen and Saudi Arabia expressed a mutual willingness to settle their border dispute peacefully.[9] Encouraged by the U.S. government, which exercised a strong leverage over both countries,[10] the two countries finally agreed to initiate direct formal contacts to settle their long-standing border dispute.[11]

The 1992 Geneva Talks

Yemen and Saudi Arabia held their first formal boundary talks following the 1990 crisis in July 1992 in Geneva. These eventually culminated in the signing of a memorandum of understanding in February 1995. On July 20, 1992, a "preparatory" Saudi-Yemeni meeting was held in Geneva, where the two sides agreed to establish a joint "committee of experts" to create a framework for bilateral negotiations on their dispute.[12] During the talks, the Yemeni and Saudi governments exchanged a series of proposals and counterproposals reflecting their sharply different positions on border issues, their territorial claims and the legal means by which to resolve them.

The Yemeni Position

The Yemeni government's position was repeatedly reiterated in its public statements on border negotiations with Saudi Arabia. It called for negotiations on the basis that the whole boundary issue constituted a single unit. The ultimate objective was to reach a comprehensive, final settlement of the entire Saudi-Yemeni land and maritime border area through a bilateral treaty or third-party arbitration, in accordance with the principles of international law as applied to Yemen's "historical and legal rights."[13]

Theoretically, Yemen's understanding of its "historical and legal rights" was derived from the pre-Islamic and medieval notion of *bilad al-yemen* (Land of Yemen) or *al-yaman al-kubra* (Greater Yemen), which extended almost in a straight line eastward from the Red Sea port of Al-Lith, south of the holy Hejaz city of Mecca, encompassing almost the entire southern half of the Arabian Peninsula.[14] This boundary represented Yemen's maximum territorial claim against Saudi Arabia.

Yemen proposed 1900 as the critical legal date in the border dispute. This would not only predate the 1934 Treaty of Taif and the 1926 Mecca Treaty, but also the existence of the Saudi state itself. More importantly, it would allow the Yemeni government to present several important legal documents as evidence in support of its historical territorial claims, including the 1914 Saudi-Ottoman agreement[15] and the Violet Line embodied in the 1914 Anglo-Ottoman Convention[16] from which the 1935 British Line was derived.[17] The Yemeni claim in the eastern sector was represented by the 1935 British Line, as modified in 1955. Extending from Jabal Al-Thar to the intersection of the Yemeni-Omani border, it became known as the Riyadh Line and was later renamed by Yemen as the Independence Line.[18]

In the Yemeni government's view the Treaty of Taif was legally void or voidable. It had been imposed on Yemen by force and had in any case expired in 1974 under the terms of its 20 year duration clause.[19] The existing Saudi-Yemeni boundary, of which the eastern part extended south of the British Riyadh Line, constituted a *de facto* boundary, not a legal one. It was based on *fait accompli* and the forced occupation of Yemeni territory, and thus without legal merit in terms of international law.[20]

The Saudi Position

Saudi Arabia, for its part, strongly rejected Yemen's historical and legal arguments. It rejected Yemen's notion of a Greater Yemen on the grounds that such a construction did not exist historically or geographically.[21] It regarded Yemeni proposals for comprehensive talks on the entire boundary as one unit as implicit Yemeni non-recognition of the Taif Treaty's 1934 boundary demarcation and Saudi sovereignty over the three southern provinces of Asir, Jizan and Najran, as well as the Farasan islands in the Red Sea.

Instead, the Saudi government proposed a piecemeal approach to the resolution of the border dispute based on 1934 as the critical date. It argued that the Treaty of Taif was a valid agreement under international law. As a result, the 1934 boundary and territorial cession, which was executed in line with the treaty, could not be subject to further negotiations, agreements without prejudice, judicial decision or arbitral settlement.[22]

The Saudis held that the initial step needed was the establishment of a joint committee to restore the obliterated boundary pillars established by the Taif Treaty's joint demarcation commission in 1937. Second, another committee was needed to "demarcate" the eastern part of the 1934 boundary, extending from Jabal Al-Thar to the intersection of the Saudi-Yemeni-British Protectorate of Aden as "delimited" in Article 4 of the Treaty. The remaining boundary not covered by the Treaty of Taif, including the area extending from the 1934 line's easternmost point to the intersection of the Saudi-Yemeni-Oman border, that is, the Saudi boundary with former South Yemen and the maritime boundary in the Red Sea would be settled through separate negotiations and agreements between the two countries.[23]

While both parties apparently agreed to delimit their maritime area in accordance with international maritime law, Saudi Arabia proposed a modified form of the Hamza Line as the basis of delimiting the eastern part of its border with Yemen. The so-called 1984 claim boundary shown on official Saudi maps extended from the intersection point of the Saudi-Omani border in the east to Jabal Al-Thar, the starting point of the 1934 line.[24]

The competing Saudi-Yemeni territorial claims outside the scope of the 1934 treaty resulted in overlapping boundary claims.[25] It appeared as though Saudi Arabia accepted Yemen's stand on Radm Al-Amir in the east as the starting point of the disputed boundary and the intersection of the Omani-Saudi-Yemeni border at coordinates 19 degrees North 52 degrees East as its terminus point.[26] Neither state seemed to have any viable alternative regarding the exact location of the intersection, as it was more or less dictated by the Saudi-Omani boundary agreement of March 1990 and the Yemeni-Omani agreement of October 1992.

The 1995 Memorandum of Understanding

The two years of bilateral negotiations failed to significantly narrow the gap between the widely divergent positions of Saudi Arabia and Yemen on solutions to their border dispute. The apparent deadlock led to a dangerous deterioration in their relations that brought the two neighbors to the brink of war by the end of 1994.[27] Arab[28] and, most importantly, American mediation moved the two sides to hold marathon talks in the holy city of Mecca in early 1995, which resulted in the signing of a limited but significant Memorandum of Understanding (MOU) on February 26, 1995.[29] The MOU, also called the Mecca agreement, was the first formal agreement since the 1953 agreement to extend the Treaty of Taif.

Like the Treaty of Taif, the MOU served to regulate the relations between the two signatories in the political, economic, security and cultural spheres. The MOU expressly confirmed the Treaty of Taif as valid and binding on both countries. It also provided, for the first time, a framework for the comprehensive settlement of the entire land and maritime boundary issue between Saudi Arabia and the newly unified Yemeni state, including the areas not covered by the Treaty of Taif.

The MOU contains a preamble and 11 articles. Article 1 of the MOU stated that "the two parties affirm and uphold the validity and binding force of the Treaty of Taif...and its annexures." Article 10 provides that: "nothing in this memorandum constitutes an amendment to the Treaty of Taif and its annexures including boundary reports." Accordingly, Article 2 in the MOU called for the formation of a joint committee with equal representation by each side. Such a committee would be entrusted with the task of dealing with a specific border issue, such as the "restoration" of the "erased" boundary markers, which start from the land terminus point on the coast of the Red Sea in accordance with the 1937 joint boundary commission reports attached to the treaty.

Article 3 stipulated that another joint committee should delimit the remaining land boundary extending from Jabal Al-Thar to the point where the Saudi-Yemeni-Omani frontiers converge. The same article entrusted the task of "agreeing on the means of arbitration in case of a dispute between the two countries" to the committee. However, since the arbitration clause appeared in an article exclusively focused on the issue of the eastern land boundary, which is not covered by the Treaty of Taif, its application seemed to be restricted to that part of the border, excluding the 1934 line.

Article 4 called for the creation of a joint committee to delimit the maritime boundary in the Red Sea, starting from the defined coastal land terminus "in accordance with international law." Article 5 called for the creation of a joint military committee to monitor new military and other installations along the common border area. Article 8 prohibited both parties from "allowing their territory to be used as a base for carrying out aggression against the other or conducting any form of political, military or propaganda activity against the other party." Article 6 called for the formation of a joint ministerial committee to "develop economic, trade and cultural relations" between the two countries, and stated that the committee should commence its work within 30 days of the date of signing of the MOU. In accordance with Article 11, the MOU entered into force from the date of exchange of the instrument of ratification on March 22, 1995.

The MOU appeared to satisfy the basic demands of both sides. Yemen, conceding the main Saudi demand, implicitly recognized the Treaty of Taif and its 1934 boundary as being valid and binding on both parties, the first time it had done so formally since the controversial Saudi-Yemeni joint communiqué in 1973. In return, Saudi Arabia agreed to the Yemeni demand to negotiate and conclude a comprehensive land and sea boundary agreement within a reasonable time limit. In addition, Yemen, by virtue of recognizing the Treaty of Taif, including its provision on arbitration, procured a new Saudi agreement to submit to arbitration any potential dispute arising from the territorial and maritime boundary, whether or not this was covered by the Treaty of Taif.

The apparently major concession by Yemen regarding the legal status of the Treaty of Taif and the boundary established under it appeared to have been less influenced by the political good offices of Arab and American mediators than by legal considerations emanating from certain contemporary international judicial decisions. It was perhaps a coincidence that the Saudi-Yemeni 1995 MOU was signed on almost the exact date of the first anniversary of the ICJ decision in the Chad versus Libyan case; the case's implications clearly did not escape the attention of the Yemeni government.

In its judgment, the ICJ reaffirmed the doctrine of the inviolability, permanency and finality of territorial settlements and boundaries, irrespective of the fate or legal status of agreements establishing them. The Court declared the boundary, though established only "implicitly" under the 1955 Chad-Libya agreement, as valid, permanent and finally assuming "a legal life of its own." This was irrespective of the clause indicating that it had a duration of only 20 years.[30] Another international judicial decision had similar implications for the Yemeni view that the 1973 Saudi-Yemeni joint

Communiqué did not reconfirm the 1934 treaty and its boundary. In the Qatar versus Bahrain Case on Jurisdiction and Admissibility in July 1994, the ICJ, reaffirming a 1978 decision,[31] declared that a "communiqué" issued by or "minutes" signed between senior officials, that is, foreign ministers of two countries, which established "rights and obligations in international law" for the parties, did in fact "constitute an international agreement."[32]

However, the Yemeni government declared that its recognition of the Taif Treaty in the MOU was conditional on the conclusion of a final and comprehensive border treaty with Saudi Arabia within a reasonable period of time. More significantly, the Yemen government also re-emphasized that the Treaty of Taif, being a comprehensive regulatory instrument, contained other non-territorial provisions, especially the "special exemptions" clauses. These clauses granted Yemeni nationals in Saudi territory certain privileges, related to their entry, work, residence and other social and economic issues.[33]

Shortly after the signing of the MOU, the Yemeni president publicly stated that Yemen did not consider the MOU as constituting an agreement, but merely as "a first step in the right direction involving the basis and principles for the resolution of the border dispute." To emphasize this view, he explained that the MOU was not ratified by the Yemeni parliament as required in the case of other agreements mandating rights and obligations.[34]

Numerous meetings of the various joint Saudi-Yemeni committees were held in the following years, but with little or no real progress being achieved in the implementation of the MOU provisions. Although the legal status of the Treaty of Taif no longer seemed to be in question, other basic differences on boundary issues remained. The first dispute involved their widely differing interpretations of the geographical dimension of Article 4 of the Treaty of Taif. In an apparent attempt to support its comprehensive approach to the settlement of its border dispute, Yemen introduced a new interpretation of the geographical scope of the boundary contained in Article 4 of the Treaty of Taif. Yemen asserted that Article 4 distinguished between "the Kingdom of Yemen" and "Yemen." It argued that some references in Article 4 to the word "Yemen" alone meant that the boundary stretched beyond the "Kingdom of Yemen" and into the northern area of the then British Aden Protectorate.[35]

Saudi Arabia rejected Yemen's new proposition as lacking any supporting evidence in the text of the article. Article 4 specifically established the geographical limits of the tribal homelands as the criteria for defining the extension of the land boundary under the 1934 Treaty of Taif, and the tribes mentioned in Article 4 lived as far as the eastern limits of the British Aden Protectorate. Furthermore, in the 1934 Anglo-Yemen treaty, Yemen recognized that a legal dispute over the common border area had existed between the two contracting parties.

In addition, it would seem from the text of the article and the contemporaneous circumstances under which the Taif Treaty was drafted that neither party to it intended that Article 4 would cover the area extending eastward all the way to the present intersection of the Saudi-Oman-Yemeni borders. This was the case, especially in light of the fact that Saudi Arabia, like Yemen, had a separate dispute with Great Britain over the same territory.[36]

After apparently reversing their stand on the geographical scope of Article 4, Yemen and Saudi Arabia agreed to restrict their disagreement on this issue to the exact location of the almost 300 boundary markers, particularly the starting and finishing points of the 1934 boundary. Yemen rejected the Saudi assertion that the Treaty of Taif and its Article 4 delimited or otherwise covered the border area east of Jabal Al-Thar, which extended to the intersection of the Yemeni-Saudi-British Aden borders. Third, the two parties were in dispute over the Saudi boundary with the former South Yemen. Both states refused to compromise on what amounted to their respective minimal territorial claims, represented for Saudi Arabia by the Hamza Line and for Yemen by the British Riyadh (or Independence) Line.

By 1997, it became apparent to Saudi and Yemeni officials alike that the issues involved in the border conflict were too complicated to be resolved by a piecemeal approach entrusted to technical joint committees with limited negotiating power. The prospect of reaching a comprehensive settlement seemed to require a joint political decision taken at the highest level of government in both countries.

The 1997 Lake Como Agreement

In the summer of 1997, a high-powered Yemeni delegation led by President Saleh held secret border talks with Prince Sultan, the Saudi deputy premier and defense minister, at the latter's summer residence at Lake Como in northern Italy.[37] The two sides reached a provisional agreement, proposed by Yemen and accepted by Saudi Arabia, which constituted a major breakthrough in the prolonged border negotiations.[38]

Although both countries acknowledged the agreement's existence, only Yemen appeared forthcoming in making some of its main provisions public. In retrospect, the main territorial stipulations of the 1997 Como Agreement were adopted with minor modifications in the subsequent Treaty of Jeddah, signed on June 12, 2000.[39] Under its terms, Yemen agreed to relinquish its historical claim to a vast area stretching to parallel 23 and encompassing the Saudi southern provinces of Asir, Jizan and Najran, as well as most of the Empty Quarter. Instead, it proposed a comprehensive boundary, starting from the official point of intersection of the Yemen-Oman boundary at coordinates 19 degrees North 52 degrees East, and extending in a westerly direction until it connected with the starting point of the Treaty of Taif's 1934 boundary at Jabal Al-Thar.[40]

The proposal was accepted by Saudi Arabia, which, according to Yemen, agreed to cede sovereignty over almost all of its disputed land and maritime territory outside the 1934 boundary settlement. The Como boundary, at least as understood by the Yemeni government, ran well to the north of the 1955 Riyadh or Independence boundary. The latter more or less represented Yemen's minimum boundary claim, which Saudi Arabia had hitherto vehemently rejected.[41]

However, the Como Line appeared to be a political compromise between competing and overlapping minimum boundary claims by Yemen and Saudi Arabia in the disputed eastern border area. It fell far short of Yemen's maximum boundary claim, based on historical and legal rights embodied in either the geographic notion of Greater Yemen or the relatively less ambitious 1914 Violet Line.

Yemen effectively conceded that it was difficult to legally defend the historical basis of its territorial claim against Saudi Arabia, which it had abandoned while negotiating and concluding its border treaty with neighboring Oman in October 1992.[42] Yemen also appeared to recognize that its position on the 1955 Riyadh Line would be legally untenable. Until 1995 at least, successive Yemeni governments in both North (royalist and republican) Yemen and South Yemen were on record that they had repeatedly rejected the Violet Line of the 1914 Convention[43] and the 1955 Riyadh Line derived from it as illegal.[44]

Moreover, the British government had consistently rejected calls to submit the border dispute with either Saudi Arabia and Yemen over the boundary of the former Aden Protectorate to international arbitration. This was on the advice of the British

Foreign Office's legal advisor, who concluded that both the 1914 Violet Line and the 1955 Riyadh Line contravened international law and that neither boundary could legally be defended before any arbitral or judicial body.[45]

Likewise, Saudi Arabia also prejudiced its position vis-à-vis Yemen by agreeing in its 1990 border treaty with Oman that their boundary ended at 19 degrees North 52 degrees East, well north of the 1935 Hamza Line. If Yemen would raise the issue of the Saudi-Omani boundary, which was probable, Saudi Arabia would find it difficult to legally maintain its boundary claim against Yemen, which corresponds to the Hamza Line in an area that is demographically and geographically homogeneous, even though Saudi Arabia had abandoned it in its 1990 treaty with Oman.[46]

Moreover, Saudi Arabia appeared to have further prejudiced its legal position with respect to the 1935 Hamza Line in the 1948 'Abr agreement, which it concluded with the British government to "regulate the relations of border tribes."[47] Under its terms, Saudi Arabia had disclaimed authority over the tribes, such as the Sei'ar, Karab and Manahil, and recognized them as part of the Hadhramout in the Aden Protectorate.[48] Most of these tribes and their homelands were situated well north of the Saudi Hamza claim line, itself based almost exclusively on tribal allegiance, as manifested in the tribe's payment of the Islamic taxation of *Zakat* to the Saudi rulers.

Controversy over the 1934 Boundary

Just after the Como agreement appeared to finally settle the Saudi-Yemeni border conflict, a serious dispute arose between the two countries over the exact position of the 1934 boundary, as delimited in Article 4 of the Treaty of Taif and demarcated in the joint commission's 1937 report attached to the treaty.[49] From the Yemeni point of view, the Treaty of Taif and its attached demarcation report indicated that the 1934 boundary started at the top of Jabal Al-Thar.[50] The boundary ended on the Red Sea coast at the northern tip of Duwaimah, which formed R'as Al-Mu'waj, referred to in Article 4 of the Treaty of Taif.[51] For its part, Saudi Arabia argued that the boundary started on top of the true *Jabal Al-Thar*, a shorter hill located near the one claimed by Yemen.[52] In the Saudi view, the land terminus point was at the southern tip of the Duwaimah island, "three-quarters" of which belonged to Saudi Arabia.[53]

The two sides were completely aware of the full implications of the exact location of the 1934 line on the allocation of sovereignty over the disputed land and sea territory. Thus, the Yemeni government, according to President Saleh, made its acceptance of the Como territorial settlement conditional on Saudi Arabia's unconditional acceptance of Yemen's position on the location of the 1934 boundary.[54]

In July 1998, frustrated by this serious obstacle to the acceptance of the Como agreement and the lack of progress in the work of the MOU joint committees, the Yemeni government issued a strongly-worded public statement that implicitly threatened to reject both the Treaty of Taif and the MOU, and reiterated the fact that Yemen was still "sticking to all its legal and historical rights."[55] The statement also repeated Yemen's accusation that Saudi Arabia continued to "slice off" Yemeni territories as part of a policy "to create a situation of *fait accompli*," and called for an end to the "Saudi presence in Yemen's territories."[56]

In response, the Saudi government issued a statement of its own, in which it denied occupying Yemeni territory and accused Yemen of waging anti-Saudi "propaganda activity." The Saudis also reaffirmed the validity of the Taif Treaty's 1934 boundary. Moreover, in July 1998, Saudi Arabia sent a note to the UN and the Arab League, belatedly protesting that the border agreement concluded between Yemen and Oman in 1992 constituted an encroachment on Saudi "rights and interests."[57]

The Saudi-Yemeni differences on the exact location of the starting and finishing points of the 1934 boundary soon deteriorated into military confrontations along their common border. The most serious incident occurred at the end of July 1998 over the Red Sea coastal area of Duwaima, the disputed location of the 1934 boundary's land terminus.[58]

The Sana'a Protocol of 1998

In an attempt to diffuse the tense situation in mid-1998, Yemen and Saudi Arabia held urgent talks in the Yemeni capital, Sana'a. At the end of the talks, on July 29, 1998, they signed a joint declaration. The Sana'a Protocol reaffirmed, yet again, the two parties' commitment to the validity of both the Treaty of Taif and the 1995 MOU. It also established a timetable to speed up the work of the various joint boundary committees formed under the terms of the provisions of the MOU. In addition, a joint military committee was formed to prevent further armed clashes and ensure that no new installation, settlement or military presence was established near the disputed border area.[59] The Sana'a talks aimed at overcoming the impasse that had been reached. Despite more than 100 meetings of the MOU's joint border committees since 1995, and countless letters exchanged between the leadership in the two countries, no tangible result had been achieved.[60]

Saudi Arabia consequently proposed the conclusion of a separate border agreement, based on the 1997 Como Agreement, while postponing negotiations over the exact location of the beginning and the end of the 1934 line to a later date. Yemen rejected this piecemeal approach and reiterated its long-standing position that the whole land and sea border issue had to be negotiated and settled as one indivisible unit, either bilaterally through a comprehensive agreement or through third-party arbitration.[61]

Dissatisfied with the slow pace of the MOU negotiations, the Yemeni government asked Saudi Arabia to agree to a time limit for negotiations, after which the two parties would be allowed to pursue other venues to settle their dispute.[62] More specifically, the Yemeni foreign minister warned that if negotiation "continues at the same pace and manner, arbitration will be the only viable alternative."[63] The parties, disinclined to choose international arbitration, both agreed to third-party mediation by the United States, which finally succeeded in persuading them to reconcile their differences and reach a settlement of their long-standing conflict.

US Mediation and the Signing of the Treaty of Jeddah

The United States, motivated by its own concern for regional stability in the Arabian Peninsula, traditionally enjoyed significant leverage with both Saudi Arabia and Yemen. The United States appeared to be the ideal mediator, whose good offices would be welcomed, if not indeed sought, by the political leadership of both governments as a means of ending their long and fruitless quest to resolve their border conflict.

During a visit to both countries in early 2000, Edward S. Walker, U.S. Assistant Secretary of State for Near Eastern Affairs, declared that the United States "would like to see" the Saudi-Yemeni border dispute solved. He expressed U.S. willingness to do "anything" that would "help the process" of reaching Saudi-Yemeni agreement on boundary issues, which the American government had "favored for years." Such an agreement, he declared, was essential to the stability and economic development of the region. He sought to "understand the position" of both governments during his talks with the two Arabian states and "the state of play within the negotiations."[64]

Aware of the special US leverage over the Saudi government, Yemen wholeheartedly welcomed the American role in the border dispute as "the only state able" to provide concrete assistance in that direction.[65] The Yemeni president explained in detail to the U.S. envoy the Yemeni position on the border dispute, including the "knot" of the Como issue concerning the exact beginning and end of the 1934 boundary.[66]

The US mediation effort appeared to have a decisive role in the eventual final settlement of the Saudi-Yemeni border conflict, at least from the Yemeni point of view.[67] Shortly after the American emissary's visit, Crown Prince Abdullah, the *de facto* ruler of Saudi Arabia, led a high-powered delegation on his first ever visit to Yemen in May 2000, the purpose of the visit ostensibly being to participate in the tenth anniversary of the Yemen Republic's unification. Also attending the celebration was a special envoy of U.S. president Bill Clinton, who declared in the Yemeni capital that the American government had made "its position clear" to Saudi Arabia, that it supported "settlement (of the border issue) by pacific means" and called on both parties to "speed up" their ongoing bilateral efforts to resolve their dispute peacefully.[68] The Yemeni president declared afterwards that there was a "convergence" between Yemeni and Saudi views in this respect, which he intended to consolidate during his visit to Saudi Arabia in the following month.

3

The International Boundary Treaty of Jeddah on June 12, 2000

On June 11, 2000, almost two weeks after the Saudi Crown Prince's visit, the Yemen president, heading a high-level delegation, arrived in the Saudi Red Sea port of Jeddah. Less than 24 hours later, the two governments made a surprise joint announcement, rather unexpectedly, that they had reached a formal settlement of their long-standing border dispute.[1] On June 12, 2000, the foreign ministers of Saudi Arabia and Yemen signed "the treaty of international land and maritime boundaries" between the two countries,[2] known informally as the Treaty of Jeddah. The treaty was ratified by both countries on June 26 in accordance with their respective procedures,[3] and came into operation on July 4, 2000, the date of the formal exchange of the instruments of ratification.[4]

Soon afterwards, the two contracting state parties jointly deposited copies of the ratified treaty instruments as a public document at the secretariats of the UN[5] and the League of Arab States.[6] Both parties praised the treaty as an "historic" achievement, which provided "a peaceful and satisfactory" settlement of the border issue that would be preserved by "future generations" of the two countries' populations and serve the quest for regional peace and security.[7]

Salient Features of the Treaty of Jeddah

The Treaty of Jeddah consisted of two complementary components. The first component was the 1934 Treaty of Taif, as well as the 1995 MOU reaffirming it. The Treaty of Jeddah expressly incorporated these documents without modification or amendments, including the 1934 boundary as demarcated in the 1937 report. The second component defined the previously undetermined common land and maritime border area not covered by the Treaty of Taif.

The latter, which sought to build on the previous agreements, was an all-embracing document regulating all components of bilateral Saudi-Yemeni relations. In addition to establishing peace and creating a territorial settlement, it contained provisions and attachments on political, military, security, economic, social and cultural ties between the two signatories. In effect, if not in law, the new Treaty of Jeddah, by integrating the 1934 treaty instead of abrogating it, constituted a subsidiary border agreement to resolve border issues that the earlier instrument had failed to address.

Before reconsidering the main provisions of the Treaty of Taif, it would perhaps be more appropriate to first outline the terms of the new treaty, which was intended to be the final territorial settlement of the Saudi-Yemeni border dispute.

Boundary Demarcation in the Treaty of Jeddah

The territorial provisions contained in the Treaty of Jeddah constituted, as stipulated in its preamble, a comprehensive and "permanent settlement of the maritime and land border issue" between Saudi

Arabia and Yemen.[8] The boundary, defined in Article 2 as "final and permanent," stretched from the intersection of the Yemeni-Omani-Saudi land boundaries in the east at 19 degrees North with 52 degrees East, extending in a western direction to the land terminus on the Red Sea coast at the coordinates 16 24 14 8 North 42 46 19 7 East. From there it extended in a southwestern direction to the intersection of the Yemeni-Eritrean-Saudi maritime border in the Red Sea.[9]

The Treaty of Jeddah consisted of five articles and four attachments. Three of the attachments contained sets of geographical coordinates, while the fourth dealt with tribal grazing and watering rights in the eastern common border area. In the Preamble and Article 1 of the Treaty of Jeddah the two contracting states reaffirmed as "valid and binding on both parties the 1934 Treaty of Taif and its annexures, including the boundary demarcation reports (of the 1937 joint commission) attached to it," as well as the 1995 MOU confirming it.[10]

Article 2 of the Treaty of Jeddah divided the maritime and land borders between Yemen and Saudi Arabia into three segments corresponding to the three disputed border sectors.[11] The first segment covered the 1934 boundary already defined in Article 4 of the Treaty of Taif and largely demarcated in the boundary report of the 1937 joint commission.[12] Article 2 of the Treaty of Jeddah also provided precise modern geographical coordinates not mentioned in the Treaty of Taif. These coordinates indicated the physical markers forming the 1934 boundary, starting from the Red Sea coastal boundary marker called the quay of R'as Al-Mu'waj, north of the Radif-garad crossing, and extending in an eastern direction to the marker on Jabal Al-Thar in the east.[13]

If one links the geographical coordinates between the starting point and endpoint, as indicated in Appendix 1 of the treaty, it should produce a line corresponding to the 1934 boundary. Article 2 of the Treaty provided that the Saudi or Yemeni nationality of villages straddling the line would be determined in accordance with the provisions of the Treaty of Taif, "including tribal pedigree," and the boundary would then be amended accordingly.[14]

Article 3(1) provided for a joint commission and a survey company to demarcate the entire area and boundary. With respect to the 1934 boundary, it committed the two signatories to "adhere precisely to the distances and directions between the points and other descriptions" contained in the Treaty of Taif's 1937 demarcation report.[15]

The second border segment dealt with the remaining and previously undefined land sector not covered by the Treaty of Taif. It ran from Jabal Al-Thar to the intersection point of the Saudi Arabian, Yemeni and Omani borders, in accordance with a set of geographical coordinates described in Appendix 2 of the treaty.[16]

The third and final segment concerned delimitation of the maritime boundary between the adjacent states in the Red Sea. Article 2(c) defined R'as Al-Mu'waj as the land terminus from which the maritime boundary extended westward to the open sea, along a set of geographical coordinates listed in Appendix 3.[17]

Article 3 also provided for the creation of a joint Saudi-Yemeni commission to supervise the implementation of the Treaty of Jeddah's provisions. The implementation process would include the demarcation of the whole land and maritime boundary by a qualified surveying company and the production of detailed land maps that would, upon formal signature, become an integral part of the treaty as the official boundary maps.[18]

The Treaty of Jeddah declared certain areas on either side of the boundary to be demilitarized zones. Article 4 confirmed Article 5 of the Treaty of Taif, which prohibited any military installations within five kilometers of the demarcated 1934 boundary.[19] Regarding the second land sector extending eastward from Jabal Al-Thar, paragraph 5 of Appendix 4 stipulated that the distance be fixed at 20 kilometers on either side of the boundary.[20] Any military presence in this zone would be restricted to mobile police patrols armed with ordinary weapons.[21]

Appendix 4 of the Treaty of Jeddah declared the demilitarized zone in the second land segment of the boundary to be a common pasture area for local shepherds on both sides, their grazing and watering rights defined in accordance with "the prevailing tribal customs" and their movement across the border regulated by special permits and mutually agreed border posts.[22] If extractable natural wealth of commercial quality were discovered along their common land boundary line, the two countries would negotiate the necessary agreements for joint exploitation.[23]

Pursuant to Article 3 of the Treaty of Jeddah, the two state parties appointed their respective ministers of the interior as co-chairmen of the joint commission and entrusted them with the task of implementing the provisions of the Treaty of Jeddah. The commission held its first meeting at the end of July 2000, during which it agreed to a timetable for implementation that should not "exceed two years as a maximum." During this period the two sides would complete the dismantling of their military installations and the withdrawal of troops in a way jointly agreed upon in the Treaty of Jeddah.[24] The commission's work would also commence with the demarcation of the maritime area, which, since it was only used by a few seasonal fishermen, would clearly be the least controversial and complex of all three border sectors to resolve.[25]

Territorial Compromise in the Treaty of Jeddah

The relevant provisions of the Treaty of Jeddah represented a compromise between the two contracting states with respect to their rival legal and territorial claims. For Saudi Arabia, the gain was more legal than territorial. It had finally realized its long-sought principal demand for Yemen's explicit recognition, in a fresh agreement, of the validity of the Treaty of Taif of 1934, specifically Article 2, which established Saudi sovereignty over the regions of Asir, Jizan and Najran, and Article 4, which created a boundary defined as final and permanent.

In the eastern sector, Yemen recognized Saudi sovereignty over the border towns of Al Kharkhair, Al Wadi'ah and Sharorah. Previously, Yemen had claimed that these towns were removed from the territory of the former South Yemen without justification. In return, Saudi Arabia renounced almost all its other claims and conceded Yemen's substantial territorial claims.

Under the Treaty of Jeddah, Yemen acknowledged that it would "regain" more than 50,000 square kilometers of economically viable maritime and land territory,[26] which subsequently formed the northern part of the "new oil map of Yemen."[27] In the east, Saudi Arabia abandoned its 1984 boundary claim based on the modified 1955 Hamza Line in favor of a line redrawn well to the north of both the 1955 Riyadh boundary and the 1997 boundary, which had been proposed by Yemen and already accepted by both parties in the Como agreement.[28] Under this territorial adjustment, Yemen "regained" more than 40,000 square kilometers of a potentially oil- and gas-rich area extending from the intersection of the Saudi Arabian, Yemeni and Omani borders in the east to Jabal Al-Thar in the west.[29]

In this sector, the northwestern direction of the agreed line briefly swerved in order to skirt the southern limits of the border towns of Al-Kharkhair, Al-Wadi'ah and Sharorah,[30] before resuming its original course. The treaty established that these towns would remain under Saudi sovereignty, while awarding most of the disputed central area between Radm al-Amir or Al-Akhasheem and Jabal Al-Thar to Yemen.[31] A joint Saudi-Yemeni military committee issued a statement in which Saudi Arabia pledged to withdraw from and "return" to Yemen by February 2001 the territory that came under Yemeni sovereignty in terms of the treaty.[32] This implied Saudi recognition that the area had been Yemeni all along.

With respect to the first land segment, which covers the 1934 boundary from Jabal Al-Thar to the Red Sea coast, Saudi Arabia acceded to Yemeni demands regarding the exact location of the boundary's starting point and endpoint. By placing the starting point on the peak of Jabal Al-Thar, Yemen not only gained more populous and fertile land, but also a strategic commanding position over Saudi territory in the area, which included the ancient city of Najran. As for the land terminus point on the Red Sea coast,[33] under the terms of the treaty its location was repositioned northward on the southern edge of the Saudi port of Al-Muwassam.[34]

The new location was well to the north of both the contested Saudi and Yemeni claims, as shown in their respective official maps.[35] As a result, Yemen not only gained complete sovereignty of the disputed coastal Duwaimah islet, but also obtained a strategically and economically important coastal strip with an even longer coastline than it had originally consented to under the Como agreement.

Moreover, under the new agreement, the new location of the land terminus became the baseline from which the maritime boundary line was drawn in a western direction, increasing Yemeni territorial waters by around 4,000 square kilometers and giving Yemen sovereignty over several important islands, including the strategic Dhu-Hirab, which controlled free and direct access to the open sea and international shipping lanes.[36]

As a result of the treaty, Saudi Arabia abandoned its last chance of gaining a sovereign territorial corridor to the Arabian Sea and thus a direct outlet to the Indian Ocean in return for a substantial territorial concession. Since Saudi Arabia is a semi-enclosed country, its trade, including oil exports and basic food imports, could only be routed through the financially costly and politically dangerous maritime Straits of Hurmuz, Bab Al-Mandab and Suez. With regard to this issue, Saudi Arabia found it difficult to obtain from Yemen what it could not obtain or did not ask for in its previous 1974[37] and 1990 border agreements with the United Arab Emirates and Oman respectively.[38]

Moreover, by accepting the 1955 Riyadh Line as the general basis of its 1974 and 1990 boundary agreements with the UAE and Oman respectively, Saudi Arabia found it exceedingly difficult to legally sustain its arguments against the validity of the same boundary in its negotiations with Yemen. The 1995 Riyadh Line, originating in the south-eastern corner of Arabia, stretched in a westerly direction to connect with the starting point of the 1934 line. Saudi Arabia had so consistently and publicly committed itself to the 1934 line that it had precluded any further opportunity to secure direct access to the open seas.

Finally, it is important to note that the territorial settlement between Saudi Arabia and Yemen as embodied by the Treaty of Jeddah remains incomplete. The two states still have to conclude agreements with both Oman and Eritrea to fix the exact location of the two points marking the starting point and endpoint of their agreed land and maritime boundary. Although both Saudi Arabia and Yemen have already concluded and ratified separate border treaties with Oman, Saudi Arabia has yet to follow Yemen in concluding a maritime boundary agreement with Eritrea.[39]

4
Yemeni Arguments regarding the Treaty of Taif

Until the signing of the Treaty of Jeddah, Saudi Arabia and Yemen held sharply different views on the status of the Treaty of Taif under international law. The territorial boundary provisions in the 1934 treaty were the legal basis for Yemeni arguments that the Treaty of Taif was legally void or voidable and for Saudi counter-arguments that it was a legally valid international agreement.

When the legal status of the Treaty of Taif and its territorial settlement no longer seemed in question because of the terms of the Treaty of Jeddah, the two state parties adopted distinctly different and potentially risky legal positions on the fundamental purpose and object of the new treaty. Saudi Arabia appeared to regard the Treaty of Jeddah, like the Treaty of Taif, as essentially, even if not exclusively, a territorial agreement establishing a boundary defined as final and permanent.

The Yemeni government, on the other hand, repeatedly declared in its public statements that its acceptance of the Treaty of Taif was only made with reference to the implementation of the non-territorial, but equally important, provisions under which Saudi Arabia granted "special privileges" to Yemeni nationals in perpetuity. These privileges covered rights of entry into Saudi Arabia and residency and work in Saudi territory.

To compound this legal dilemma, the Treaty of Taif further contained some controversial, ambiguous and downright contradictory provisions that, separately or together, had been used at one time or another by both parties to question the treaty's legal status. Since the Taif Treaty had been incorporated without change into the Treaty of Jeddah, the legal status of the latter and the boundary settlement created under it could also be questioned in future by one of the parties. Consequently, the same legal arguments used by both parties to support their opposing claims regarding the status of the Treaty of Taif could be used by them with respect to the Treaty of Jeddah.

Yemen's Legal Case

Yemen has never fully accepted the Treaty of Taif, its dissatisfaction being evident since the conclusion of the Treaty after the short 1934 war with Saudi Arabia, which Yemen lost. A dispatch from the British Legation in Taiz, Yemen's second largest city, reported that the Yemeni government:

> …consider that the Treaty was negotiated and signed under duress and they have not been satisfied with some parts of the frontier as it has been defined.[1]

This attitude towards the treaty remained unchanged and hardened with the passage of time, particularly after the 1962 revolution. In Yemen's view, the Treaty of Taif was legally voidable, if not void *ab initio*.

The historical and legal circumstances under which the Treaty of Taif was formulated have provided the Yemeni government with many strong legal arguments against the Treaty of Taif. The arguments are that the treaty is void or voidable, either in whole or in part, as a result of procedural matters. It is also void or voidable in terms of legal doctrines applied to the legal and historical circumstances of the treaty's conclusion and subsequent implementation.[2]

The following is an appraisal of arguments that Yemen has used or could have used under international law to invalidate the Treaty of Taif. These arguments could be developed primarily on the basis of the customary and positive law on treaties, contained *inter alia* in the relevant provisions of the Vienna Convention on the Law of Treaties (VCT).[3]

Duress and Coercion of the State Representative

Yemen has always maintained that the Treaty of Taif was signed under duress because of the threat and actual use of force.[4] Neither the Yemeni state nor its representatives gave their consent voluntarily, and hence the resulting treaty was null and void under customary and conventional law.

According to Yemen, King Ibn Saud detained the Yemeni negotiating delegation, headed by Ahmad Al-Wazir, in order to force Imam Yahya, the king of Yemen, to sign a treaty containing provisions that had been mainly drafted by King Ibn Saud himself. The latter issued "an ultimatum" to this effect to the Yemeni king, who "did not reply."[5] The Saudi action, according to the Yemeni argument, constituted personal coercion of the Yemeni government's negotiator. Hence, within the context of the principles of international law, the treaty was null and void.

This argument was largely based on article 51 of the VCT, which declared that consent procured by "coercion of the state representative through acts or threats directed against him" is "without any legal effect."[6] Many distinguished scholars assert that for the consent to be valid it must be expressed freely and voluntarily by each of the contracting parties.[7]

However, there are two basic problems with this argument, both in terms of historical evidence and law. First, there is no historical record that independently confirms Saudi Arabia's confinement of Yemeni representatives. On the contrary, Saudi Arabia's own records tend to refute the Yemeni allegations. According to these records, the Yemeni representative, Mr. Al-Wazir, appeared to give his consent freely in the presence of various mediating Arab delegates when signing the Treaty of Taif, which the Yemeni king himself voluntarily ratified soon afterwards.[8] As mentioned before, his son and successor, Imam Ahmad, who as the heir apparent strongly opposed the treaty, further confirmed it by personally initiating its formal extension in 1953.

Second, the relevant article of the VCT does not expressly declare that treaties resulting from coercion are void. Instead, article 51 merely describes such treaties as "without any legal effect." This might render the Treaty of Taif voidable, rather than void *ab initio*. The *onus probandi* or burden of proof that the state representative had been coerced would fall on the accusing party, in this case Yemen. Within the same principles of international law, Yemen would have to obtain the agreement of the other party, that is, Saudi Arabia, to discuss the issue of the treaty's voidability. In the meantime, the treaty itself would continue to be valid. The Yemeni government had not formally sought Saudi agreement in this respect nor had Saudi Arabia refused to grant it.

The Treaty of Taif as an Imposed Treaty

According to Yemen, Saudi Arabia was the aggressor when it declared a war in 1934 that Imam Yahya could not avert and eventually lost.

As a result, Yemen, the vanquished party, was forced to sign the Treaty of Taif on the victor's terms, and in the process it relinquished claims to the territory in dispute.[9]

According to Yemen, Saudi Arabia violated the provisions of all existing international conventions prohibiting state acts of aggression, including the 1919 Covenant of the League of Nations, the 1928 General Treaty for the Renunciation of War, otherwise known as the Kellogg-Briand Pact, the 1945 UN Charter and the 1969 VCT. The Treaty of Taif was concluded under the coercion of Saudi military power. As a result, the treaty was imposed and void *ab initio*.

However, the rationale behind the Yemeni claim must be assessed in terms of the tenets of international law. To claim that the Treaty of Taif is void or voidable, the claimant has to show that rules to that effect existed in international law at the time of the conclusion of the treaty.

Legal scholars have differed over the issue of whether modern laws against force are *retroactive*. Article 52 of the VCT, for example, stipulates as follows: "A treaty is void if its conclusion has been procured by the threat or use of force in violation of the principles of international law embodied in the Charter of the United Nations." Some scholars assert that modern law against the use of force is retroactive. According to this view, the Treaty of Taif and the resulting acquisition of territory claimed by Yemen were procured by force at a time when force was illegal, that is, under the 1928 Kellogg-Briand Pact. As a result, the treaty was null and void when it was signed.

It is generally believed that, by inserting this provision, the state parties intended to make the clause applicable to treaties concluded before the adoption of the Charter of the United Nations. The provision in the UN Charter particularly relevant to article 52 is found in article 1(1), which states that the purposes of the United Nations Organization are:

> To maintain international peace and security, and to that end: to take effective measures for the prevention and removal of threats to the peace, and for the suppression of acts of aggression or other breaches of the peace, and to bring about by peaceful means, and in conformity with the principles of justice and international law, adjustment or settlement of international disputes or situations which might lead to a breach of the peace.[10]

This clause clearly prohibits all "acts of aggression or other breaches of the peace." In this sense, the Treaty of Taif, at least from Yemen's point of view, clearly was in breach of the principles embodied in the UN Charter.

However, the principle's retroactive effect, a point of serious contention among legal scholars, should be examined cautiously. Some authors, particularly those from the (former) USSR, eastern European and Third World countries, supported its retroactivity. Some international court cases have also upheld clauses contained in treaties that were clearly intended to have a retroactive effect, such as the decision of the PCIJ in the 1924 Mavrommatis Palestine Concessions Case[11] and in the 1973 Fisheries Jurisdiction Case.[12]

However, neither the 1945 UN Charter nor Article 52 of the 1969 VCT makes any reference to the retroactivity of their relevant provisions with regard to treaties concluded before 1945. Moreover, the provisions of the VCT, in terms of its own Article 4, are not applicable to treaties concluded before the VCT came into force. Thus, the principle of intertemporal law prevails in the case of the

Treaty of Taif, which was concluded in 1934, and the treaty should be evaluated accordingly.[13]

The doctrine of intertemporal law says that the validity of legal rights must be determined within the terms of the law in effect when the rights were created. Thus, a treaty that was concluded legally according to the international law in effect at the time remains valid.

The international prohibition of the use of force, which constitutes the basis of the "principles of international law" mentioned in article 52 of the VCT, is old enough to make the 1934 Treaty of Taif voidable. Immediately after the end of the First World War, several steps were taken to de-legitimize aggression by imposing strict limitations on the right of states to wage war.[14] The Covenant of the League of Nations, adopted on June 28, 1919, and the Treaty for the Renunciation of War as an Instrument of National Policy,[15] the so-called Kellogg-Briand Pact, which was adopted on August 27, 1928, were the most significant documents imposing legal restrictions on war before the acceptance of the UN Charter on June 26, 1945.

The Covenant of the League of Nations obliged member states to submit their disputes to the Permanent Court of International Justice, established by the Covenant, or the Council of the League of Nations.[16] Under the Briand-Kellogg Pact, contracting state parties agreed to renounce war as a means to settle international disputes and as an instrument of national policy.[17]

Both conventions were in effect during the Saudi-Yemeni war and the subsequent Treaty of Taif. However, neither of the two states was a member of the League or subject to the provisions of the Covenant at that time, at least in terms of conventional law. Unlike Yemen, Saudi Arabia, as the consulted records show, did in fact join the Briand-Kellogg Pact on December 10, 1931, about two years before the outbreak of the Saudi-Yemeni war.[18]

In terms of the Covenant of the League and the Kellogg-Briand Pact in particular, to which Saudi Arabia was a party, the 1934 war constituted an act of aggression by Saudi Arabia against Yemen. In terms of contemporary international law principles, this state of affairs apparently made the resulting Treaty of Taif void *ab initio.*

However, there are several legal problems inherent in such a contextual interpretation. First, since the Covenant of the League was applicable only to member states, neither Saudi Arabia nor Yemen was subject to its provisions. The Covenant had a limited membership, restricted largely to Western and Central Europe, and could hardly be said to amount to customary law and an international norm binding on non-member states.

In addition, the Covenant and the Pact did not by themselves create a legal obligation on member states to refrain from exercising military pressure. Indeed, member states of the League were permitted to resort to war when the Council of the League failed to reach a unanimous recommendation on the resolution of conflict between them. Likewise, the Kellogg-Briand Pact provided only for a "general prohibition of war" and was restricted to war *stricto sensu.*[19] The only valid legal reasoning in terms of intertemporal law would be to argue that the Treaty of Taif and subsequent territorial concessions claimed by Yemen were null and void at the moment of signature, because they had been procured by force at a time when war was illegal under the Kellogg-Briand Pact, to which Saudi Arabia was a party.

There are, however, at least equally strong arguments by the dominant school of authors. They reject both the legal effect of intertemporal law and the retroactivity of those articles in the 1945 UN Charter and the 1969 VCT that relate to treaties emanating from state coercion and aggression and concluded before the adoption of the UN Charter in 1945. In their opinion, to give legal precedent to the 1945 UN Charter and the 1969 VCT in terms of *lex posterior derogat priori* would be tantamount to rejecting the validity of a whole host of peace treaties concluded at the end of the Second World War. These treaties would include the Potsdam Declaration of July 26, 1945, whose acceptance by Japan formally ended the war,[20] and most if not all previous peace treaties, including those concluded long after the Second World War and the adoption of the UN Charter.

The Iraq-Kuwait boundary agreement imposed by the UN Security Council in 1991, and the forced territorial settlements of NATO and the European Community in the former Yugoslavia in the 1990s were also post-war peace treaties imposed by the victors on the vanquished, whose consent was secured involuntarily. The coercion involved did not negate the validity of the treaty. The defeated state could still refuse to consent to the treaty, but this would only lead to the extension of hostilities or the state of war.

The consent of the vanquished state is required to make a peace treaty valid, but there are some instances when it is not required. The consent of Japan was required to secure the 1951 peace treaty, while the consent of defeated Italy was not necessary for the Italian peace treaty to come into effect after the Second World War.[21] Yemen, as discussed before, freely consented when its representative, Mr. Al-Wazir, in the presence of various Arab mediating delegations invited by Yemen itself, signed the Treaty of Taif. The Imam ratified the treaty soon afterwards and his son and successor, Imam Ahmad, initiated and signed the treaty's extension in 1953.[22]

Likewise, the Treaty of Taif, being a treaty concerned with peace and territory, and regardless of the conditions under which it was concluded, is as valid as any other similar peace treaty. Its validity is not affected by subsequent changes in customary and positive international law, according to which the use of force is illegal and treaties obtained by force void.

Finally, Yemen may face an equally strong argument, consistently asserted by the Saudis, that the 1934 war, far from being an aggressive war as Yemen claims, was in fact defensive in nature and forced upon Saudi Arabia by Yemen's acts of armed aggression against its territories. According to Saudi Arabia, Yemen occupied the "neutral" Najran area in 1931 and then invaded the southern mountain areas of Al-'Abadilah, Fayfa and Bani-Malik, all of which formed part of the former independent Idrisi emirate that had been legally and peacefully incorporated into Saudi territory by the 1926 Mecca Treaty.[23]

During the Saudi-Yemeni negotiations that preceded the war of 1934, Ibn Saud repeatedly accused Yemen of being the aggressor and occupier. He demanded an immediate Yemeni withdrawal from Saudi territory, the evacuation of Yemeni forces from the disputed Najran area and the conclusion of a boundary treaty that would in effect mean Yemen's recognition of Saudi Arabia's southern boundary as indicated in the 1926 Mecca agreement. When Imam Yahya asked for the clarification of Saudi demands regarding, *inter alia*, the issue of frontiers, Ibn Saud gave the following reply:

> First, the settlement of the issue of the boundary…in the same legitimate manner agreed upon by fixing the points along the boundary line on either side starting from (the Red) sea coast to the hinterland…evacuation of the mountain areas and elimination of all acts violating the concluded covenants…Second, the settlement of the issue of Wadi Najran where our soldiers and your soldiers are stationed, in a manner honorable to both sides. By one of two ways (1) the return of Najran to its previous status of neutrality…(2) show us an alternative method whereby the pride and rights are maintained…[24]

Significantly, Ibn Saud referred in another instruction to his acceptance of the Imam's suggestion to "set a fixed period of twenty years for the treaty."[25] This indicated that the controversial Article 22 of the Treaty of Taif was later inserted at the request of the Yemen government, most likely as a basis for reclaiming the territory ceded under the treaty if circumstances changed.

The Fixed Duration Provision as a Ground for Termination

Yemen claimed that ownership of the Yemeni territory ceded to Saudi Arabia had, by virtue of the fixed duration clause in the Treaty of Taif, become "suspended" during this period. With the expiration of the period, the territory would automatically revert to Yemen, its original owner.[26] Thus, the Treaty of Taif, according to the Yemeni position at the time, was legally terminated in 1974 through the expiration of the first and only formal 20 year extension agreement signed in 1953. Such a termination would appear to be in accordance with international law, Article 22 of the Treaty and the provisions of the VCT.[27] Article 54(a) of the VCT provides that the "termination of a treaty or the withdrawal" of a state party may take place "in conformity with the provisions of the treaty."

Most modern treaties contain provisions for their termination upon the expiration of a fixed period, unless the contracting parties agree to extend it in accordance with its provisions for extension.[28] Nevertheless, under Article 67(2) of the VCT, the termination of such treaties must first be communicated to the other party in a formal instrument, without necessarily giving any reasons other than a reference to the impending termination of the treaty under the terms of its own provisions and given the absence of any wish to renew it.

Accordingly, the Treaty of Taif, in the light of conventional law, would have been terminated according to its Article 22.

Subsequent Yemeni governments did not agree to Saudi proposals for formal extension agreements of the Treaty of Taif upon the expiration of the first renewal agreement of 1953. They did, however, sign the 1973 MOU and the 1995 MOU, which expressly recognized the Treaty of Taif as a continued valid and binding agreement on both parties.

As discussed earlier, Yemen rejected the Saudi argument that the Memorandums of Understanding constituted at least second and third extension agreements of the Treaty of Taif. The Yemeni government argued that the two instruments did not constitute international agreements on future rights and obligations. A joint press statement in 1973 stated that the Treaty of Taif was made without legal authority: the MOU was a legal "framework," not an agreement to conclude a final border treaty in future. Nevertheless, as far as is known, Yemen had always refrained from taking the legal steps necessary to terminate the treaty, by communicating written notification to the Saudi government as required by the VCT.

The reasons behind Yemen's reluctance appeared to be political and legal. Being essentially a peace treaty, the termination of the treaty under Article 22 or on any other legal ground would have meant an almost immediate renewal of the state of hostility that both countries seemed inclined to avert. In addition, Yemen was apparently aware of the inherent weakness of the legal basis for invoking the fixed duration clause to seek the termination of treaties stabilizing territorial rights and obligations, such as the Treaty of Taif.

Positive law and recent international decisions, as discussed in this study, confirm the notion of the finality and permanency of boundaries established under agreements, irrespective of the legal circumstances under which they were concluded. The VCT expressly states that certain principles cannot be invoked to terminate treaties establishing boundaries. In the Chad versus Libya Case, the ICJ upheld the sanctity and finality of boundaries established only implicitly by the 1955 treaty, which, like the Treaty of Taif, contained a fixed duration clause of 20 years. Furthermore, Article 22 of the Treaty of Taif might have been rendered legally inoperative, if not amended, by the 1973 Saudi-Yemeni joint communiqué that confirmed the "finality and permanency of the boundary line" contained in Article 4 of the treaty, and by the 1995 MOU's reaffirmation of the same treaty as being "valid and binding on both parties."

As far back as 1992, the Yemeni government itself appeared to recognize the fixed duration clause's legal irrelevance to the Treaty of Taif. The Yemeni Deputy Premier and Foreign Minister, Mr. Adbulkarim Al-Iryani, was asked in an interview whether the Yemeni government intended to inform the Saudi government of its desire to terminate the treaty by not renewing it upon its expiration later that year, according to the Islamic lunar calendar. He replied that "no decision" had been made in this regard. He then proceeded to give what could be viewed as Yemen's realistic and legal assessment of the Treaty of Taif in 1992:

> Neither side has the right to say that they do not want to renew the treaty. The legal text is clear; there is no text that stipulates this. Talking about the right of renewal or otherwise is an incorrect interpretation of the agreement. It does not say that any party has the right to renew or not to renew. The agreement says that at the end of twenty years, or six months prior to that time, either party has the right to inform the other of its desire to review any of the agreement's clauses. If one party does not inform the other of this, then the treaty will still be valid and remain so even six months after one party has expressed its desire to review the agreement. This means that this could take place 100

years from now. It is not linked to 20 years as is commonly thought. This is the text of the agreement. One is committed to the text.[29]

This public comment by a senior Yemeni official amounted to an implicit official recognition by Yemen of the indefinite validity of the Treaty of Taif, a few years before the ICJ award on the 1994 Chad versus Libya Case and the 1995 MOU. In practice, at least, both the Saudi and Yemeni governments seemed to regard the 1973 and 1995 Memorandums of Understanding as constituting second and third renewal agreements of the Treaty of Taif, since the dates of the two instruments corresponded very closely to the second and third expiration date of the 1934 treaty according to the Gregorian calendar.

A New Peremptory Norm (*Jus Cogens*) and the Taif Treaty

It can also be argued that the 1934 Taif Treaty violated the doctrine of *jus cogens*. Under the provisions of the VCT, a treaty becomes void if it contravenes this principle of international law. Article 53 of the VCT states that this is the case if a treaty, at the time of its conclusion, violates a peremptory norm of general international law, which Article 53 defines as a rule universally accepted and recognized by the world community of nations. Prohibition of slavery, piracy and genocide are examples of the rule of *jus cogens*. Most authors also agree with Article 64, which states that if "a new peremptory norm of general international law…emerges, any existing treaty which is in conflict with that norm becomes void and terminates."[30]

The Treaty of Taif contains several provisions that potentially contravene the international law principle of *jus cogens*. Yemen had a potential claim that the doctrine of *jus cogens* was applicable to the Treaty of Taif, since the treaty had been the result of the Saudi declaration of war in 1934, an act that was prohibited under intertemporal law, the Covenant of the League and the Kellogg-Briand Pact to which Saudi Arabia adhered in 1931. In addition, the 1963 International Law Commission (ILC) expressly confirmed in a draft article the "retroactive effects (of the new peremptory norm) on the validity of treaties concluded prior to the establishment." However, the effect of *jus cogens*, the ILC qualifies, "is not to render it void *ab initio*, but only from the date when the new rule of *jus cogens* is established."[31] More significantly, in a revised draft of the same article, the 1966 ILC commented that it:

> ...cannot therefore be properly understood as depriving of validity *ab initio* a peace treaty or other treaty procured by coercion prior to the establishment of the modern law regarding the threat or use of force.[32]

Based on the context if not the text of Article 64 of the VCT on *jus cogens*, the Treaty of Taif, a treaty establishing peace and a territorial boundary, can be declared voidable, but probably not void *ab initio*. Article 64 of the VCT is further restricted by Article 71. In effect, Article 71 stipulates that the voidability of a treaty will not affect the rights, obligations and legally established situations, that is the state of peace and territorial settlement, created by the implementation of that treaty before its presumed abrogation, provided that the continuation of those subsequent rights, obligations and situations do not in themselves operate against the emergent peremptory norm of general international law. The continuation of the state of general peace and territorial rights established by the Treaty of Taif can hardly be considered a situation operating against an emergent *jus cogens*.

In addition, the retroactive effect of Article 64 appears to be in conflict with the non-retroactive effect of Article 4, which stipulates that the provisions of the VCT apply "only to treaties which are concluded by states after the entry into force of the present Convention with regard to such States." Hence, its provisions on *jus cogens* appear to be inapplicable to the 1934 Treaty of Taif.

Moreover, Yemen's potential argument about the voidability of the Treaty of Taif through application of the doctrine of *jus cogens* can be constrained further by the equally powerful legal doctrines of acquiescence and estoppel. Saudi Arabia may and perhaps did invoke the principle of estoppel, in that Yemen's post-1934 behavior constituted acquiescence in the legality of the Treaty of Taif and "estopped" Yemen from rejecting its validity *ab initio*.

Saudi Arabia's Revocation of Exemptions Granted to Yemeni Nationals

According to Yemen, the Saudi government's repeal in 1960 and 1990 of exemptions granted to Yemeni nationals in Saudi Arabia violated certain provisions in the Treaty of Taif. They were embodied in Article 4, side letter number 5 and the 1936 General Agreement between the Kingdom of Saudi Arabia and the Kingdom of Yemen Concerning the Settlement of Matters relating to the Subjects of the two Kingdoms, which was attached to the Treaty of Taif.[33]

From the Yemeni point of view, unilateral Saudi revocation of the privileges granted in these letters constituted a material breach of the Treaty of Taif. Yemen consequently retained the right to renounce the treaty in part or in whole. In an emergency session, the Yemeni cabinet referred to these exemptions as the "legitimate and acquired rights of the sons of the Republic of Yemen."[34] Soon afterwards, "responsible Yemeni sources" were quoted in press reports as saying that the Yemen government not only "opposed the renewal" of the treaty that was due shortly, but would soon:

> ...demand termination of the Treaty of Taif and would also demand compensation from Saudi Arabia for its support of the royalists during the civil war, as well as for losses suffered by Yemenis who left Saudi Arabia following the rescission of their special privileges.[35]

However, there appears to have been serious legal flaws in this argument. The relevant paragraph in Article 4, the side letter and the 1936 General Agreement each expressly provided for reciprocal cross-border movement privileges related to inter-tribal customary visitation rights and social interaction. These provisions were restricted to Yemeni and Saudi subjects inhabiting the common border area along the 1934 line.

Article 4, which defined the 1934 boundary, expressly restricted these privileges to certain tribal elements inhabiting particular border areas. It granted the disputed starting point of the 1934 line to Saudi and Yemeni subjects who belonged to the Wa'ilah tribe that inhabits the hinterland area of the Najran valley at and immediately east of the Jabal Al-Thar.[36]

Side letter number 5 concerning the movement of subjects between the two countries was exchanged and signed on the same date as the Treaty of Taif. During the negotiation of the treaty the Saudi Arabian plenipotentiary, Prince (later King) Khalid ibn Abdulaziz, signed the following letter, which was acknowledged by the Yemeni plenipotentiary, Abdullah Ahmad al-Wazir:

> On the occasion of the signature of the Treaty of Taif between our Kingdom and that of Yemen, I hereby confirm our agreement concerning the movement of subjects of the Kingdom of Saudi Arabia and of the Kingdom of Yemen in

the two countries, that the movements at present shall continue as in the past until a special pact is drawn up between the two countries regarding the method that both governments jointly agree to adopt with regard to the regulation of movement, whether for pilgrimage or for trade, or for any other purpose or vocation. I await your reply in the positive in this regard.[37]

Yemen's claim of a material breach by Saudi Arabia as a ground for its right to renounce the Treaty of Taif appears to have its basis in the relevant articles of the VCT, which stipulate that the material breach of a bilateral treaty is a ground for terminating it. Article 60(1) states that a "material breach of a bilateral treaty" by one of the parties "entitles" the other "to invoke the breach" as a reason for terminating it "in whole or in part." However, Article 60(3) requires that the breach must be material and that the violated provision must be "essential to the accomplishment of the object or purpose of the treaty."

In the Yemeni view, the Saudi action of revoking these privileges constituted a serious breach of those articles that were essential to accomplish the purpose of the Treaty of Taif. Thus, the action granted Yemen the right to unilaterally terminate the whole treaty. Furthermore, the right of the injured party to invoke material breach as a ground for terminating or suspending the operation of the treaty is only one of several options. The wronged party can also claim "compensation" instead of or in addition to exercising its rights under Article 60 of the VCT.[38]

However, due to several reasons, it was exceedingly difficult for Yemen to legally sustain this argument. Even if the Saudi action supposedly constituted a serious breach, it was difficult to build a sound legal case presenting either document as being "essential to the accomplishment of the object and purpose" of the Taif Treaty.

Article 4, which established the 1934 boundary, is essential to the accomplishment of the object and purpose of the Treaty of Taif, but its last paragraph related to cross-border privileges would probably not be relevant. If this were the case, Yemen, as alleged by Saudi Arabia, would be in serious breach of the article, since it has consistently refused to carry out its obligations in this respect.[39]

The six side letters attached to the Treaty of Taif could be regarded as reservations stated by Saudi Arabia and accepted by Yemen. As a rule, reservations included in a treaty do not constitute an integral part of the treaty under conventional law, unless expressly specified. Second, Saudi Arabia clearly made its acceptance of the treaty's validity conditional on Yemen's consent to the first letter, which deals with the evacuation of troops and the repatriation of prisoners.[40] No similar express condition is stated in the remaining letters, whose texts merely imply that both contracting parties had no intention to this effect.[41]

Even if the Saudi revocation of privileges granted to the Yemenis constituted a breach under Article 60 of the VCT, it nevertheless was not a sufficiently "material" breach of a provision of the Treaty of Taif to be deemed essential to the accomplishment of its fundamental object. This purpose presumably was a cessation of hostilities, the establishment of perpetual peace and a permanent territorial settlement. The only viable legal option available to Yemen was to seek some form of mutually agreed compensation instead of the Taif Treaty's termination.

Finally, there appeared to be no legal link in the text of Article 4, side letter number 5 and the 1936 General Agreement to the exemptions that the Saudi government had long granted to Yemeni nationals. These documents only regulated the century-old movements of subjects across the boundary of 1934 and in the areas adjacent to the boundary. They involved certain privileges that were granted reciprocally and exclusively to Saudi and Yemeni subjects inhabiting the common border area. These border privileges did not appear to be affected by the Saudi government's decision in 1990 to cancel exemptions granted to Yemeni nationals residing in Saudi Arabian territory. Moreover, Saudi Arabia maintained that Yemen, unlike the Saudis themselves, had consistently failed to fulfil its legal obligations regarding these privileges.

Thus, the relevant provisions in Article 4, side letter number 5 and the 1936 General Agreement appeared to form a non-integral and non-essential part of the Treaty of Taif that did not have any legal link with the Saudi exemptions annulled in 1990. The Yemeni government seemed to be aware of the apparent legal weakness of its case. When questioned in an interview in 1991 on whether the Saudi rescission of privileges was a "legal Saudi measure," Mr. Al-Iryani declined to depict the action "as illegal and failed to assert any legal right of Yemenis to their former privileges."[42]

Rebus sic stantibus as a Ground to Terminate a Treaty

Yemen could invoke the doctrine of a fundamental change of circumstances *(rebus sic stantibus)* as a ground to withdraw from or terminate the Treaty of Taif. However, Saudi Arabia could also invoke the doctrine under different circumstances. According to this principle of international law, a state's obligations as expressed by a treaty cease when a fundamental change of circumstances occurs after the treaty's conclusion. Article 62 of the VCT sanctions this principle and lays down the rules under which *rebus sic stantibus* can be invoked as "a ground for terminating or withdrawing from a treaty."[43]

One eminent author gives an example of this rule, namely, when a state party to a treaty has a "change of government" deemed incompatible with the basis of the treaty.[44] Yemen could claim that the 1962 revolution and the 1990 unification, and the aftermath of these events, constituted a fundamental change of circumstances that gave it the right to terminate or withdraw from the Treaty of Taif.

Saudi Arabia, not Yemen, was the first party to question the legal status of the Treaty of Taif. In 1960, two years before the revolution in Yemen, Saudi Arabia had formally decided to unilaterally abrogate the Treaty of Taif. It invoked the principle of a fundamental change of circumstances as a ground for its decision. In the summer of 1960, it was reported that Saudi Arabia had notified the Yemeni government of its decision to "abrogate" the Treaty, citing Yemen's decision to join the political union of the United Arab Republic between Egypt and Syria, which was perceived at the time as an anti-Saudi axis.[45] Saudi Arabia had reportedly invoked the principle of *rebus sic stantibus* as a reason for its intended renunciation of the treaty.[46] The Yemeni foreign ministry confirmed receipt of a Saudi note renouncing the "whole" treaty, with the consequence that "Yemenis would now be free to reassert their territorial claims to certain of the border area."[47]

However, after being personally approached by Imam Ahmad of Yemen, the Saudi Arabian government soon rescinded its decision to terminate or otherwise amend the Treaty of Taif and the two states agreed to return to "the *status quo ante*."[48] Under positive law, the Saudi renouncement of its earlier intention to terminate the Treaty was possible with the consent of the other party and provided that the rescission would take place before the earlier declared intention had any legal effect.

However, in reality Yemen (and Saudi Arabia) would both find it exceedingly difficult, if not impossible, to apply the principle of a fundamental change of circumstances as a basis for terminating or withdrawing from the Treaty of Taif. Customary and conventional law excludes "treaties fixing boundaries from the operation of the principle" of fundamental change of circumstances "in order to avoid an obvious source of threats to the peace."[49] Article 62(2)(a) of the VCT is more explicit, for it states:

> A fundamental change of circumstances may not be invoked as a ground for terminating or withdrawing from a treaty: if the treaty established a boundary;

It is for this reason that the application of this principle is largely confined to non-territorial treaties[50] or perhaps non-territorial provisions in territorial treaties, for example the provisions regarding fixed duration or special privileges in the Treaty of Taif.

On May 26, 1990, the Yemen Arab Republic (North Yemen) and the People's Democratic Republic of Yemen (South Yemen) united into "a single international entity" called the Republic of Yemen.[51] Given the doctrine of the inviolability of international boundaries[52] in Article 62 of the VCT and the 1978 Vienna Convention on the Succession of States in Respect of Treaties, Vienna (VCS), this act of political and legal unification cannot be invoked by Yemen or by Saudi Arabia as a fundamental change of circumstances. In fact, the new Republic of Yemen declared that it was "a party to all treaties which had been concluded by one of the predecessor states with effect from the date which the first of the two had become party to the treaty."[53]

Article 4 of the Treaty of Taif, which established the 1934 boundary, constituted the *raison d'être* for Saudi Arabia to maintain the validity of the treaty, and for Yemen to want to terminate it. Thus, it was unlikely in the aftermath of unification that either of the two countries would have attempted, out of political and legal considerations, to alter the *status quo* of their common borders by invoking this doctrine or any other legal principle.

The 1926 Mecca Agreement

The Treaty of Taif was based on the 1926 Mecca Agreement, under which the Idrisi emirate, claimed by Yemen, became a Saudi protectorate.[54] At the time of signing the Mecca agreement, both the Idrisi[55] and Ibn Saud,[56] unlike the independent Imam of Yemen, each maintained the relationship of a protectorate with Great Britain.[57]

It could thus be argued that the 1926 agreement was null and void because it was ultimately an unequal "colonial" treaty procured through coercion and duress brought to bear upon the Imam Idrisi. He, like Ibn Saud himself, lacked the legal status under international law to conclude treaties concerning territories claimed by Yemen. Since the provisions of the Treaty of Taif, particularly those pertaining to territorial cession and boundaries, were expressly based on the 1926 agreement, the Treaty would as a consequence likewise become null and void.

First, the Yemen claim, made by Imam Yahya himself, was that the Idrisi and their territory had "always been Yemeni" and that Idrisi "occupation" would not change such a historically and legally established status.[58]

Second, Yemen also asserted that the Idrisi, though not Ibn Saud, never possessed international legal personality under international law and thus lacked the jurisdiction and capacity to cede territory by means of a treaty. Consequently, the Treaty of Taif, or at least Article 4, which pertains to territorial cession, was void because it was based on the 1926 treaty, which lacked legal force from the moment of its signing.

Third, Yemen might have claimed that the 1926 Mecca Treaty was void because it was an unequal "colonial" treaty signed under duress and unfair conditions.[59] To support this claim, Yemen could have pointed to the circumstances under which the Idrisi signed a letter dated October 16, 1930, that transferred the remaining control of internal affairs of the emirate to King Ibn Saud, the colonizing power.

Yemen could also have pointed to the ensuing rebellion in 1931 by the local population against Saudi rule and the subsequent Idrisi escape to Yemen.[60] More significantly, Yemen could have argued that Article 2 of the Treaty of Taif indicated an implicit Saudi recognition that the Idrisi emirate, in whole or in part, had once been Yemeni. The article required that King Ibn Saud:

> ...abandons by the treaty any right of protection or occupation or others he claims over the territory which by this treaty belongs to Yemen and which formerly was in the possession of the Idrisi and others.[61]

However, these Yemeni arguments, actual or hypothetical, would face serious obstacles with regard to the legal status of the Idrisi emirate. Apart from Yemen's shaky historical claim, there was no evidence in the available historical sources of Yemen's effective control of the Idrisi territory in the period immediately before 1926, nor evidence of the Idrisi's legal allegiance to the Imam of Yemen.[62] For example, Article 2 of the Treaty of Taif required that both Imam Yahya and Ibn Saud abandon "any right he claims in part or parts of the other party's territory beyond the definite boundary defined in the text of this treaty." It also called on Yemen to abandon any right to claim "in the name of Yemen unity" or any other notion the territory that once "belonged to the Idrisi or the Al-'Aayidh or in Najran and Yam country" and had become part of Saudi Arabia under the Treaty of Taif.[63]

[74]

Furthermore, prior to the conclusion of the 1926 Mecca Treaty, the Idrisi emirate appeared to meet at least the minimum requirements for an independent state with a legal personality in the context of international law at that time. It had concluded international if unequal treaties with Turkey, Great Britain and Italy.[64] In fact, the British government acknowledged in a report that before 1926 the Idrisi emir was "an independent ruler exercising sovereignty over certain territories in South-West Arabia."[65]

The Idrisi emirate's complete surrender of Asir to Ibn Saud in the Mecca agreement of 1926 resulted in Asir legally becoming a part of Ibn Saud's dominions, since the Idrisi "ceased to possess the status of an international person under international law."[66] More important, in 1933 the British government formally informed the Italian government, Yemen's ally, that "Asir has become, both *de facto* and *de jure*, an integral part of Ibn Saud's territories" as a result of the 1926 and 1931 agreements. As a result, Britain decided to grant a formal expression of its recognition of Ibn Saud's sovereignty over Asir (including the Farasan Islands)."[67]

Thus, in the opinion of the British government:

> [Saudi] sovereignty over these territories was effective in international law and did not require any express or implied recognition by any other Power to render it legally complete and effective.[68]

In this international view, or at least the British government's view, the Yemeni occupation in 1932 of the mountainous areas of Bani Malik and Jibal Fayfa, part of the former Idrisi territory, could have constituted aggression as Ibn Saud asserted. As a result, the subsequent 1934 war became an act of self-defense sanctioned by international law at the time, namely the Covenant of the League of Nations and the Kellogg-Briand Pact, which Saudi Arabia had joined in 1931. Thus, the resulting Treaty of Taif would not be an unequal, imposed colonial treaty, nor could any of its provisions relating to territorial settlement be subsequently void or voidable.

The Effect of the Doctrines of "Ancient Title" and "Reversion"

Yemen's legal arguments against the validity of the Treaty of Taif were based almost wholly on the notion of "ancient title as the principal source of Yemen's territorial sovereignty" over virtually the entire southern half of the Arabian Peninsula. This area constituted the historical *bilad al-yaman* of the land of Yemen or *al-yaman al-kubra* (Greater Yemen), that extended far beyond the 1934 boundary of the Treaty of Taif and deep into Saudi territory.[69]

Successive Yemeni governments have continuously propagated the approach of "historical rights" emanating from pre-Islamic and medieval times since at least the end of the First World War. The current Yemeni president and senior officials repeatedly emphasized that this notion was central to Yemen's territorial claims against Saudi Arabia. They insisted that any bilateral negotiations would have to "guarantee the legal and historical rights" of Yemen as known to every Arab.[70] Specifically, they demanded the "return," not only of the Saudi southern administrative provinces of Jizan, Asir and Najran, which had been ceded under the Treaty of Taif,[71] but also the territory beyond the "very large geographical expanse of Al-Rub' al-Khali (the Empty Quarter)."[72]

However, since at least 1992, certain acts to which Yemen had been a party seriously weakened the notion that historical and legal rights provided a basis for its territorial claim against Saudi Arabia. Yemen had employed the historical argument in its boundary dispute with Oman. However, negotiations leading to the conclusion of the 1992 Yemen-Oman border treaty were distinctive in that they were not based, as Yemen publicly admitted, on Yemen's geographical notions of a "Greater Yemen" or on preceding historical agreements like the 1914 Violent Line or the 1965 agreement.[73]

As a result, Yemen would have great difficulty in sustaining its arguments about historical and legal rights against Saudi Arabia after it had abandoned them as the basis of its border agreement with Oman. This argument was further undermined by a public statement of the Yemeni president in Saudi Arabia. During an official visit after the conclusion of the 1995 MOU, he declared Yemen's readiness to negotiate a comprehensive boundary agreement with Saudi Arabia that would be based on neither "historical nor *de facto*" considerations.[74]

The Implications of the Eritrea-Yemen Arbitration Award of 1998

However, it was the Eritrea-Yemen Arbitration Award of 1998 that expressed Yemen's notion of historical and legal rights best. The Eritrea-Yemen Arbitration Award (First Phase) of October 9, 1998, articulated the Yemeni emphasis on its legal and historical rights as the main source of its territorial claim against Saudi Arabia.[75] The tribunal expressed its "awareness" that Yemen "attaches great importance" to the question of "ancient title" and has "especially …placed 'particular' emphasis on historical title as a source of territorial sovereignty" over the historical "*bilad el Yemen*," or Greater Yemen.[76] In the Agreement of Arbitration, Yemen asked the Tribunal to resolve the question of the disputed Red Sea islands' sovereignty "…on the basis in particular of historical titles" and to expressly apply "the principles, rules and practices of international law…in confirmation of its ancient title."[77]

Yemen also asserted that it "enjoys an ancient title" to the islands in question. The "title existed before the hegemony of the

[77]

Ottoman Empire and indeed emanates from medieval Yemen."[78] Furthermore, Yemen contended that the notion of "ancient title" still existed in international law at the time of the Ottoman defeat in 1918. Thus, when Turkey renounced its territorial title in the Treaty of Lausanne in 1923, along with the title to the islands, "the right to enjoy that title in possession 'reverted' to Yemen."[79]

Similarly, Yemen's territorial claim against Saudi Arabia was based on the notion of "ancient title" emanating from Arab and Islamic history and the doctrine of "reversion" under which the right of possession of former Ottoman "territorial titles" in the Arabian Peninsula (i.e., the area south of the Violet Line in the 1914 Anglo-Ottoman Convention) would have reverted to Yemen in 1923.[80]

However, in its judgement, the Tribunal rejected Yemeni notions of historical title and reversion, a conclusion that would have direct and serious legal ramifications for its territorial claim against Saudi Arabia. While recognizing the concept as a principle of international law, the Tribunal stated that Yemen was unable to prove the "actual existence" of an historical title. In this respect, Yemen had failed:

> ...to persuade the Tribunal that the history of the matter reveals the juridical existence of an historic title, or of historic titles, of such long-established, continuous and definite lineage to these particular islands...as would be a sufficient basis for the Tribunal decision.[81]

Moreover, it rejected as a "sheer anachronism" Yemen's attempt to link "the modern Western concept of a sovereignty title" to "medieval" notions like *bilad al-yaman* (land of the Yemen).[82]

With respect to the doctrine of "reversion," the Tribunal was inclined to support the Eritrean assertion that there was not "such a doctrine of reversion in international law."[83] It added:

> ...nor is the Tribunal aware of any basis for maintaining that reversion is an accepted principle or rule of general international law. Moreover, if the doctrine were valid, it could not apply in this case. That is because there is a lack of continuity. It has been argued by that in the case of historic title no continuity need to be shown, but the Tribunal finds no support for this argument.[84]

Commenting on the decision, a prominent author wrote:

> The Tribunal rejected Yemen's argument for a reversion of title on the basis of law and facts. Yemen had not established that the doctrine was part of international law, nor had it persuaded the Tribunal that historic *bilad el Yemen* had exercised territorial control over coastal areas and perforce over the islands.[85]

Significantly, the Tribunal, in explaining its rejection of Yemen's historical title argument, also seriously undermined the basis of Yemen's land and maritime territorial claims against Saudi Arabia. Firstly, it distinguished between the "territorial extent" of the Ottoman "*vilayet* (province) of Yemen" and that of the Imamate of Yemen "as an autonomous entity" within the former.[86] Secondly, it stipulated that during "the entire period" from the middle of the 19th century until 1925, the Imam of Yemen had "neither sovereignty nor jurisdiction over the Tihamah and the Red Sea coasts."[87]

The Imam administered "an exclusively landlocked territory, limited to high mountains" within the terms of his 1911 Da'an accord with the Ottoman government.[88] The Tribunal's statement thus constituted an international legal precedent undermining the basis of Yemen's claim to the Asir coastal territory of the Idrisi emirate and its islands, including the Farasan archipelago[89] and the eastern hinterland in the Najran valley.

Interestingly, the Tribunal acknowledged the possible relevance of an historical argument in the case of a nomadic territory, so that the claimant could theoretically demonstrate "socio-political power over that geographic area" to secure title.[90] It was the "relatively recent history of use and possession that ultimately proved to be a main basis" of the Tribunal's decision to award sovereignty over the disputed islands of the Hanish group and Zugar to Yemen. In making its award, the Tribunal was guided, *inter alia*, by the legal precedents of the Palmas[91] and Minquiers and Ecrehos[92] cases.

The disputed territory in the Saudi-Yemeni eastern land border area that was not covered by the Treaty of Taif could still be regarded as *res nullius*. It was indeed defined as *res nullius* by the British government's legal advisor back in 1934, albeit privately.[93] Any party would be free to acquire a sovereign title to the territory by occupation or prescription through the simple presumption of *effectivités* or an international plebiscite, as in the case of the Western Sahara.[94]

Saudi Arabia appeared to have a better chance of establishing a solid claim to territorial sovereignty over at least part of the disputed territory outside the border area of the 1934 line by applying any of these principles. Since the 1930's, as acknowledged by Yemen, Saudi Arabia unilaterally acquired and continuously held large parts of territory in the disputed territory, including the Sharorah, Al-Wadi'ah and Al-Kharkhair areas. Saudi Arabia could claim to have demonstrated "socio-political power" in these areas since at least the 1950's. Such power perhaps amounted to a peaceful display of the functions of the state and other means of possession gradually consolidated into a title by prescription, or by revealing the legal existence of an historical title to most if not all of the disputed eastern hinterland.[95] This might explain the Yemeni government's consistent refusal to agree to a referendum on self-determination for the indigenous tribal population as an option to settle the sovereignty question in the disputed territory.[96]

On the other hand, the whole legal basis of this strong hypothetical Saudi argument could be seriously jeopardized by the 1948 'Abr agreement. Saudi Arabia itself had apparently sought and concluded this agreement with the British government to "regulate relations of border tribes" between Saudi Arabia and the then Aden Protectorate.[97]

Within the terms of this agreement, Saudi Arabia recognized certain tribes as forming part of the Protectorate's province of Hadhramout.[98] The position of most of these tribes and their tribal homelands was well to the north of Saudi Arabia's own Hamza Line, which was drawn exclusively on the basis of tribal allegiance. Since Saudi Arabia and the British Aden government had consented to the 1948 agreement, this agreement would apparently continue to be binding on both Saudi Arabia and Yemen (as the successor state) and, as a result, immensely enhance the latter's legal claim to the territory in question.

This analysis is supported by the recent international case of Qatar versus Bahrain (Merits) of March 2001. In its judgment, the ICJ ignored the presumption of the *effectivités* principle and awarded the sovereignty of the disputed Hawar island to Bahrain, a judgement primarily based on the 1939 British "decision" consented to by both parties, even though the Court acknowledged that it was "a political" decision, not an arbitral one, lacking the authority of *res judicata* but not devoid of legal effect.[99]

Apparently encouraged by the potential impact of the Eritrea-Yemen Award on its possible arbitration case involving Yemen, the Saudi government, long opposed to arbitration as a method to settle the border dispute, suddenly reversed its stand on the issue. Shortly after the announcement of the award, the Saudi foreign minister declared that his government had communicated to Yemen its "readiness to submit" the border dispute to judicial or abitral arbitration if that was "what Yemen wanted." Moreover, he added confidently, "the Yemenis, under all circumstances, would not obtain better results from arbitration than they would under friendly (bilateral) negotiations."[100]

Yemen's traditional position had been to opt for a unilateral request for arbitration to settle its border dispute with Saudi Arabia. Fully recognizing the potentially adverse impact of the Eritrea-Yemen Award of 1998 on its territorial dispute with Saudi Arabia, Yemen quickly began to back down from this position.[101]

Indeed, subsequent Yemeni statements appeared to suggest that the Yemeni government did not only decide to abandon arbitration as a viable option, but actually deemed the whole idea as undesirable. Shortly after the announcement of the decision, Yemen's president declared that neither Yemen nor Saudi Arabia "has the inclination to resort to arbitration" and that both would seek to settle their border issue amicably and among themselves.[102] The Saudi government, never enthusiastic about arbitration as a method, welcomed Yemen's change of heart. It declared that the two states had "ruled out" arbitration and that the "political leadership" in both countries had decided to bilaterally reach "a final settlement" of their long-standing dispute.[103]

5

Saudi Arabian Arguments regarding the Taif Treaty

The Treaty of Taif as a Valid International Agreement

The 1934 Treaty of Taif and its attachments, including the 1936 General Agreement and the 1937 demarcation report, appear to conform to the definition of international "convention" contained in the VCT. Thus, it constitutes "an international agreement concluded between states in written form and governed by international law."[1] Article 2(1)(a) of the VCT defines a treaty as:

> ...an international agreement concluded between States in written form and governed by international law, whether embodied in a single instrument or in two or more related instruments and whatever its particular destination.[2]

However, there exists an exception to this rule regarding both the contracting parties, the Treaty of Taif and all the relevant subsequent Saudi-Yemeni agreements concluded before the Convention's entry into force in 1980. Firstly, neither Yemen nor Saudi Arabia is a signatory or party to the VCT. Secondly, Article 4 of the VCT stipulates that the Convention "applies only to treaties which are concluded by States after the entry into force of the present Convention with regard to such states."[3]

Since the Treaty of Taif was signed and ratified in 1934 by two non-signatories to the VCT, it would appear that the treaty, as a matter of law, is subject to international customary law rather than conventional law as embodied in the articles of the VCT. However, the VCT itself was but a codification of existing rules of customary law. Consequently, in evaluating the legal status of the Treaty of Taif, in addition to the articles of the VCT itself, the relevance of the other customary sources of international law stipulated in Article 38 of the ICJ Statute becomes equally apparent.[4]

The Treaty of Taif is both a peace and boundary treaty creating territorial rights and obligations. Thus, customary law doctrines like the *priori* principle of *pacta sunt servanda* and the rule of *rebus sic stantibus*, both codified in the VCT, are relevant to the Treaty of Taif as a whole and in relation to specific clauses pertaining to cession of territory, the creation of a boundary, definite duration and renunciation.

The Capacity to Conclude the Treaty of Taif

Historically, in terms of customary law, the conclusion of treaties is the prerogative of a sovereign state only and constitutes one of the most fundamental characteristics of its sovereignty. In recognition of the general international rule, Article 6 of the VCT stipulates that every "state possesses the capacity to conclude treaties."[5] Both Saudi Arabia and Yemen were sovereign states as defined by the prevailing customary law. Hence, each possessed the capacity to enter into the negotiation and conclusion of the Treaty of Taif and related agreements.

The Authority to Conclude the Treaty of Taif

In an era of absolute monarchical rule and slow communication, which was the case in both Saudi Arabia and Yemen at the time of concluding the Treaty of Taif, it was of paramount importance to confirm the authority of the representatives of the state or states with which one wished to negotiate and conclude a treaty. This authority was established by the reciprocal production of a formal document entitled "full power," which designates a person or persons to represent the state for the purpose of negotiating, concluding, signing and sealing a binding treaty.[6] Like their European counterparts of previous centuries, the Treaty of Taif was concluded, both in form and in substance, in the name of King Ibn Saud and Imam Yahya, as an expression of the personal will of two absolute rulers.

The preamble of the Treaty of Taif specifically states that King Ibn Saud and Imam Yahya had entrusted their respective representatives, mentioned by name, with documents indicating their "full power." These documents were properly produced for reciprocal examination and mutually acknowledged by negotiators.[7] It states that King Ibn Saud of Saudi Arabia and Imam Yahya of Yemen:

> ...have accorded to their respective representatives (mentioned by name) full powers and absolute authority; and their above-mentioned representatives, having perused each other's credentials and found them to be in a proper form, have, in the name of their Kings, agreed upon the following articles contained in the Treaty of Taif.[8]

Mutual Consent to be Bound by the Treaty of Taif

Article 22 of the Treaty of Taif lists ratification as the means by which both Saudi Arabia and Yemen would mutually express their consent to be bound by the treaty, which was signed by the authorized representatives of Saudi Arabia and Yemen on May 20, 1934. The article specified that the treaty would be "ratified and approved by their Royal Majesties" and that it "shall come into force as from the date of the exchange of the instruments of ratification." It was duly sealed by the rulers of the two states, and the instruments of ratification were formally exchanged between the two parties at the Yemeni port city of Hodiedah on June 22, 1934.

Ratification also happened at the municipal level, in the constitutional sense. Both Saudi Arabia and Yemen were at the time absolute hereditary monarchies lacking any form of legislating parliamentary system. King Ibn Saud and Imam Yahya were the heads of state invested with the full authority to ratify treaties under Article 7(2) of the VCT, which they duly exercised with regard to the Treaty of Taif. Thus, it appears from the available evidence that the legal requirements relating to negotiation, signature and ratification by a formal exchange of notes had been satisfied, which consequently made the Treaty of Taif legally binding upon the two parties.

The Treaty of Taif's Entry into Force

In conformity with Article 24 of the VCT, Article 22 of the Taif Treaty specified that it "shall come into force from the date of exchange of the instruments of ratification." The instruments of ratification were formally exchanged between the two parties on June 22, 1934. On this date the treaty entered into force, except for the termination of the state of war, which, pursuant to the same article, took effect on the date of signing of the treaty, May 20, 1934.

The legal force of the Treaty of Taif was displayed by the subsequent administrative and legal measures carried out by both parties in the execution of the treaty's terms. Yemen formally recognized Saudi sovereignty over regions previously claimed by Yemen. Saudi Arabia, in turn, pulled back its troops from Yemeni territories, including the town of Hodiedah, which was occupied in the course of the war, to the boundary drawn in Article 4 of the treaty. The boundary was demarcated by the 1937 joint commission established by both countries under the same article. The 1953 exchange of notes extending the duration of the Treaty, the 1973 Joint Communiqué, the 1995 MOU and the 1998 protocol all expressly reaffirmed joint Saudi-Yemeni recognition of the validity of the Treaty and the boundary indicated in it.

Registration of the Treaty of Taif

Neither Saudi Arabia nor Yemen was a member of the League of Nations in 1934 or at any time.[9] Thus, neither was under the obligation in Article 18 of the League of Nations' Covenant to register the Treaty of Taif with the League's Secretariat.[10] In addition, the Treaty was concluded long before the UN came into existence. When both states became signatories to the UN Charter in 1945, neither of them sought to register the treaty subsequently.

Nevertheless, a treaty that is not registered with the UN is not void under the terms of the Charter. Article 102(20) merely specifies that "no party to any such treaty...may invoke that treaty...before any organ of the United Nations," that is the ICJ.[11] The Charter remains silent on the retroactive effect of these provisions, but there are several international court cases that recognized the validity of pre-Charter agreements as evidence.

The Side Letters and the 1936 General Agreement

As discussed above, the Treaty of Taif also contains in its attachments six side letters exchanged between the plenipotentiaries of Ibn Saud and Imam Yahya and signed on the same date as the treaty. Under international law, these side letters seemed to constitute formal declarations or reservations made by Saudi Arabia, which were acknowledged and accepted by Yemen.[12]

Saudi Arabia expressly made its acceptance of the treaty's validity conditional upon Yemen's consent to the first letter, which deals with the evacuation of troops from Tihamah, the exchange of prisoners and the extradition of wanted Idrisi rebels that had revolted against Saudi rule and had sought refuge in Yemen. It also required that "the contents of this treaty be kept secret and not be published by either party" until after the safe withdrawal of Saudi troops in the Tihamah.[13]

However, no similar explicit condition was made by Saudi Arabia with respect to other side letters like numbers 5 and 6, which deal with the all-important issue of the "movement of subjects." The Yemeni government invoked this issue in the aftermath of the 1990-1 Gulf War as justification for renunciation of the Treaty of Taif.

Saudi Arguments: The Legal Basis of the Treaty of Taif

Modification Clauses of the Treaty of Taif: Articles 8 and 22

Most treaties sanctioned by customary and conventional law contain provisions relating to duration, modification and revision as a peaceful means of change in international relations.[14] Article 22 of the Treaty of Taif contains clauses providing for the modification and duration of the treaty's provisions and the method of their implementation. It states that the treaty "shall remain in force for a period of twenty complete lunar years," during which it may not be subject to any form of modification. However, it "may be renewed or modified during the six months preceding the expiration of its force." If the treaty is not renewed or modified by that date, it will automatically "continue to remain in force for six months after the date of notice given by one party to the other party of his desire to modify it."[15]

Although the article implied that the whole treaty would cease to be in force six months after the notification, the text does not expressly use any term equivalent to the Arabic word for termination, renunciation or suspension. Article 22 clearly refers to *tajdid* (renewal) and *ta'dil* (modification), which is clearly not the same thing as termination or cancellation.

In addition, Article 8 of the Treaty of Taif appears to open the door for the two states to conclude bilateral agreements in the future to peacefully settle any dispute that may arise, whether within or outside the framework of the treaty. It requires that the two parties "mutually undertake to refrain from resorting to force in all difficulties between them, and to do their utmost to settle any disputes which may arise between them, whether caused by this treaty or the interpretation of all or any of its articles or resulting from any other cause, by friendly representations."[16]

The 1973 Joint Communiqué, 1995 MOU and the Sana'a Protocol

The 1953 renewal agreement was concluded by an exchange of diplomatic notes and in accordance with the relevant provisions of VCT and the renewal clause in Article 22 of the Treaty of Taif. However, this agreement extended the force of the treaty for a period of another 20 years, which ended in early 1973, according to the Islamic lunar calendar. Since no formal extension agreement was made after that date, the treaty was terminated according to its own Article 22, as claimed by Yemen on several occasions.

The 1973 Joint Saudi-Yemeni Communiqué, issued a few days before the formal expiration of the 1953 Renewal Agreement's first extension period, was directly related to the subject matter of the Treaty of Taif and the 1953 Renewal Agreement. It expressly reaffirmed the validity of the Treaty and the "finality and permanency of the boundary line" indicated by it. Likewise, the 1995 MOU and 1998 Sana'a Protocol reaffirmed the validity of the treaty and its attachments.[17]

The relevant provisions of the VCT provided for the modification of an existing treaty through the conclusion of a mutual agreement without resorting to the procedural formalities required to express such an agreement.[18] Given the interpretation of the relevant clauses in Articles 8 and 22, whether read separately or together, Saudi Arabia could argue that the conclusion of these four related instruments constituted a proper modification of the provisions of the Treaty of Taif within the terms of its own clauses and those of the VCT.[19]

However, this argument, based on an interpretation that modification has occurred, would appear to be in direct conflict with identical clauses in the 1995 MOU and 1998 Protocol, which expressly state that neither of the two agreements constitute any "amendment to the Treaty of Taif. It may be more prudent legally to view these instruments as renewal agreements that are not formulated under Article 22, but under Article 8, which requires the two parties to seek bilateral methods to settle any dispute arising from the interpretation and application of the Taif Treaty. Saudi Arabia appears to have done this.[20]

The Interpretation of various Subsequent/Subsidiary Agreements

Article 31(3) of the VCT states that "any subsequent agreement" concluded between the parties, as well as "any subsequent practice" by either of them in the application of its provisions should be used to interpret the treaty.[21] The subsequent interpretation and practice of the contracting parties regarding the provisions in Articles 8 and 22 of the Treaty of Taif are important for the application of the Treaty in part or whole.

Saudi Arabia may view the 1936 General Agreement, the 1953 renewal agreement extending the duration of the Treaty of Taif, the 1973 Saudi-Yemeni Joint Communiqué, and the 1995 MOU and the 1998 Sana'a Protocol as related instruments constituting "subsequent agreements" and "subsequent practice" under the terms of Articles 8 and 22 of the Treaty and the VCT. They can be seen as an application of the provision in Article 8 for both parties to seek bilateral agreement on any dispute arising from the Treaty of Taif or from outside its framework.

International Agreements creating Future Rights and Obligations

Customary and conventional law dictates that treaties should be interpreted *uberrima fides*, in utmost good faith, and assumes that they were not intended to be absurd or without effect. Article 31 (1) of the VCT says:

> A Treaty shall be interpreted in good faith in accordance with the ordinary meaning to be given to the terms of the treaty in their context and in light of its object and purpose.[22]

In order to define "good faith," "ordinary meaning" and "object and purpose," a treaty should be interpreted *effet utile*, that is, contextually, in order to give practical effect to its provisions.[23] Accordingly, the 1936 General Agreement, 1953 Renewal Agreement, 1973 Joint Communiqué, 1995 MOU and 1998 Sana'a Protocol might all be seen as separate, valid and binding international agreements under international law that create future rights and obligations and can be registered under the depository guidelines of the UN Secretariat.[24] Each one meets the definition of the term international "treaty" in Article 1(2)(a) of the VCT, which defines a treaty as:

> ...an international agreement concluded between States in written form and governed by international law, whether embodied in a single instrument or in two or more related instruments and whatever its particular destination.

No legal significance is attached to the different names of treaties (for example, agreement, accord, communiqué or minutes). In the Draft Article of the International Law Commission, a treaty is defined as being:

> Any international agreement in written form, whether embodied in a single instrument or in two or more related instruments and whatever its particular designation (treaty, convention, protocol, covenant, charter, statute, act, declaration, concordat, exchange of notes, agreed minutes, memorandum of agreement, *modus vivendi* or any other appellation), concluded between two or more States or other subjects of international law and governed by international law.[25]

In the Aegean Sea Continental Shelf Case (Greece versus Turkey) the ICJ upheld the possibility of a joint communiqué constituting an international agreement:

> ...the Court need only observe that it knows of no rule of international law which might preclude a joint communiqué from constituting an international agreement.[26]

In its 1994 judgement on the jurisdiction case between Qatar and Bahrain concerning maritime and territorial questions, the ICJ recognized that the 1987 exchange of letters and "minutes" between Qatar, Bahrain and the mediator state, Saudi Arabia, and the 1990 tripartite "minutes" signed by representatives of the three states, constituted binding international agreements creating rights and obligations. In its Judgment, the Court decided:

> ...that the exchanges of letters between the King of Saudi Arabia and the Amir of Qatar dated 19 and 21 December 1987, and between the King of Saudi Arabia and the Amir of Bahrain dated 19 and 26 December, and the document headed 'minutes' and signed at Doha on 25 December 1990 by the Ministers for Foreign Affairs of Bahrain, Qatar and Saudi Arabia, are international agreements creating rights and obligations for the Parties.[27]

Subsequently, a strong argument could be put forth that the 1973 Joint Communiqué, 1995 MOU and 1998 Sana'a Protocol, in addition to independently confirming the Treaty of Taif, may at least implicitly and separately or in combination supercede or amend the fixed duration clause in Article 22 of the Taif Treaty. This would effectively render the treaty as a whole, or at least its boundary provisions, valid for an indefinite period.

Hence, it would be difficult to sustain a legal argument that the Treaty of Taif had been terminated due to its own clause at the end of a fixed duration period in 1973, when neither party had apparently given the mandatory six months' notice of its intention to amend or otherwise terminate the treaty, a decision which would in any case have required the consent of the other contracting party.

Alternatively, in freely signing the 1973 Joint Communiqué, which coincided with the expiration date of the 1953 renewal agreement, the "intention" of the two contracting parties, as confirmed by their subsequent state practice, appeared to signify the permanence of the Treaty of Taif and effectively render its fixed duration clause indefinite. This is the case, especially in view of the fact that the subsequent 1995 MOU appears to be an amendment, a subsidiary or even an independently superceding agreement.

The Intention of the Parties to the Treaty of Taif

A debate on "the intention of the parties" in a disputed peace treaty involving territorial settlement becomes merely academic in the opinion of one distinguished author, who wrote:

> As a matter of fact, no special arguments have to be advanced to prove that in treaties concerning territorial settlement, which have to be executed immediately, the intention of the parties could not have been directed to the creation of a temporary situation. Here as the parties have had in mind a definite settlement of the problem, a right of denunciation is out of the question. In fact, a denunciation would in this case mean the unilateral annulment of a settlement already in being. The abrogation of a peace treaty by one of the parties to it would bring about a still graver situation. Consequently, here the presumption must that the intention off the parties could not have been directed to such a contingency.[28]

In the 1962 Temple of Preah Vihear Case (Cambodia versus Thailand), the ICJ commented that:

> It is a general principle of law...that a party's attitude, state of mind or intentions at a later date can be regarded as good evidence...in relation to the same or closely connected matter...of his attitude, state of mind or intentions at an earlier date also; provided of course that there is no direct evidence rebutting the presumption thus raised.[29]

Nevertheless, any attempt to interpret the provisions of the Treaty of Taif should also examine Articles 1, 4 and 22 together. This would establish that both Yemen and Saudi Arabia also intended the boundary settlement to remain in force until they would conclude an agreement to the contrary.

In 1933, shortly before the outbreak of the war, according to the Saudi view, the Imam of Yemen agreed in writing to recognize Saudi sovereignty over Asir for 20 years. This would, however, "preclude" Yemen from "contesting Ibn Saud's rights in Asir at any future time" after the expiration of the fixed duration period.[30] The British minister in Jeddah quoted a statement from Fuad Hamza, the Saudi Acting Minister of Foreign Affairs, dated December 29, 1933:

> ...the Imam of Yemen had then expressed his readiness to recognize this (Saudi sovereignty over Asir) and to conclude a treaty for twenty years, a limitation which would not, however, in Fuad Bey's view, leave the Imam free to reopen the frontier question at the end of that time.[31]

Furthermore, one important piece of evidence on the intention of the parties regarding the duration clause in Article 22 would be a textual interpretation of the article itself. Although the Treaty of

Taif was for 20 lunar years, the treaty would automatically remain in force for another 20 years, if no contracting party declared its intention to amend, modify or otherwise renounce the treaty at least six months before its original or second date of expiration.

The 1937 Agreement for the Settlement of Frontier Questions and for the Regulation of Movement, the 1953 Renewal, the 1973 Joint Communiqué, the 1995 MOU and the 1998 Sana'a Protocol[32] can also be considered as a "supplementary means" to interpret the text of Article 22 and "the intention" of the parties, in accordance with the relevant provisions of the VCT. In the 1994 case of Libya versus Chad, which concerned a land boundary dispute, the ICJ resorted to previous agreements as "a supplementary means in order to seek a possible confirmation of its interpretation of the text."[33]

Acquiescence and Estoppel

In addition to or instead of the aforementioned arguments, Saudi Arabia could hypothetically also claim that the legal doctrines of acquiescence and estoppel applied when the Treaty of Taif was concluded in 1934. Yemen's acts after 1934 could constitute Yemeni state acquiescence in the legality of the Treaty of Taif and, at the same time, estop Yemen from rejecting the treaty's validity *ab initio*.

Acquiescence implies that one state recognizes the sovereignty of another state and its acquisition or cession of territory. In a territorial dispute, as in the case here, acquiescence arises from the attitude, "conduct, absence of protest when it might reasonably be expected" of a "losing" state.[34] Although, in general, acquiescence does not constitute "a complete foundation for the title in the holder," it nevertheless adds significance to a *de facto* control of territory and various "acts of state authority" where there are no competing acts of possession.[35] Article 45 of the VCT provides that a state "must by reason of its conduct" be "considered as having acquiesced in the validity of the treaty or in its maintenance in force or in operation, as the case may be."[36]

In the Temple of Preah Vihear case between Cambodia and Thailand, the ICJ upheld the doctrine of acquiescence. It based its decision to uphold the "map line" on the fact that "both Parties, by their conduct, recognized the line and thereby in effect agreed to regard it as being the frontier line" determined by the 1904 Mixed Delimitation Commission.[37]

Estoppel refers to the legal doctrine that one can hold a party to a statement it has made and preclude it from denying the statement even when it may not correspond with the real intention of that party.[38] It is particularly relevant to cases involving territorial disputes. The principle is based on good faith and consistency in inter-state relations and constitutes an important indicator of state sovereignty.

In the famous Eastern Greenland Case, the Permanent Court of International Justice ruled that Norway, through an oral statement by its foreign minister, had "debarred herself" (was estopped) from contesting Danish sovereignty over Greenland. The statement had conceded Denmark's sovereignty and promised not to contest the latter's sovereignty, with Norway accepting binding "bilateral and multilateral agreements" that reaffirmed Norwegian recognition of the whole of Greenland as Danish territory.[39]

Thus, it can be argued that in terms of the doctrine of *uti possidetis juris*, the intertemporal law in effect from at least the time of the treaty's conclusion in 1934 to the adoption of the UN Charter in 1945, which invalidated treaties imposed after 1945, there exist certain principles of international law. These principles still seem capable of rebutting any other grounds one party might invoke to assert the invalidity or voidability of the Treaty of Taif and contest the boundary established by it.

The history of the Taif Treaty's application appears to be sufficient to develop a relatively strong Saudi argument based on customary law doctrines like acquiescence, estoppel, *effectivités*, *in precario possessionis* and *uti possidetis juris*. For example, if Yemen questioned the validity of its consent to the Treaty of Taif or deemed such consent vitiated, as it actually did, the Treaty of Taif would, in terms of the principle of *uti possidetis juris* and in conjunction with other relevant criteria, such as estoppel and *effectivités*, extend legal validity to disputed territory not covered by the treaty. This would happen irrespective of the strength of Yemen's claim of historic title and *animus possidendi*. In this case, Saudi Arabia had traditionally exercised actual *corpus possessionis* or *in precario possessionis* over the territory in question.

One international judicial decision tends to support by analogy not only the validity of the Treaty of Taif, but also the relevance of these customary law doctrines. In its Judgment of March 16, 2001 in the Qatar-Bahrain case, the ICJ acknowledged that the 1939 British decision to award possession of the disputed Hawar islands to Bahrain did not have a *res judicata* character, but the court nevertheless recognized its status as a valid international agreement binding upon both parties.[40] In addition, the ICJ based its judgment on the relevant principles of customary law in order to at least implicitly decide on this and other issues of the territorial dispute, at least implicitly.[41]

Since 1934, the Yemeni state has taken several voluntary actions in accordance with the provisions of the Treaty of Taif, thereby reflecting continued and consistent endorsement of the treaty. Article 22 of the Treaty of Taif and the relevant suspension clauses in the VCT require a formal notification by one party informing the other of its intention to suspend, renounce or terminate the Treaty in whole or in part. As far as can be ascertained from the public record, none of the successive Yemeni governments since 1934 has ever sent a formal notification to the Saudi government.

In addition, the 1937 joint boundary commission report demarcating the boundary in accordance with Article 4 of the 1934 treaty had been unanimously approved "in the most friendly manner, and…no disputes arose."[42] Other indicators would be the 1937 general agreement concluded under Article 7 of the Treaty of Taif, the 1953 renewal agreement in terms of Article 22, the 1973 joint communiqué, the 1995 MOU and the 1998 Sana'a Protocol, which affirmed the Treaty.

Other examples demonstrating the Yemeni state's acquiescence in the Treaty of Taif might also be mentioned. The first one relates to Yemen's voluntary accession on August 26, 1937 to the Treaty of Arab Brotherhood and the Alliance between Iraq and the Kingdom of Saudi Arabia. Article 2 of the trilateral Saudi-Iraqi-Yemeni treaty explicitly referred to the provisions of the Treaty of Taif's arbitration covenant as the means to settle future disputes. It states that:

> The important contracting parties undertake to settle any differences that may arise between them by means of amiable negotiations and, in case settlement of such a dispute by negotiations has proved difficult, they shall resort to the means of arbitration provided for in Article 8 of the Treaty of Taif concluded between the Kingdom of Yemen and the Kingdom of Saudi Arabia.[43]

The second and perhaps more important example of Yemen's acquiescence was demonstrated in 1963 when the new revolutionary government of republican Yemen formally accepted the establishment and stationing of the United Nations Yemen Observation Mission in a demilitarized zone "on each side of the demarcated Saudi Arabia-Yemen border." On April 29, 1963, the Secretary General of the United Nations, in a report to the Security Council on Saudi and Egyptian support of opposing factions in the raging Yemeni civil war, stated that he had:

> (3) Received from each of the three governments concerned, in separate communications, formal confirmation of their acceptance of identical terms of disengagement in Yemen...
> (4)...a demilitarized zone to a distance of twenty kilometers on each side of the demarcated Saudi Arabia-Yemen border is to be established from which military forces and equipment are to be excluded...[44]

The Yemeni government thus formally agreed to the establishment of the UN mission along its border with Saudi Arabia. However, it is significant to note that at the same time the Yemeni government rejected a US-UK suggestion to similarly establish an international observation mission along its border with the British Protectorate of Aden, on the grounds that such an agreement would amount to Yemen's recognition of the boundary with the British colony.[45]

The Finality and Permanence of Boundaries

The vast majority of modern treaties contain specific provisions relating to their duration. The term of the expiration period may be fixed by the parties in various forms, for example, in terms of calendar years, during which the treaty generally remains in force from the day when it comes into operation to the expiration of the last day of the year.[46] The expiration of the duration period envisaged by the parties in the text of the treaty constitutes one of the principal reasons for the rejection of the treaty by one party.[47] Article 54 of the VCT provides that the termination of or withdrawal from a treaty may take place "in conformity with the provisions."[48]

Article 22 of the Treaty of Taif contains a clause stipulating the duration of the legal force of the treaty. It states that the treaty "shall remain in force for a period of 20 complete lunar years," during which it may not be subject to any form of modification. However, it "may be renewed or modified during the six months preceding the expiration of its force."

If it is not renewed or modified by that date, the treaty will automatically "continue to remain in force for six months after the date of notice given by one party to the other party of his desire to modify it."[49] The fixed duration clause implies that the treaty in whole will cease to be in force upon the expiration date, though no express use is made of any Arabic term equivalent to termination, renunciation or suspension in the text of the provision.

Article 22 expressly refers only to "*tajdid*" (renewal) and "*ta'dil*" (modification), which is clearly not the same thing as termination or cancellation. The Treaty of Taif was only once formally renewed according to the terms of Article 22, namely in 1953. The Yemeni government argued that the treaty had expired *proprio motu* due to the operation of its fixed duration clause and the expiration date of its only formal renewal under Article 22.

However, Saudi Arabia rejected the Yemeni view and insisted that the 1973 joint communiqué and 1995 MOU respectively constituted a third and fourth formal extension of the Treaty of Taif.

[101]

This was the case under Article 8, which requires that the two parties pursue bilateral methods to settle any dispute arising from the interpretation and application of the Treaty.[50] Nevertheless, treaties with a fixed duration establishing boundaries appear to be exempted from the rule, or at least the provisions containing the territorial settlement.

The 1994 Chad versus Libya case established an international judicial precedent to this effect. Like the Treaty of Taif, the 1955 Chad-Libya treaty was concluded "for a period of 20 years," after which, "or at any other time," it "can be terminated by either Party."[51] Unlike the Treaty of Taif, the 1955 Libya-Chad treaty did not contain provisions expressly establishing boundaries or making any territorial adjustments.

Libya argued that the 1994 treaty had been terminated by the force of the fixed duration provision in Article 2 and that whatever boundary had been established, by implication or otherwise, was likewise no longer in existence. Nevertheless, the ICJ's judgement of the case rejected the Libyan arguments.[52]

In its judgment, the Court supported the doctrine of the inviolability and permanency of boundaries established under international agreements. According to the court, treaties referring to peace and territory that involve two states presuppose the existence of a boundary between the two states that is final and permanent, separate from and irrespective of the temporary nature of the treaty itself. Because of the significance of the Libya-Chad case and its serious implications for the Treaty of Taif or the Treaty of Jeddah in any potential arbitral or judicial case, it may be relevant to quote at some length the following key points from the Court's Judgement:

> These provisions notwithstanding, the Treaty must, in the view of the Court, be taken to have determined a permanent

frontier. There is nothing in the 1955 Treaty to indicate that the boundary agreed was to be provisional or temporary; on the contrary it bears all the hallmarks of finality. The establishment of this boundary is a fact which, from the outset, has had a legal life of its own, independently of the fate of the 1955 Treaty. Once agreed, the boundary stands, for any other approach would vitiate the fundamental principle of the stability of boundaries, the importance of which has been repeatedly emphasized by the Court. A boundary established by treaty thus achieves a permanence which the treaty itself does not necessarily enjoy. The treaty can cease to be in force without affecting, in any manner, the legal status of the boundary line created under it. In this instance the state parties have not exercised their option to terminate the Treaty, but whether or not the option can be exercised, the boundary line remains. This is not to say that two States may not by mutual agreement vary the border between them; such a result can of course be achieved by mutual consent, but when a boundary has been the subject of agreement, the continued existence of that boundary is not dependent upon the continuing life of the treaty under which the boundary is agreed.[53]

This judicial precedent, as well as others like the Temple of Preah Vihear[54] and the Aegean Sea Continental Shelf case,[55] serves to support the principle of international law that sanctions the permanence and finality of a boundary established by treaties. Such permanence and finality are established, whether explicitly or implicitly, where the stability of borders has proved essential to regional and international peace, irrespective of what restrictive clauses (i.e., definite duration) these agreements may contain.

The Treaty of Taif as a Peace and Boundary Treaty

Although it was common for treaties to have clauses on fixed duration, it was rather unusual to include them in international agreements establishing peace and territorial settlements. Prominent authors have long been aware of the various functions of a treaty and have sought to classify international agreements into various types.[56] Peace and boundary treaties are closely linked, as they often involve both the termination of a state of war and territorial settlement. Some authors have argued that the right to reject treaties, for example, after the expiration of their fixed period of duration, only remains when such treaties are not classified as executed treaties or peace treaties.[57]

Executed treaties are those implying a single obligation to be discharged, such as the creation of a territorial arrangement. By their very nature, such treaties cease to be in force upon the execution of their provisions, regardless of any duration clause.[58] By the same token, treaties with multiple recurrent obligations are not terminated by the fulfillment of an obligation.[59] Although the executed treaty becomes extinct, it nevertheless remains of legal significance. It may attest to the status of executed actions, such as territorial cession, and provide guidance for the settlement of future disputes.[60]

The Treaty of Taif also appears to be a multiple agreement implying recurrent international obligations that need to be implemented. It is at once a peace, territorial and executed treaty. As a peace treaty, it formally ended a state of war. As a territorial treaty that allocated territorial rights, it clearly established a boundary between the two contracting states. As an executed treaty, the provisions establishing a boundary were duly executed with the approval of the joint commission report in 1937, which was attached as an integral part of the Treaty, demarcating the boundary as stipulated in Article 4.[61]

The principal objective of peace treaties is to provide for the immediate termination of a state of war between parties. In addition, they also contain fundamental provisions regarding the settlement of territorial and boundary issues, often the cause of conflict in the first place. While Article 4 stipulates a territorial adjustment, the Preamble and Article 1 of the Treaty of Taif call for the immediate cessation of hostilities and permanent peace and goodwill between Yemen and Saudi Arabia. Article 1 states:

> The current state of war between the Kingdom of Saudi Arabia and the Kingdom of Yemen ceases upon the signing of this treaty. A state of perpetual peace, strong fraternity, permanent Islamic and Arab brotherhood that will not be infringed upon in part or whole, shall be established between their two Majesties, their countries and their peoples. The two contracting parties pledge to resolve all disputes and differences that may occur between them in the spirit of Arab and Islamic camaraderie, at all situations and circumstances, and God is the witness of their good faith and intention, and sincere desire for conciliation and agreement in private and in public.[62]

A treaty whose principal provisions have been duly executed, that is, the termination of a state of war and the establishment of territorial rights, may not be rejected in terms of other provisions like the expiration of the duration period.[63] This is especially true for peace and territorial treaties, as the unilateral rejection of the treaty under any legal pretext would amount to a return to the *status quo ante natura*, that is, a renewal of the state of war that was declared illegal under international law.

In order to avoid an obvious source of threats to regional and world peace, International Law Commission reports and the VCT expressly exclude "treaties fixing boundaries" from the operation of the principle of a "fundamental change of circumstances."[64] For this reason, Article 62(2)(a) of the VCT stipulates as follows:

> (2) A fundamental change of circumstances may not be invoked as a ground for terminating or withdrawing from a treaty: (a) if the treaty established a boundary;[65]

If the established customary law doctrine of *rebus sic stantibus* does not apply to territorial and boundary treaties, a clause on fixed duration in such treaties would likewise be without legal effect. Prominent authors also affirm the sanctity of treaties establishing territorial rights. Oppenheim notes that:

> …it is clear in law that a boundary established by treaty is not to be called into question by the mere fact of a succession of states, or by a fundamental change in circumstances since the treaty was made…[66]

Furthermore, he comments that treaties expressly concluded to establish a permanent state are:

> …as a rule not terminable by notice, although they can be dissolved by mutual consent of the contracting parties. All treaties of peace, and all boundary treaties, belong to this class.[67]

The fact that Article 22 of the Treaty of Taif contained a fixed expiration date would not, under international law, affect this exception. The eminent author Haraszti comments that in treaties simultaneously establishing a boundary and a fixed expiration date, the presence of restrictive clauses such as a period of fixed duration has no legal relevance. He says that the "differentiation between treaties concluded for definite and indefinite periods is arbitrary and unjustifiable."[68]

6

Yemeni Views on the Treaty of Jeddah

In Yemen, the conclusion of the Treaty of Jeddah generated an apparently genuine public approval and universal support from all sectors of political and social life, including opposition parties.[1] Moreover, in an apparent turnabout, the Treaty of Taif, hitherto disliked in public and official circles, all of a sudden seemed to become the crown jewel of the boundary settlement agreed in the Treaty of Jeddah.

Like Saudi Arabia, but for different reasons, Yemen had come to regard the Treaty of Taif as the *raison d'être* of its acceptance of the Treaty of Jeddah. Saudi Arabia was motivated almost exclusively by its strong desire to obtain Yemen's formal recognition of the 1934 boundary settlement created under the Treaty of Taif, and viewed the Treaty of Jeddah as essentially a territorial protocol defining a boundary for the border area not covered by the 1934 treaty.[2] Yemen, on the other hand, was motivated by actual and potential territorial and non-territorial gains through the application of the Taif Treaty under the aegis of the new treaty.

There are several legal factors that may account for the apparent change in Yemen's official and public position on the 1934 treaty.

Previously, Yemen appeared to see the treaty from a positive perspective. The initial reason for the change in attitude was related to the Yemeni government's apparent realization, discussed earlier, that it could not possibly hope to "regain" through a judicial or arbitral settlement body any significant part of the territory it had "lost" to Saudi Arabia under the terms of the Treaty of Taif. Secondly, Yemen regarded the substantial land and sea territory gained under the Treaty of Jeddah as comparable compensation for those areas lost in 1934.[3]

Third, and more important, from the moment of signing of the Treaty of Jeddah, the Yemeni government started to emphasize certain non-territorial provisions of the Treaty of Taif, which, it asserted, granted specific social benefits to Yemeni citizens.

Public statements by the Yemeni government, parliament and political opposition parties during the signing of the Treaty of Jeddah emphasized the legal preeminence of the Treaty of Taif as the driving force behind Yemen's wide support for the Treaty of Jeddah.[4] The Treaty of Jeddah recognized the Treaty of Taif as valid and binding on both parties and incorporated all of its articles and attachments in it wholly and without modification.

The Treaty of Jeddah henceforth became a comprehensive agreement embodying territorial and non-territorial articles with the same legal force and effect, and regulating all aspects of bilateral relations in the political, military, economic, social and cultural fields. These included certain provisions under which Saudi Arabia, as Yemen had always maintained, granted in perpetuity "special privileges" to Yemeni nationals residing in Saudi Arabia, and perhaps even committed the Saudi government to finance development projects in Yemen itself. On the government level, various ministers expressed Yemen's understanding of the legal relationship between the two treaties. The Yemeni minister of legal and parliamentary affairs described the Treaty of Jeddah:

> ...as comprehensive for, in addition to covering all maritime and land boundaries, it affirms the Treaty of Taif as valid and binding on both parties. Thus, it embodies peaceful methods of settling border issues (arbitration in Article 8 of the Treaty of Taif).[5]

The Yemeni Minister of Planning and Development declared that the new treaty:

> ...makes the Treaty of Taif the legal basis of regulating relations between the two countries, in addition to the delineation of the remaining boundary agreed to. Therefore, the Treaty of Jeddah is not merely an agreement to draw a boundary, but it is also a complete system regulating political, security, social and economic relations between Saudi Arabia and Yemen.[6]

The chairman of the parliamentary Committee on Constitutional and Legal Affairs asserted:

> ...the legal indivisibility and integration between the Treaty of Jeddah and the Treaty of Taif have been expressed in the text of the Treaty of Jeddah and the MOU pursuant to the intention and concurrence of the two contacting parties, who did not agree on anything contrary to the text of the Treaty of Taif. Neither party absolved itself from any provision or commitment contained in the Treaty of Taif, which stipulates the reactivation of bilateral cooperation in various political, social, economic and cultural fields beneficial to both countries.[7]

On a legislative level, a parliamentary deputy, speaking on behalf of his colleagues while debating the treaty, declared that parliament would agree to ratify the treaty primarily on the basis of its "confirmation of the Treaty of Taif and the MOU as valid and binding" on both parties.[8] Another deputy emphasized "the necessity of Yemen's commitment to the privileges provided in the Treaty of Taif, especially those relating to Yemeni immigrants living there (Saudi Arabia) as our minimum demand to ensure that they experience an atmosphere of security, tranquility and stability."[9]

For this purpose, the Treaty of Taif was explicitly cited in the Yemen parliament's resolution no. 16/2000, which unanimously approved the Treaty of Jeddah. It read in part:

> ...[the Council of Deputies] has ascertained through the report of the experts and the new map before the Deputies the return of more than forty thousand square kilometers of land in the eastern region and three thousand square nautical kilometers of maritime territory including the islands of Dhu-Hirab, al-Duwaimah, Syoul, Rab and Marin...the Council of Deputies instructs the government to exert its utmost efforts to guarantee the Saudi government's full implementation of all provisions of the Treaty of Taif, its annexures and letters as ratified by the governments of the two countries and which covers political, security and economic aspects in addition to work, travel for the purposes of pilgrimage, trade and other purposes, constructing paved roads in the areas located in the second land sector of the border...as well as exchange of educational and cultural expertise.[10]

In this respect, even Saudi Arabia appeared to accept Yemen's view of the Treaty of Jeddah as a comprehensive agreement because it incorporated the Treaty of Taif. Prince Naef, the Saudi Minister of the Interior, a principal participant in the negotiations leading to the Treaty of Jeddah and co-chairman of the Saudi-Yemeni joint commission charged with implementing its provisions, told the

Yemeni armed forces newspaper that in the Saudi government's view, the Treaty of Jeddah was not restricted to the border issue, but "in fact covers everything contained in the Treaty of Taif and all its annexures, as clearly expressed in the Treaty of Jeddah."[11]

The Taif Treaty's Provisions on "Special Privileges"

At least since the early 1950s, Saudi Arabia traditionally exempted Yemeni nationals from certain requirements of its law on foreign labor law, namely those related to residency and work in the country, including the so-called Saudi employer sponsorship.[12] On at least two occasions, in 1960[13] and in 1990, Saudi Arabia decided to formally revoke these special exemptions granted to Yemeni citizens.

In both cases, the Yemeni government condemned the Saudi action as a violation of rights guaranteed by the Treaty of Taif. From this perspective, Saudi conduct constituted a material breach of the treaty, giving Yemen legal grounds to reject it in whole or in part. In the 1960 case, for example, the Yemeni government interpreted the Saudi action as a unilateral renunciation of the Treaty of Taif, therefore creating a situation whereby "Yemenis would now be free to reassert their territorial claims to certain parts of the border area"[14] before the two sides agreed to return to "the status quo ante."[15]

When Saudi Arabia again repealed the Yemeni privileges in 1990, the Yemeni government denounced the Saudi decision as depriving those Yemenis of their "legitimate and acquired rights" under the provisions of the Treaty of Taif.[16] Consequently, Yemen acquired the legal right to refuse a second "renewal" or seek the termination of the Treaty when it was due to expire in September 1992 according to the Islamic lunar calendar and, moreover, to seek compensation for losses suffered by the nearly one million Yemeni citizens who left Saudi Arabia after the rescission of their special privileges.[17] Although Saudi Arabia rejected Yemen's assertion of a legal link with the terms of the Treaty of Taif, it never explained the legal basis of its decision to rescind these privileges or to grant them in the first place.[18]

The official view of the Yemeni government was that these "special privileges" provisions should be restored under the terms of the Treaty of Jeddah, which incorporated the Taif Treaty. As explained earlier, these privileges, as contained in the Taif Treaty, constituted the basis of Yemen's acceptance and ratification of the Treaty of Jeddah.

Consequently, the Yemeni government repeatedly argued that the Saudi government would be required under the new treaty to restore the rescinded privileges to Yemeni nationals, permit the "return" of those who were expelled and compensate them for the material loss they had incurred. The Saudi government also had to amend the Saudi labor and investment laws to conform to the provisions of the treaty.[19]

Dissatisfied by the Saudi government's steps with respect to the special privileges provisions, the Yemeni president, prime minister and speaker of parliament collectively made telephone calls to their Saudi counterparts in early August 2001, urging them to speed up the "rearrangement" process of "regulating the status of the Yemeni community and labor force" residing and working in Saudi Arabia. In those conversations, reported on the front page of the influential Yemeni armed forces weekly, the Yemeni leadership "reiterated the importance of taking into account that Yemeni labor should be treated in accordance with the relevant treaties and agreements… and especially since the signing of the historic Jeddah treaty" between the two countries.[20]

A month later, the Yemeni president declared that "the treaties of Taif and of Jeddah accorded preferential treatment to Yemenis" in the Saudi labor market.[21] Moreover, he appeared to imply that the Yemeni government had signed the Treaty of Jeddah on the assumption of a Saudi commitment to accept Yemen as the seventh member of the regional Gulf Cooperation Council.[22] The potentially adverse legal implications of Yemen's continued assertion, along with Saudi Arabia's denial of the special privileges in the Treaty of Jeddah and the boundary settlement created under it, became readily apparent.

The Yemen government indicated that these special privileges were contained in certain provisions of the Treaty of Taif, later incorporated with equal legal force into the Treaty of Jeddah, namely in Article 4, side letter number 5 and the 1936 General Agreement between Saudi Arabia and Yemen concerning the settlement of matters relating to the subjects of their counties.[23] However, barring the existence of secret agreements, which both sides publicly denied,[24] careful examination of the clauses emphasized by Yemen does not appear to reveal explicit or even implicit legal links to the Yemeni argument in this regard.

The crux of Yemen's legal argument and the basic flaw inherent in it has already been discussed in the chapter dealing with Yemen's hypothetical arguments against the Treaty of Taif. However, all the provisions discussed earlier expressly stated that the reciprocal privileges regarding cross-border movement should be accorded exclusively to Yemeni and Saudi subjects traditionally inhabiting the common border area on either side of the 1934 boundary.

Article 4 of the Treaty of Taif granted both Saudi and Yemeni subjects belonging to the Wa'ilah tribe in and around the eastern hinterland area of Najran equal rights regarding their customary inter-tribal communication and visitation.[25] In the controversial side letter number 5, signed on the same date as the treaty, the two signatories agreed that cross-border "movement at the present time" of subjects of both countries "whether for pilgrimage, or for trade, or for any other purpose or reason" would "continue as in the past until a special agreement" was drawn up between them to regulate such movement.[26]

In 1937, pursuant to the side letter, the two sides concluded "a general agreement concerning the settlement of matters relating to the subjects" of the two countries.[27] If anything, the subsequent agreement tightened the previously relaxed rules concerning cross-border movement even further. The preamble stipulated that the provisions of the agreement were exclusively applicable to the age-old seasonal and customary tribal movements of the "the subjects of the parties inhabiting the area adjacent to the border." They were required under Article 7(1) to obtain an "official permit" to cross the border for the purpose of "grazing, attending farms they owned on the other side of the boundary line or were accustomed to visit in order to attend markets there."[28]

Moreover, the article stated that "in case of emergency," either of the two parties was allowed to "restrict, totally or partially" the cross-border movement or to ask for additional identification papers. If people wanted to venture beyond the common border zone as "traders, tourists and pilgrims," they were required under Article 7(3) to obtain formal valid travel documents (i.e., passports) issued by their own governments, as required by the nationals inhabiting other parts of the country.[29] Furthermore, Article 12 of the Treaty of Taif required that "the subjects of each of the two parties, when in the country of the other party, shall be treated in accordance with municipal law."[30]

In this respect, Saudi Arabia maintained that, unlike Yemen, it had implemented Article 7 of the 1936 General Agreement. The Saudi government exempted Yemeni and Saudi subjects inhabiting the adjacent border area from travel requirements and accepted special travel permits issued for this purpose, while Yemen's government always required the same subjects to carry regular passports.[31]

However, Yemen accused Saudi Arabia of advancing the location of its cross-border points well south of the 1934 boundary and inside Yemeni territory. Yemen could not reciprocate, whether by establishing border posts or by accepting special travel permits, since such steps would be tantamount to *de jure* recognition of an otherwise *de facto* boundary.[32] The problem was further compounded by the fact that neither the Treaty of Taif nor subsequent agreements, including the Treaty of Jeddah, designated or called for the establishment of a regulatory border authority[33] or border-crossing points along the Saudi-Yemeni border.[34]

Despite Article 4, side letter number 5 and the 1936 General Agreement, it remained a fact that Saudi Arabia had traditionally and unilaterally granted all Yemeni nationals certain exemptions related to entry, residency and work in any part of Saudi Arabian territory. While such privileges did not appear to emanate, as Yemen asserted, from any of the relevant provisions or attachments contained in the Treaty of Taif, the Saudi state's subsequent behavior may have suggested an implicit acknowledgement of the Yemeni claim, therefore lending it at least a quasi-legal credibility.

Firstly, Saudi Arabia had been granting these privileges to Yemeni nationals for a long time, possibly dating back to the conclusion of the 1934 Treaty of Taif. Secondly, the Saudi government had inexplicably and repeatedly failed to justify the legal rationale of granting as well as repealing these long-established exemptions, especially in the face of Yemen's continued public and official assertions that they were inalienable, legal rights guaranteed in perpetuity in bilateral agreements, including the Treaty of Jeddah.

Thirdly, since the signing of the Treaty of Jeddah, the topic of Yemeni "special privileges" has always been discussed within the legal framework of the Treaty of Jeddah. The topic had been adopted by both sides as part of the official agenda during the periodical meetings of the Saudi-Yemeni joint commission, whose sole responsibility was the implementation of the provisions of the treaty.[35] In this context, the Saudi government made statements and initiated acts that showed its apparent agreement with Yemen's claim regarding special privileges.

Initially, the Saudi government appeared to shift from its general position that the treaties of Taif and Jeddah were basically boundary agreements.[36] After the ratification of the Treaty of Jeddah, Prince Naef, the Saudi Minister of the Interior, a principal negotiator of the treaty and co-chairman of the Saudi-Yemeni joint commission for the treaty's implementation, told the influential mouthpiece of the Yemeni armed forces that, in the Saudi government's view, the Jeddah Treaty was "not merely linked to the border issue…but in fact covers all provisions and annexures of the Treaty of Taif."

When asked about "the restoration of the former privileges granted to Yemenis in the fields of health, education and residency," Prince Naef replied that it was "as you know, the Treaty of Taif" that involved granting an "entry facility" to Yemeni nationals presently numbering "more than a half a million," who "are still exempted from deportation" regulations applied to other foreign workers. He also declared the Saudi government's intention to amend "sponsorship" provisions in its labor laws, and its wish to deport other nationalities "in order to replace them by Yemenis who, of all other nationalities, are the most favored…and to whom we have an obligation."[37]

The Yemeni minister of the interior and co-chairman of the joint commission declared that the two sides had "agreed on a way to deal with the problems and status of Yemeni immigrants residing in Saudi Arabia."[38] Likewise, during the formal exchange of the instruments of ratification in the Yemeni capital, the Saudi Foreign Minister, who initialed the Treaty of Jeddah on behalf of his government, declared that Yemeni labor would be "welcome in Saudi Arabia," and that the government no longer opposed Yemen's membership of the regional Gulf Cooperation Council.[39]

Measures introduced by Saudi Arabia indicated the first concrete steps on the road to full restoration of the former privileges claimed by Yemeni citizens. In December 2000, the high-level Saudi-Yemeni Coordination Council, suspended since 1989, resumed its first meeting "within the framework of and as a result of the conclusion" of the Treaty of Jeddah.[40] As in almost all previous and subsequent bilateral meetings on the implementation of the Treaty of Jeddah, the topic of special privileges was, at the insistence of Yemen, accorded top priority in the official agenda of the SYCC meeting. Yemen's definition of "special privileges" was apparently widened to include not only the traditional demand for exemptions regarding the entry, work and residence of Yemeni expatriates, but also huge Saudi investment in development projects in Yemen itself, as well as relaxing restrictions on imports of Yemeni labor and agricultural products.[41]

The Saudi chairman of the SYCC's preparation committee stated that the "Saudi vision of the exemptions demanded by Yemeni side" was essentially the same as that of Yemen. However, due to economic difficulties and the high unemployment rate in Saudi Arabia, he suggested that the Saudi government should implement Yemen's "innovative idea" of large-scale Saudi investment in Yemen, at least for the time being. In this way, Yemeni labor would be employed at home without prejudicing the status of the nearly one million expatriates already in Saudi Arabia.[42]

At the conclusion of the SYCC meeting, Saudi Arabia in effect agreed to cancel Yemen's huge debt, which amounted to around $300 million,[43] and to grant a new loan of $350 million to finance massive development projects in health, education, training and electricity.[44] More specifically, the Saudi and Yemeni governments signed a cultural agreement stating that Saudi Arabia would grant preferential treatment to almost 200,000 Yemeni students in Saudi Arabia, so that they would be "treated the same as their Saudi counterparts."[45]

Soon afterwards, the Saudi government amended its foreign investment and labor law and repealed the "Saudi employer's sponsorship" clause, which Yemen had long regarded as incompatible with the terms of the complementary treaties of Taif and Jeddah. In this context, the Saudi government also decided in August 2001 to "postpone" the implementation of its policy to indigenize the economically powerful gold and jewelry market, which was traditionally dominated by Yemeni nationals.[46] Furthermore, at the end of the sixth meeting of the Saudi-Yemeni joint committee for the implementation of the Treaty of Jeddah, which followed the regular meeting in Sana'a in October 2001, the Saudi government instructed its embassy in Yemen to "grant the necessary exemptions regarding the entry of Yemeni citizens into Saudi Arabia."[47]

These Saudi decisions came after senior officials in the Yemeni leadership, including the president, made a direct appeal to their Saudi counterpart to "rearrange the status of the Yemeni community and labor" in Saudi Arabia in order to make it compatible with the terms of the international treaties and agreements between the two countries, including the "historical Treaty of Jeddah."[48]

It is clear that Saudi Arabia is in the process of formally restoring exemptions previously granted to Yemeni nationals, albeit gradually. This restoration seems to be within the framework of implementing the provisions of the Treaty of Jeddah. Judging from past experience, it is also clear that any future cancellation of such privileges by Saudi Arabia, under whatever pretext, would almost certainly be interpreted by Yemen as a violation of the provisions of the Treaty of Taif as incorporated in the Treaty of Jeddah. This would have potentially adverse legal implications for the entire boundary settlement in the Treaty of Taif, the status of which is still far from clarified.

7

Controversial Provisions under Municipal and International Law

The Treaty of Jeddah's Provisions on Territorial Adjustment

Contrary to its official name, the boundary established under the terms of the Treaty of Jeddah is not yet "final and permanent." The Treaty of Jeddah simply defined a set of fixed geographical coordinates, but not the line linking them together and with no apparent attention to geographic features or demographic factors. With respect to the 1934 treaty, the Treaty of Jeddah stipulated that the resulting line linking the geographical coordinates should produce a boundary corresponding precisely to the 1934 boundary defined in Article 4 of the Treaty of Taif and demarcated in its 1937 report.

However, the actual course of the line will be known only after the joint commission has completed its demarcation work, which is expected to last for four years. It will probably propose a radical amendment of the course of the 1934 line, that will significantly affect the legal status of the territory and population in the common border area.

Article 2 of the Treaty of Jeddah stipulates that the "nationality of villages" located on the course of the new line will be determined by the "tribal affiliation" of their inhabitants, as defined in Article 4 of the Treaty of Taif and its joint boundary demarcation report that identifies the nationality of the tribes along the common border by name. In the event that any of the fixed geographical coordinates are located in a village identified in the Treaty of Taif as belonging to the other state party, Article 2 seems to suggest that the nationality of such a village would be decided by the villagers and the course of the boundary would be "amended accordingly" by the survey company erecting boundary markers.

This implies that the geographical coordinates, at least those linking the starting point and endpoint of the 1934 boundary, were not based on the boundary markers contained in the 1937 demarcation report, due perhaps to the two parties' disagreement as to their exact location. Indeed, the text of Article 2 itself appears to confirm this, stipulating that only the lines linking the spaces between the coordinates, but not the positions of the coordinates themselves, should conform to the boundary markers defined in Article 4 of the Treaty of Taif and demarcated in the report attached to it.

Thus, on theoretical and practical grounds, it seems impossible that the resulting boundary would conform exactly to the line of 1934 as required in Article 2 of the Treaty of Jeddah. There appears to be a conflict between Article 2 of the Treaty of Jeddah and Article 4 of the Treaty of Taif, each of which categorically describes itself as final and permanent. This creates an apparent contradiction in Article 2, further compounded by the fact that the two signatory states have maintained two substantially different conceptions of the course of the 1934 line.

By allowing inhabitants of villages located on any of the coordinate points to choose between belonging to Saudi Arabia or belonging to Yemen, Article 2 of the Treaty of Jeddah appears to recognize the principle of a plebiscite or self-determination. However, the plebiscite clause in Article 2 seems to be in direct conflict with Article 12 of the Treaty of Taif, which expressly denied the population of the common border area the right of referendum. Article 12 stipulated the two parties' recognition that:

> ...the people of all areas accruing to the other party by virtue of this treaty are subjects of that party. Each one of them undertakes not to accept as its subjects any person or persons who are subjects of the other party, except with the consent of that party.[1]

This apparent contradiction in the provisions of the two articles contained in the two complementary treaties could lead to a legal dispute concerning their interpretation and application. A legal question may arise as to whether Article 2 of the Treaty of Jeddah superceded Article 12 of the Treaty of Taif. In addition, it is not clear whether the plebiscite clause in Article 2 would also be applicable to villages and tribes inhabiting the second land sector east of Jabal Al-Thar, although Yemen has rejected this method as a way of settling the territorial dispute in that area.[2]

More significantly, the Treaty of Jeddah appears to define the land boundary in absurd geographical terms without sufficiently taking into account the important human elements involving inhabitants of the large villages and tribal settlements adjacent to the boundary.[3] In an ominous sign of the problems that may arise, virtually all Yemeni and some Saudi tribes inhabiting the densely populated common border areas declared their rejection of the Treaty of Jeddah's proposed amendment of the 1934 boundary.

These include the powerful tribes of Wa'ilah,[4] Dahm-alhamra,[5] Dhu-Yahya and Al-Zawalima straddling the Saudi-Yemeni frontier area along and east of the 1934 line.[6]

The tribes described the boundary under the new treaty as "unjust," since it would cut across their tribal territory and vowed to thwart by force the work of the demarcation commission and survey company. The Yemeni Wa'ilah and Saudi Yam tribes claimed that their tribal territory was regulated by a 241-year-old treaty,[7] acknowledged by the 1934 Treaty of Taif, while the new treaty threatened to split off a large part of the territory in favor of Saudi Arabia.[8]

Although the two states publicly dismissed tribal opposition as mere transient "bubbles,"[9] the frequent armed confrontations between these tribes and both Saudi and Yemeni troops[10] were serious enough to force the two states to postpone the scheduled date of contracting the surveying company.[11] Ultimately, their declared mandate to complete the demarcation work was extended by another two years and wisely left the volatile sector near the 1934 line to be finished last.[12]

Saudi Arabia and Yemen apparently failed to notice the potentially serious implications of the radical demographic transformation in the common border agreed in 1934. The protests from the tribes and villages primarily emanated from this proposed demographic transformation. On both sides, new villages and towns had sprung up, and small tribal settlements of no more than a few huts had increased substantially in terms of population growth and geographical size to extend well beyond the common border zone along the 1934 line.[13]

To compound the problem, most of the former physical markers of the 1934 boundary have either vanished or been made redundant by changes in names and locations.[14] A new *de facto* boundary that hardly showed any resemblance to that defined in the Treaty of Taif or the Treaty of Jeddah has been established.

In addition, the post-1934 period witnessed slow, but steady Yemeni (and Saudi) tribal migration northwards. It was primarily driven by economic factors that created new facts on the northern (Saudi) side of the 1934 line that the Treaty of Jeddah apparently ignored. Members of the tribes, identified as Yemeni nationals in the Treaty of Taif, permanently settled in territory that was identified in the same treaty as belonging to Saudi Arabia. Since the 1934 boundary was exclusively defined on a tribal basis, the question immediately arose as to whether this territory could no longer be considered as Saudi Arabian. This appears to have been the interpretation by Yemen.[15]

Yemen alleged that Saudi Arabia, in order to counter a possible Yemeni claim to the territory, began to grant the population Saudi citizenship.[16] It also granted Saudi nationality papers to Yemeni citizens residing on Yemeni territory, possibly in order to support its territorial claim in the disputed border area.[17]

An example of the consequences of this alleged Saudi policy was that the inhabitants of entire villages located within the tribal homeland of the large border tribe of Wa'ilah sometimes held dual Saudi and Yemeni nationality, although the tribe itself and its territory were expressly defined as Yemeni in the Treaty of Taif and the 1937 demarcation report.

If there was a covert Saudi policy of tribal assimilation, it did not have the desired effect, since the tribe of Wa'ilah spearheaded Yemeni northern tribal opposition to the Treaty of Jeddah. Its paramount chief, Shaykh Muhammad bin Shaji,' explained that his tribesmen, including himself, had obtained Saudi nationality purely for economic reasons, which "does not give Saudi Arabia the right to say this land is Saudi. The land, people, trees, soil and water are still Yemeni and will remain Yemeni forever."[18]

Nevertheless, the post-1934 demographic situation as a whole is bound to raise complex legal questions that the Treaty of Jeddah failed to address. How, for example, can Article 2 of the Treaty of Jeddah be applied to the post-1934 population and territory, including the very recent settlements built on both sides of the border?[19] Under the Treaty of Jeddah, what will be the legal status of people defined as Yemenis under the Treaty of Taif, who have moved northward since 1934, permanently settled in territory defined as Saudi Arabian in the 1934 treaty and adopted Saudi citizenship?

Likewise, under the new arrangement, what will be the status of the people and territory defined as Yemeni under the Treaty of Taif, when those people have since held Saudi or dual citizenship? Could the principle of a plebiscite, recognized implicitly in Article 2 of the Treaty of Jeddah, be applicable in these cases? And if so, will the applicability of a plebiscite extend beyond the 1934 line to cover the more sparsely populated second land sector in the east and the Red Sea islands? How can one legally reconcile the plebiscite clause in Article 2 of the Treaty of Jeddah with the apparently conflicting provision in Article 12 of the Treaty of Taif, which stipulates that nationality is linked to territory?

It also is questionable whether the latter provision would be applicable to the post-1934 demographic changes along the common border. There are two possible ways to deal with the problems created by the newly demarcated border. One option would be to seek an avenue to legalize the status of one country's citizens that are permanent residents in the other. However, adopting this choice would require an amendment of the relevant articles of the Treaty of Jeddah. The other option would require large-scale population exchanges. In this regard Yemen, though not necessarily Saudi Arabia, could also find itself in conflict with its own municipal law.

The Treaty of Jeddah and Yemeni Municipal Law

Under the Yemeni constitution of 1994, the legislative body, the Council of Deputies, only ratifies treaties in their final form.[20] The treaty, in its present form, which has already been ratified by the Yemeni parliament, cannot legally be regarded as final since it contains provisions providing for future territorial adjustment and the preparation of official border maps. These will become integral parts of the treaty after completion and joint approval by the two countries.

Consequently, in terms of the constitution, parliamentary approval of the Treaty of Jeddah may become "null and void," as some Yemeni legislators have suggested.[21] Furthermore, if the final demarcation process requires a territorial adjustment of the 1934 line, as stipulated in Article 2 of the Treaty of Jeddah, Yemen would have to cede a part of the territory recognized as Yemeni in the Treaty of Taif. However, in terms of its relevant articles, the constitution of 1994 would first have to be amended in order to legally effect any territorial adjustment by Yemen.[22]

It was partly due to this potential constitutional dilemma that the Yemeni government, despite strong political opposition, quickly moved to amend the relevant provisions of the constitution. They wanted to ensure that the provisions conform to the articles of the Treaty of Jeddah dealing with territorial affairs. On August 23, 2000, one month after its ratification of the Treaty of Jeddah, the Yemeni Council of Deputies approved a presidential bill proposing the amendment of certain articles of the constitution, including Article 91, which introduced the necessity of a "boundary adjustment" of the Yemeni state for the first time.[23]

Previously, only the elected unicameral legislative body of the Council of Deputies had the authority, under the terms of the 1994 constitution, to ratify treaties. However, Article 91, as amended by the new constitution, states that the Council of Deputies, in joint session with a newly-established upper chamber, the Council of *Shura* (Consultation), composed of presidential appointees, can ratify "treaties and agreements relating to defense, alliance, settlement, peace or adjustment of the boundary."[24] The proposed amendments, including Article 91, were incorporated into the new constitution of 2001.

The final demarcation of the Saudi-Yemeni boundary under the Treaty of Jeddah will almost certainly entail territorial adjustment of the boundary, particularly along the politically most volatile and populous 1934 boundary. Such an adjustment would require parliamentary approval within the framework of the constitution. It was perhaps for this reason that Article 91 in its amended form was intended to ensure such approval in case the elected Council of Deputies proved to be unwilling to agree to the new territorial changes.

However, the appointed Council of *Shura* is essentially an extension of the executive branch of government. Granting it legislative power under the amended Article 91 will arguably cause a serious legal conflict given the Yemeni constitution's express support for a separation of powers. Indeed, many political opposition groups and Yemeni legal experts have criticized the validity of the new constitution's form and substance resulting from these amendments.[25]

By casting doubt on the legitimacy of state legislative bodies, the legality of their acts, such as the Treaty of Jeddah itself, can be seriously questioned. Yemen has relied on precisely the same arguments in the past to undermine the legal force of previous boundary agreements, including the Treaty of Taif and the territorial settlement created under it, as well as the related 1973 joint communiqué.[26]

The Treaty of Jeddah and Saudi Municipal Law

Unlike the Yemeni case, Saudi municipal law does not currently or potentially clash with the terms of the Treaty of Jeddah, even in the event of additional Saudi territorial cession to Yemen in accordance with the adjustment provisions of the 1934 line. The Saudi constitution of 1992, formally called the Basic Law of Governance and inspired by an Islamic framework, is simply a written codification of what King Fahad has called the "existing status quo."[27]

According to the constitution, the king is at once the head of state, prime minister, chief legislator, chief judge, chief executive and commander-in-chief of the armed forces.[28] Article 44 declares the king to be "the point of reference for all" judicial, legislative and executive powers.[29] He rules absolutely by issuing royal decrees and orders and, under Article 70, he alone has the power to conclude, ratify, amend and abrogate treaties, including those involving the cession of state territory.[30]

Unlike most other states' constitutions, including that of Yemen, the Saudi constitution does not contain provisions pertaining to state territory or notions of its inviolability and integrity. The *Shura* (Consultative) Council, as mandated by its own statute, is just that, a government consultative committee legally responsible to the cabinet.[31]

Thus, contrary to the misleading depiction in local government media, the Consultative Council does not constitutionally amount to a separate or even nominal legislative body, nor does it have such a legal status.[32] Composed of royal appointees, the council's principal task is advisory. As defined in Article 15 of its statute, its task is to merely "express opinions on the general policy of the state referred to it by the Council of Ministers" headed by the king himself.

The ratification procedures of the Treaty of Jeddah under Saudi municipal law were swift and almost in a reverse order to those followed in Yemen. After the initial joint signing of the treaty in Jeddah on Saturday evening, June 12, 2000, the treaty was rushed to the Consultative Council in Riyadh the next day. After listening to a prepared written government report on its benefits, the Council approved[33] the treaty on Sunday afternoon in the form of a resolution.[34]

The resolution was duly "submitted," as prescribed by the Council's statute, to the general secretariat of the Council of Ministers, where it was approved during the regular Monday session presided over by the prime minister, King Fahad.[35] The latter, in his capacity as chief legislator and head of state, ratified the treaty in the form of a separate royal decree containing the full text of the Treaty of Jeddah's articles and attachments.[36]

A Fixed Duration Clause and the Treaty of Jeddah

Article 22, which stipulates a period of fixed duration for the treaty with a possibility of renewal or modification, was one of the most controversial clauses of the Treaty of Taif.[37] Incorporation of the Taif Treaty into the Treaty of Jeddah could provide either party with a legal basis, sanctioned under international law, to seek suspension or termination of the new treaty in whole or in part, should a dispute over the article's interpretation and application arise.[38]

Although duration clauses are not uncommon in general treaties, they are rarely included in peace treaties or in treaties resolving boundary disputes. The Treaty of Taif is a rather unusual instrument in the annals of modern legal history in that it serves both as a peace treaty and a boundary agreement, and as a general agreement regulating various aspects of Saudi-Yemeni relations, including political, military, economic and social matters.

On the one hand, it aims to be a timeless treaty that creates future rights and binding obligations involving the ending of an existing state of war (Preamble and Article 1), a cession of territory (Article 2) and the establishment of a boundary (Article 4). On the other hand, it contains a clause limiting its legal force to a fixed period of "twenty lunar years" from the date of ratification.

Article 22 of the Taif Treaty provides for the duration, renewal and amendment of the provisions of the treaty and the method by which this is to be achieved. If the treaty is not renewed or amended during the six months preceding its expiration, it will continue to remain in force, terminating six months from the date when one party notifies the other of its desire to amend it.[39] However, the general question in international law is whether the boundary-related components of the treaty are permanent or subject to a duration clause and options to renounce them, as parts of the Treaty of Jeddah may be.

Article 2 of the Treaty of Jeddah categorically confirms that all the articles and provisions contained in or attached to the Treaty of Taif are valid and binding on both Saudi Arabia and Yemen, without any modification, amendment or extension. Thus, irrespective of Article 22's previous disputed status, under the Treaty of Jeddah Article 22 assumes a new legal life of its own for 20 lunar years, commencing from the ratification of the new Treaty of Jeddah on July 4, 2000.

The remaining questions that may need to be addressed largely relate to the scope of Article 22's application. Could this scope be restricted to the provisions of the Treaty of Taif or extended to cover the Jeddah Treaty, including the provisions in the Jeddah Treaty not covered by the original and incorporated treaty of 1934.

However, Article 22 would appear to be applicable only to those articles in both complementary treaties involving non-territorial issues like the so-called "special privileges" clause. As explained above, provisions in either treaty that create territorial rights and establish boundaries would appear to be executed rights and subject to the doctrine of the sanctity and permanency of boundary treaties, which is sanctioned under conventional and customary law and evident in recent international judicial decisions. Thus, they would be excluded from the application of Article 22.[40]

Either way, international law and arbitration clauses contained in the Treaty of Jeddah guarantee either party the right to raise a legal dispute based on the interpretation and application of any of the articles contained in the Treaty of Jeddah and its complementary treaties. This could pertain, for example, to special privileges or an amendment or termination of the 1934 boundary upon the expiration of the treaty in 2019.

Interpretation of the Treaty of Jeddah by Arbitration

Under conventional law, interpretation of treaty provisions is the exclusive right of the parties involved who, subject to the rules of international law, may confer competence of interpretation on a judicial or arbitration body. Article 65 of the 1969 VCT gives priority to arbitration clauses in agreements that can be invoked by the parties to settle a potential dispute arising from the interpretation and application of the treaty.[41]

Both the Treaty of Taif and the 1995 MOU contain arbitration clauses. The Covenant of Arbitration, based on Article 8 of the Treaty of Taif, provides a compulsory mechanism for settlement to be invoked by either party if a dispute arises from or beyond the interpretation and application of the treaty's provisions.[42] The first article of the Covenant of Arbitration, which attaches it to the treaty as an "integral part" with "the force and authority of this treaty," states that the two parties "undertake to accept submission of the question in dispute to arbitration" within 30 days from the date of receipt of the other party's notification. The decision of the tribunal body is "considered binding on the two parties" and its execution is "obligatory and immediate" upon its announcement.[43]

Since the Treaty of Jeddah does not expressly contain arbitration clauses, it is assumed that it does contain them by virtue of its incorporation of the Treaty of Taif and the MOU. This raises important questions. The first question is whether the application of the arbitration clause is restricted to the Treaty of Taif or whether it covers the Treaty of Jeddah too.

The second and most important question is whether the arbitration clauses apply to disputes arising from territorial provisions creating the 1934 boundary under the Treaty of Taif or creating the maritime and land boundary under the Treaty of Jeddah. While both Saudi Arabia and Yemen accepted in principle the right of either party to seek arbitration under the relevant arbitration clause in the Treaty of Taif, they differed sharply and publicly on the extent of its application to the territorial provisions creating the 1934 boundary settlement.

When Yemen repeatedly insisted on the submission of the entire border dispute, including the 1934 boundary, to international arbitral or judicial arbitration,[44] Saudi Arabia consistently refused on the ground that international law precluded the territorial provisions in the Treaty of Taif from being submitted to third-party settlement.[45] Since the Treaty of Jeddah apparently failed to rectify this potentially serious problem, a similar legal dispute may very well re-emerge from the interpretation and application of non-territorial provisions, such as the clause on a period of fixed duration and territorial articles, including those relating to territorial adjustment of the 1934 line under the new treaty. Indeed, international law gives Saudi Arabia and Yemen the unhindered right to challenge, jointly or unilaterally, the validity of the Treaty of Jeddah as a whole or the interpretation or application of any of its provisions before a judicial or arbitral body.

As a general rule under international law, the Treaty of Jeddah remains valid until a contracting party claims the opposite. In such cases, it may remain in force but become voidable, rather than void. Articles 65-68 of the VCT explain the procedures to be followed with respect to invalidity, termination, withdrawal from a treaty and the settlement of disputes, these being conciliation, judicial or arbitral methods. Under article 65 of the VCT, or upon the expiration date under Article 22 of the Treaty of Taif, one party, i.e., Yemen, may invoke a ground for termination of or withdrawal from the Treaty of Jeddah, or for "impeaching the validity" of the treaty.

To this end, Yemen must first communicate to the other party the measure it intends to take with respect to the treaty, and the reason behind it.[46] The notification must be made in writing and signed by the head of state, the head of the government, the minister of foreign affairs or a representative of the state who may be called upon to produce his authorization to act with full powers.[47]

If, after no less than three months from the date of receipt of the notification, the receiving party, that is, Saudi Arabia, has not raised any objection, Yemen, as the party issuing the notification, may execute its proposed measure.[48] However, under the terms of Article 68 the notification can be revoked at any time before it takes effect.

If, however, an objection is raised by the receiving party, then both Yemen and Saudi Arabia are obliged under Article 33 of the Charter of the United Nations to seek a peaceful settlement of the dispute through conciliation. If no solution has been reached within one year after the date of the formal objection,

Yemen or Saudi Arabia may jointly or unilaterally seek a judicial or arbitral settlement under the auspices of the UN Secretary General.[49]

The potential dispute may concern the application or the interpretation of certain clauses contained in the Treaty of Jeddah and its complementary agreements, which may constitute *jus cogens* provisions as defined in Articles 53 or 64 of the VCT. In such a case, the two state parties must, under Article 66(a), refer the dispute to the ICJ in writing unless they jointly agree to submit it to arbitration.[50]

ICJ decisions have recognized the right of one state party to a dispute to unilaterally submit the dispute for judicial settlement. In the 1995 Jurisdiction and Admissibility Case concerning a territorial dispute between Qatar and Bahrain, the ICJ confirmed Qatar's unilateral decision to submit the dispute for judicial settlement and the Court's jurisdiction to adjucate "the whole of the dispute" between the two countries, who henceforth would be "bound by procedural consequences."[51]

Consequently, either Saudi Arabia or Yemen may choose to declare that, within the context of the relevant arbitration provisions contained in the Treaty of Taif and the 1995 MOU, as well as in the VCT and UN Charter, an international legal dispute with the other party exists. Either of the two governments may declare that such a dispute emanates from the interpretation of any of the provisions in the Treaty of Jeddah and its supplementary agreements and, accordingly, initiate the necessary procedures to submit the dispute to judicial or arbitral settlement.

Given the broad definition of a legal dispute under international law, the other party would find it exceedingly difficult to deny its legal existence or that it does not merit submission for arbitration by a third party. In the South West Africa Cases in 1962, the ICJ, in its

Advisory Opinion, rejected the Republic of South Africa's assertion that disagreement with the applicants in interpreting the provisions of Article 7 of the League of Nations Mandate for South West Africa was not in dispute.[52] In defining legal disputes, the Court confirmed an earlier PCIJ definition as being "a disagreement on a point of law or fact, a conflict of legal views or of interests between two persons."[53] It then proceeded to comment:

> ...the mere denial of the existence of a dispute does not prove its non-existence...there has arisen a situation in which the two sides hold clearly opposite views...confronted with such a situation, the Court must conclude that international disputes have arisen.[54]

Meanwhile, a treaty whose validity is being contested in terms of its own or any other provisions will continue to remain in force as long as the procedures for the settlement of the dispute through arbitration take place in accordance with the relevant articles of the VCT.[55]

The outcome of any potential or hypothetical judicial or arbitral settlement between Saudi Arabia and Yemen may or may not invalidate the Treaty of Jeddah in whole or in part. However, it will not in any substantial way legally affect the boundary settlement established between them by the complementary treaties of 1934 and 2000.

As discussed elsewhere in the study, this opinion is supported by customary and conventional law, as is evident in international judicial and arbitration decisions, such as the case of Cambodia versus Thailand in 1962, the case of Chad versus Libya in 1994, and the 1998 Eritrea-Yemen Award (First Phase). It is also supported by the relevant provisions in the VCT, which sanction treaties that establish boundaries, the UN Charter's maintenance of international peace and stability, and the works of prominent authors.

The Treaty and Yemeni and International Law

Since it embodies the 1934 and 1995 agreements, the Treaty of Jeddah contains certain provisions that are very contentious in terms of observance and legal status under both Yemeni municipal law and international law. The two complementary agreements require Saudi Arabia and Yemen, as the contracting parties, to prevent "with all material and moral means available," the use of their respective territories as a base for any actual or potential threat against each other in whatever form, be it "political, military or propaganda activity."[56]

Each party would also undertake "immediate measures" against any of its nationals "fomenting discord" by meting out deterrent punishment in a way that would "destroy his deed and prevent its recurrence."[57] If that person were a national of the targeted country, he would be "immediately arrested and…extradited without delay or excuse."[58] Furthermore, the Treaty of Taif prohibited both parties from granting refuge to political dissidents and stipulated their prompt and unconditional return in the event of their entry.[59]

In the MOU, provisions of non-interference also included "political and propaganda activity," which required the press and media in each country to refrain from criticism. As a result, the Treaty of Jeddah became one of the few modern international agreements containing provisions legally proscribing or restricting rights pertaining to the freedom of the press, freedom of expression and association, political asylum, and the extradition of political dissidents and refugees.[60]

These clauses, incorporated into the Treaty of Jeddah, appear to be in direct conflict with Yemeni municipal law and international law. Unlike their Saudi counterparts, the Yemeni constitution and press law both guarantee freedom of the press, freedom of expression and freedom of political association.⁶¹ More significantly, the clauses appear to be in violation of international human rights guaranteed under customary and conventional law as embodied in certain multilateral conventions. These conventions include, inter alia, the International Convention on Civil and Political Rights and its first and second optional protocols, the International Convention on Economic, Social and Cultural Rights, the Convention against Torture, and Other Cruel, Inhuman or Degrading Treatment or Punishment, and the Convention relating to the Status of Refugees.

In addition, the International Convention on the Protection of the Rights of All Migrant Workers and Members of their Families may also be relevant to Yemen's claim regarding "special privileges" and its labor force in Saudi Arabia. Although neither Saudi Arabia nor Yemen appear to be a party to any of these conventions, both countries would nonetheless be subject to them as customary law. Moreover, it is possible to argue that each of the provisions adopted in the Treaty of Jeddah pertaining to the extradition of fugitives, political dissidents, asylum and freedom of expression may also contravene the international legal principle of *jus cogens*.

Under Article 53 of the VCT a treaty becomes void if, at the time of its conclusion, it violates a peremptory norm of general international law. According to the article, a peremptory norm refers to a rule universally accepted and recognized as such by the world community of nations. Moreover, prominent authors agree with Article 64, which stipulates that if a new peremptory norm of general international law emerges "any existing treaty which is in conflict with that norm becomes void and terminates."⁶²

While prohibition of force as a means to settle disputes, slavery, piracy and genocide are established examples of the rule of *jus cogens*, one may also argue that the extradition of political and criminal fugitives without due process and the inhibition of freedom of belief and expression constitute a violation of a newly emerging peremptory norm of international law. Consequently, the Treaty of Jeddah, as well as the two complementary agreements it embodied, may be declared void or voidable in terms of the *jus cogens* principle.

Hypothetically, the *jus cogens* doctrine provides Saudi Arabia and Yemen with the legal ground to seek the termination of the Treaty of Jeddah, in whole or in part, and together or unilaterally. However, if this potential Saudi-Yemeni dispute concerned the interpretation or application of articles in the Treaty of Taif and the 1995 MOU that are likely to be *jus cogens* provisions under Articles 53 or 64 of the VCT, the disputing party would be required, under Article 66(a) of the Convention, to refer the dispute to the ICJ in writing, unless the two sides agreed to submit it to arbitration.[63]

8
Conclusions and Prospects

In form and substance, the 2000 Treaty of Jeddah is almost unique in the annals of modern treaties. It is a multiple treaty composed of separate though interrelated bilateral international agreements that were concluded at various times and places between Saudi Arabia and Yemen. By incorporating these agreements without change, the Treaty of Jeddah, despite its official name, constitutes a multipurpose treaty covering all aspects of bilateral Saudi-Yemeni relations.

It is at once a peace treaty calling for the permanent cessation of armed hostility between the two countries, a boundary treaty involving territorial cession and establishing a final maritime and land boundary, and a general instrument regulating political, military, economic and social interaction between Yemen and Saudi Arabia. Nevertheless, it contains a clause expressly limiting the legal force of the Treaty of Jeddah to 20 years.

This apparently contradictory clause is but one of several conflicting provisions in the Treaty of Jeddah that could seriously impede its operation. The inherent legal weakness in the new treaty emanates primarily, but not exclusively, from the fact that it incorporates in whole and without change the contentious Treaty of

Taif, instead of superceding or amending it. The dispute over the previous Treaty's status under international law has long neutralized its legal effect.

Nevertheless, the most innovative feature of the Treaty of Jeddah is that it provides for a comprehensive and final settlement of the boundary dispute. The dispute has marred bilateral relations between Saudi Arabia and Yemen for most of the twentieth century, making it one of the longest-running boundary conflicts in the world.

The treaty was the direct outcome of a joint decision taken at the highest levels of leadership in the two countries and thus represented a political compromise aimed at reconciling their long-standing border differences. The legal settlement is regarded by the two governments as a prerequisite for securing and maintaining political stability in their respective countries.

For Yemen, political stability could be achieved only after the "return" of Yemeni territory lost to Saudi Arabia before and since 1934. From the Yemeni point of view, the Treaty of Jeddah satisfied this demand, at least partially. Within the terms of the treaty, Yemen's territory, in the words of one Yemeni politician, "increased in size to half the area of *bilad al-yaman*,"[64] the perceived "Greater Yemen" covering the lower part of the Arabian Peninsula south of the holy city of Mecca. Yemen could not recover all of the territory, but was compensated by the substantial non-territorial social and economic benefits granted in perpetuity to Yemen and its nationals under the so-called "special exemptions" provisions contained in the new treaty.

Nevertheless, the settlement provided by the treaty is generally viewed in Yemen as less than satisfactory. According to a senior advisor to the Yemeni president, the government agreed to the treaty because it constituted "the only possible option under the prevailing circumstances," and the Yemeni government had to "accept most of what we can not obtain in whole."[65]

The legal dimensions of the prevailing circumstances were reflected in two specific and relevant international judicial and arbitral decisions. These decisions eventually forced the Yemeni government to abandon its long-standing demand, indeed threat, to unilaterally submit its entire boundary dispute with Saudi Arabia to a third settlement body. Instead, it agreed to the Saudi call for a resolution of the conflict by means of bilateral agreements.

The Yemeni government felt that the 1994 international case of Chad versus Libya had undermined its main legal argument that the 1934 boundary settlement was illegal, because it had been established under a treaty that was void or voidable under international law. The ICJ clearly stated that boundaries established under treaties were final and permanent. Such boundaries gain a legal life of their own, irrespective of the legal status or fate of the treaties that create them.

Likewise, in the international arbitration case on Eritrea and Yemen in 1998, the Tribunal rejected the grounds of Yemen's ancient title and its reversion of an historical argument in support of its claim to a sovereign title over, *inter alia*, the Red Sea Hanish group of islands. However, the Tribunal agreed to award sovereign title over the islands to Yemen on the principle of prescription and state activities.

Subsequently, the Yemeni government anticipated that it would be exceedingly difficult to legally sustain the same historical title argument that it had lost against Eritrea against Saudi Arabia too. In the former case, the Tribunal asserted that as recently as 1925, shortly before the signing of the Saudi-Idrisi Treaty of Mecca, the Imamate of Yemen was almost a semi-landlocked country whose limits did not extend beyond the central highlands in the southwestern corner of Arabia, well south of the Treaty of Taif's boundary agreed in 1934.

Consequently, if the same principle of a prescriptive title was applied in a hypothetical comprehensive arbitration, especially in connection with other principles like a *res nullius* and a plebiscite among the indigenous population, Yemen could plausibly loose substantial territory to Saudi Arabia. Such territory would include previously undisputed areas south of the 1934 boundary and 1955 Riyadh Line, which might theoretically include a direct and sovereign Saudi territorial corridor to the Indian Ocean.

Yemen recognized the potentially adverse legal implications of the two judicial and arbitral decisions on its territorial dispute with Saudi Arabia, and probably also realized that it had already prejudiced its legal position vis-à-vis Saudi Arabia by abandoning the historical title argument in the 1992 border agreement with Oman.

Saudi Arabia had a seemingly unassailable legal position compared to that of Yemen, as a result of the two relevant international judicial and arbitral decisions. Thus, it is difficult to explain the Saudi government's tenacious adherence to the 1934 boundary, its refusal to submit the dispute wholly or partially to arbitration, and the eventual generous territorial cession with apparently no comparable territorial or political compensation. According to the available public record, Saudi Arabia did not seem to realize the full potential implications of the two recent international law cases. Yemen apparently did and adapted its legal position accordingly.

Second, even if Saudi Arabia realized the potential legal benefits and reversed its long-standing position on the status of the Treaty of Taif and third-party judicial or arbitral settlement, it would be unlikely that a hypothetical arbitral or judicial arbitration would have significantly changed its existing *de jure* and *de facto* boundary with Yemen. In terms of the international legal doctrine of the inviolability and permanency of the boundary for the sake of regional stability and international peace, a third party arbiter would probably reaffirm the legal sanctity of the Treaty of Taif's boundary in 1934, even if it had been mutually or unilaterally terminated by the parties.

With respect to the eastern sector not covered by the 1934 treaty, Saudi Arabia, like Yemen, had already prejudiced its legal position in relation to Yemen in two important respects. In the 1948 Al-'Abr agreement, Saudi Arabia had recognized certain nomadic tribes, such as the Sei'ar, Karab and Manahil, as subjects of the British Aden Protectorate (and of Yemen as its ultimate legal successor). It therefore gave up its claim to the territory in which they roamed, most of which is located north of the Saudi government's own 1935 Hamza claim line. This boundary was drawn exclusively on the basis of tribal allegiance, as manifested in the payment of Islamic taxation in the form of *Zakat* to the Saudi rulers.

Likewise, in its 1990 boundary treaty with Oman, Saudi Arabia had departed from its traditional position and had accepted the British Riyadh Line of 1955 by establishing the western end of its boundary at 19 degrees North 52 degrees East. As a result, Saudi Arabia found it difficult to legally justify its continued rejection of the Riyadh Line in its dispute with Yemen after it had already agreed to it in its dispute with Oman. This ultimately forced Saudi Arabia, under the 1997 Como Agreement, to accept the same 19 degrees North 52 degrees East coordinates as in the case of the eastern end of its boundary with Yemen. Since both the Hamza and Riyadh Lines extend in a westerly direction until they cross the eastern limits of the 1934 line, Saudi Arabia virtually precluded itself from developing and sustaining any sound legal argument for a direct and sovereign corridor through Yemeni territory to the Indian Ocean.

Finally, the seemingly unilateral Saudi cession of territory to Yemen under the terms of the Treaty of Jeddah must be seen as part of Saudi Arabia's long-established policy pattern of settling border issues with neighboring states.[66] In this context, Saudi Arabia viewed internal political stability as a function of regional stability, and ceding part of the disputed or undisputed Saudi territory to a neighboring state was a worthwhile price to achieve the prime policy objective of maintaining domestic political stability.

This pattern is clearly apparent in virtually all the boundary agreements Saudi Arabia concluded with neighboring states after becoming a member of the UN in 1945.[67] Saudi Arabia declared as late as 1999 that Yemen would be "no exception to this rule" of the self-acknowledged traditional Saudi policy.[68] With the conclusion of the Treaty of Jeddah, Saudi Arabia formally settled its longest and politically most serious border dispute in the region, though by no means, as it erroneously declared, all boundary disputes with neighboring states.[69]

However, most of these boundary agreements appear to have been less than successful in providing the border stability Saudi Arabia has hoped for.[70] The Treaty of Jeddah, though intended to strengthen political stability in Yemen by "regaining" territory and in Saudi Arabia by ceding territory, appears to be no exception due to its internal contradictions.

From a strictly legal point of view, by embodying in whole and without change all the articles and attachments of the contentious Treaty of Taif of 1934, the Treaty of Jeddah has incorporated the same basic defects that had rendered the 1934 treaty legally inoperative.

While both the Saudi and Yemeni governments view the Treaty of Taif as a fundamental legal component of the Treaty of Jeddah, each emphasizes a different aspect of the treaty. Saudi Arabia emphasizes the territorial provisions under which the 1934 boundary was established,[71] while Yemen attaches importance to the non-territorial aspects of the Treaty of Taif, particularly those pertaining to economic, labor and social issues.[72]

In form, the Treaty of Jeddah and the previous agreements it incorporated meet the procedural requirements of the VCT regarding the conclusion of a valid international agreement.[73] In substance, the status of the new treaty within the terms of international law is questionable through the same arguments hypothetically employed in this study against the Treaty of Taif, which contains certain important but legally controversial, if not conflicting, articles. These articles could lead to the emergence of different Saudi-Yemeni views on their interpretation and application under the new treaty, as they have in the past.

All this is bound to have legal implications that may affect the status and implementation of the Treaty of Jeddah, including provisions stipulating a final settlement of the long border dispute between the two countries. These potential legal problems emanate primarily, if not exclusively, from the fact that the Treaty of Jeddah expressly incorporated all the provisions and attachments contained in the 1934 Treaty of Taif, including the controversial and apparently conflicting provisions on territorial boundaries, fixed duration, special privileges and extradition.

By doing so, the Saudi and Yemeni creators of the Treaty of Jeddah unwittingly infected its substantive text with the basic defects that had already rendered the Treaty of Taif a worthless legal document. This potentially serious problem that threatens the status and operation of the new treaty would have been largely avoided if the Treaty of Jeddah had expressly superceded the Treaty of Taif, instead of incorporating it.

The new treaty was the direct result of important political decisions apparently made in haste and leaving little or no space for legal teams to hammer out a sound legal document. The whole process of negotiations, formulation and signature took less than four weeks.[74] This is clearly reflected in the errors involving the principal points listed in the geographical coordinates[75] and, more seriously, in the poorly structured and confusing wording of Article 2, which is essential to the fundamental objective of the Treaty of Jeddah. On the one hand, Article 2 of the Treaty of Jeddah contained some provisions that contradicted others in its text and in Article 1. On the other hand, Article 2 appeared to be in glaring conflict with Article 4 of the Treaty of Taif and Article 10 of the MOU.

Ideally, the Treaty of Jeddah should have superceded, instead of integrated, the Treaty of Taif and all other previous agreements by including a clause expressly cancelling them. The Treaty of Jeddah should have been an exclusively territorial and boundary agreement, as indicated in its preamble and Article 2 and demonstrated in other boundary agreements that the two signatory states had concluded with their neighbors.[76] It could then have included an article calling on both parties to conclude future protocols on economic, social, cultural and other non-territorial issues.[77]

Alternatively, the two countries could have negotiated an arrangement whereby certain non-territorial provisions contained in the 1934 treaty and deemed essential by one or both of the parties were included in the Treaty of Jeddah after modification and clarification in unambiguous terms. This would have left little room for a potential legal dispute over the provisions arising from their interpretation and application under customary and conventional law. While legally canceling the former treaty, the new treaty should also have removed all other irrelevant, outdated or otherwise suspect provisions contained in the Treaty of Taif and pertaining to the 1934 state of war, such as the provisions on a termination of the war in particular.

After all, this is what Saudi Arabia and Yemen had achieved during the conclusion of the Taif Treaty back in 1934. After incorporating many of the provisions of the 1931 'Aru Agreement into the Treaty of Taif, they inserted Article 21, which explicitly declared the preceding instrument "null and void" from "the date of" the superceding treaty.[78] The 2000 treaty should also have removed all the provisions dealing with universal human rights issues, such as the extradition of political dissidents and freedom of expression. These provisions were contained in the 1934 treaty and 1995 MOU and appear to violate the emergent peremptory norm of general international law (*jus cogens*) as stipulated in Article 53 of the VCT.

Judging from the recent political history of bilateral Saudi-Yemeni relations, it seems probable that the Treaty of Jeddah, by incorporating the same fundamental legal problems that plagued the Treaty of Taif, could also become the main source of a recurrent border conflict instead of being part of its solution.

Yemen clearly reads far more into the Treaty of Jeddah than its text provides, especially with regard to the potential social and economic benefits presumably contained in the so-called special exemptions. Senior parliamentary and government officials have interpreted the provisions to mean "massive Saudi investment in Yemen as well as opening the Saudi labor market gates to Yemenis."[79]

It was perhaps such high, albeit unrealistic, expectations that a senior advisor to the Yemeni President had in mind when, days after the signing of the treaty, he wrote a telling commentary that was reminiscent of previous arguments regarding the prevailing circumstances that forced Yemen to conclude the Treaty of Taif in 1934. Yemen had agreed to sign the Treaty of Jeddah, he wrote, because it was:

> ...the only possible option under the prevailing circumstances. For Yemen, there is no other alternative to come out of this dilemma. As such it is the choice least harmful to the country and its sons. We should accept most of what we cannot obtain in whole. The coming days are pregnant with surprises for the two sides either to go forward or revert decades backwards. It depends on whether the two sides – the stronger one in particular [i.e., Saudi Arabia] - prove their credibility by translating the text and provisions of the treaty into living reality.[80]

In this light, it appears inevitable that, in the not too distant future, the two states will find themselves compelled by circumstances to initiate a whole new tortuous process of third-party judicial or arbitral decision-making or to renegotiate yet again a new and comprehensive bilateral agreement. These would be the only viable legal options to resolve by peaceful means the re-emerging Saudi-Yemeni border conflict, which is based on the two parties' essentially conflicting views on the interpretation and application of the controversial clauses contained in the two "complementary" treaties.

In the meantime, one hopes that any potential dispute will be resolved peacefully in the same spirit that led to the Treaty of Jeddah, but with more political acumen and legal competence, taking into account the primacy of strategic interests and the well-being of the respective peoples as the only certain guarantee for creating and sustaining regional and international peace and stability sanctioned by customary and conventional law.

APPENDICES

Appendix I
Sources related to the Saudi-Yemeni Dispute[1]

1926: The Mecca Agreement

The Arabic text appears in Ministry of Foreign Affairs (Saudi Arabia), *Majmu'at Al-Mu'ahadat, aljuza alawwal: Min 1341 Ila 1370 Hijriyah, Almuwafiq:1922 -1951)* (Collection of Treaties, vol. 1: 1922-1951) (Mecca: Government Printing Office, 1375h/ 1955), 23, and the English translation in Richard Schofield (editor) *Arabian Boundary Disputes: Saudi Arabia-Yemen, 1913-1992*, vol. 20 (London: Archive Editions 1993), 48-49.

1931: Al-'Aru (Abu 'Arish) Agreement

The English text appears in Penelope Tuson and Emma Quick (editors) *Arabian Treaties 1600-1960*, vol. 4 (London: Archive Editions, 1992), 153.

1934: Statement on Relations between the Kingdom of Saudi Arabia and Imam Yahya (of Yemen)

Bayan 'an Al-'Ala'qat Bayn Al-Mamlakah Al-'Arabiyah Al'Su'udiyah wa Al-Imam Yahya Imam Yahya Hamidul-Din in Ministry of Foreign Affairs, *Al-kitab al-akhdhar* (The Green Book) (Mecca: Um Alqura Press, 1934).

---

1. See bibliography for the full references.

1934: The Treaty of Taif

The Arabic text of the treaty, including the 1936 General Agreement between the Kingdom of Saudi Arabia and the Kingdom of Yemen concerning the Settlement of Matters relating to the Subjects of the two Kingdoms, and the 1937 Saudi-Yemeni Joint Commission Demarcation Report, appears in *Majmu'at*, op. cit., 152-198. For the Arabic text with an English translation, but without the 1936 and 1937 attachments, see Doreen Ingrams and Leila Ingrams (editors) *Records of Yemen: 1798-1960, vol. 8: 1933-1945* (London: Archive Editions, 1993), op. cit., 191-228; for the English text only, see *4 Arabian Treaties*, op. cit., 336-45.

1936: General Agreement between the Kingdom of Saudi Arabia and the Kingdom of Yemen concerning the Settlement of Matters relating to the Subjects of the two Kingdoms

The Arabic text appears in *Majmu'at*, op. cit., 194-198.

1937: Saudi–Yemeni Joint Commission Demarcation Report

For the Arabic text, see above; for the English translation, see "Annexure to the Taif Agreement for the Demarcation of Borders between the Kingdom of Yemen and the Kingdom of Saudi Arabia, 1937," *20 Arabian Boundary Disputes*, op. cit., 643-672.

1948: The Al-'Abr Agreement between Saudi Arabia and the Aden Protectorate

The Arabic text appears in King Abdulaziz Public Library, *Mawsu'at Tarikh Al-Malik 'Abdulaziz Al-Dublumasi* (Encyclopedia of the Diplomatic History of King Abdulaziz) (Riyadh: 1999), op. cit., 433-8.

1953: Saudi-Yemeni Note constituting a formal extension of the Taif Treaty's duration

The Arabic text appears in *Um Alqura*, March 20, 1953, 1.

1973: Saudi-Yemeni Joint Communiqué

The Arabic text appears in *Um Alqura*, March 23, 1973, 1, 8.

1990: The Agreement to Unify the Yemen Arab Republic and the People's Democratic Republic of Yemen

For the text, see *International Legal Material* (*ILM*) vol. 30 (1991).

1991: European Union: Declaration regarding the 'Guidelines on the Recognition of New States in Eastern Europe and in the Soviet Union'

European Journal of International Law (*EJIL*) vol. 4 no. 1 (1993).

1995: Memorandum of Understanding between Saudi Arabia and Yemen, signed February 26, 1995

The Arabic text of the MOU is in *Alriyadh*, February 27, 1995, and the unofficial English translation at http://www.al-bab.com/yemen/pol/mou.htm.

2000: International Boundary Treaty (Treaty of Jeddah) between Saudi Arabia and Yemen, signed on June 12, 2000

For the Arabic text, see *Um Alqura*, July 7, 2000, 1-4; *Sitta-Wa-Ishreen Septambar*, June 22, 2000, 8-9. For an unofficial English version, see *The Yemen Times*, June 26-July 2, 2000 and *Middle East Economic Survey* (*MEES*) vol. 43, no. 27 (June 2000), 25-29.

Appendix II
Full Text of the Treaty of Taif, including its Attachments, the Covenant of Arbitration and Amendments[2]

In the Name of Allah the Merciful, the Compassionate.

Treaty of Islamic Friendship and Arab Brotherhood between the Kingdom of Saudi Arabia and the Kingdom of Yemen.

His Majesty Imam Abdulaziz ibn Abdulrahman Al-Faysal Al Saud, King of the Kingdom of Saudi Arabia, and His Majesty Imam Yahya bin Muhammad Hamidaddin, King of Yemen:

Desiring to end the state of war unfortunately existing between them and their governments and peoples,

And to unite the Islamic Arab nation and elevate its status and maintain its dignity and independence,

And in view of the need to establish strong ties based on a treaty between them and their governments and countries on the basis of mutual advantage and reciprocal interest,

And wishing to fix the frontiers between their countries and to establish good neighborly relations and ties of Islamic friendship between them and to strengthen the foundations of peace and calm between their countries and peoples,

And desiring that there should be a united front against sudden misfortune and a solid structure to preserve the safety of the Arabian Peninsula, have resolved to conclude a treaty of Islamic friendship and Arab brotherhood between them and have nominated the following representatives for that purpose, to act as plenipotentiaries on their behalf: On behalf of His Majesty the King of the Kingdom of Saudi Arabia, His Royal Highness Amir Khalid

---

2. Author's translation.

Ibn Abdulaziz, son of His Majesty and Deputy President of the Council of Ministers,

And on behalf of His Majesty the King of Yemen, His Excellency Sayyed Abdullah bin Ahmed Al-Wazir,

Their Majesties the two Kings have given their above-mentioned representatives full powers and absolute authority; and their above-mentioned representatives, having perused each other's credentials and having found them to be in a proper form, have, in the name of their Kings, agreed upon the following articles:

Article 1

The state of war existing between the Kingdom of Yemen and the Kingdom of Saudi Arabia shall be terminated from the moment the treaty is signed, and a state of perpetual peace, firm friendship and everlasting Islamic Arab brotherhood, inviolable in whole or in part, shall immediately be established between their Majesties the Kings and between their countries and peoples. The two important contractual parties undertake to settle all disputes and differences that may arise between them in a spirit of affection and friendship, and to ensure that a spirit of Islamic Arab brotherhood shall dominate their relations under all circumstances. They call upon God to witness the benevolence of their intentions and their honest desire for concord and agreement, both in private and in public, and they pray to the Almighty to grant them and their successors and heirs and governments success in maintaining this proper attitude, which pleases the Creator and honors their people and religion.

Article 2

Each of the two important contracting parties recognizes the full and absolute independence of the other party's kingdom and his sovereignty over it. His Majesty Imam Abdulaziz ibn Abdulrahman Al-Faysal Al Saud, King of the Kingdom of Saudi Arabia, acknowledges to His Majesty Imam Yahya and his lawful successors the full and absolute independence of the Kingdom of Yemen and his sovereignty over it, and His Majesty Imam Yahya bin Muhammad Hamidaddin, King of Yemen, acknowledges to His Majesty Imam Abdulaziz and his lawful successors the full and absolute independence of the Kingdom of Saudi Arabia and his sovereignty over it. Each one of them gives up any right he has claimed over any part or parts of the country of the other party beyond the frontiers fixed and defined in the text of this treaty. In terms of this treaty, His Majesty King Abdulaziz waives any right of protection or occupation, or any other right that he has claimed in the territories which, according to this treaty, belong to the Yemen and were formerly in the possession of the Idrisi, and other territories. By this treaty, His Majesty Imam Yahya similarly waives any right that he has claimed, in the name of Yemeni unity or something else, to the territories that belong to the Kingdom of Saudi Arabia in terms of this treaty and were formerly in the possession of the Idrisi or the Al 'Aayidh, or in Najran, or in the Yam area.

Article 3

The two important contracting parties agree to conduct their relations and communications in a manner that will secure the interests of both parties and will cause no harm to either of them, provided that neither of the important contracting parties shall concede to the other party less than he concedes to a third party. Neither one of the two parties will be bound to concede to the other party more than he would receive.

Article 4

The boundary line that divides the countries of the two important contracting parties is explained in sufficient detail below. This line is considered to be a fixed boundary between the territories that are subject to each party. The boundary between the two Kingdoms begins at a point halfway between Midi and al-Muwassam on the Red Sea coast and runs in an easterly direction to the mountain of the Tihamah. It then turns northwards until it reaches the northwest boundaries between Bani Juma'ah and those (tribes) adjacent to them to the north and west. It then bends to the east until it reaches (a point) between the boundaries of Naqa'a and Wa'ar, both of which belong to the Wa'ilah tribe, and the boundaries of the Yam. It then bends until it reaches Marwan Narrows (Madhig Marwan) and the Riyadh Pass ('Aqabat Rifadah). It then bends east until, at the eastern end, it reaches the edge of the boundaries between Yam (on the one hand) and Wa'ilah and the other (tribes) of Hamdan bin Zayd, Yam excluded.

Everything that is to the right side of the aforementioned line, from the aforementioned point on the coast to the end of the borders of the aforementioned mountains, in all directions, belongs to the Kingdom of Yemen. Everything that is to the left side of the aforementioned line belongs to the Kingdom of Saudi Arabia. On the aforementioned right side are Midi, Haradh, some of the Al Harath tribe, Al-Mir, the mountains of Al-Dhabir, Shadha and Al-Day'a, some of the Al-'Abadil, all the territories and mountains, Razih and Munabbah, including 'Aru Al Amshaykh, all the territories and mountains of the Bani Juma'ah and Sihar al-Sham, Yabad and the apportioned areas, the area of the Muraysagha of Sihar al-Sham, all of Sihar, Naqa'a-Wa'ar, and all of Wa'ilah, hence La-Far together with the Nahuqa pass, and all the territories of the Hamdan bin Zayd, apart from those of the Yam and the

Wada'a of Dhahran. The aforementioned (tribes), their territories with their known boundaries, and everything between and beyond the said directions of which the name is not cited, but which was actually linked to or in the firm possession of the Yemeni Kingdom prior to 1352 A.H., all of that, being on the right side, belongs to the Yemeni Kingdom.

That (territory) which is on the left side, namely Al-Muwassam, Walloon, most of the Al-Harath, the Al-Chubb, the Al-Jabber, most of the Al 'Abadil, all of Fay, Bani Malik, Bani Hairs, Al-Tailed, Qahtan and Dhahran Wadi'ah, and all of the Wadi'ah of Dhathran, together with Marwan and the Rifadah pass and the territories to the north and east of Yam, Najran, Al-Hadhn and Zur Wadita, all of the Wa'ilah in Najran and everything below the Nahuqa pass to the end of Najran and Yam to the east, the aforementioned tribes, their territories with their known boundaries, and everything between and beyond the said directions of which the name is not cited, but which was actually linked to or in the firm possession of the Kingdom of Saudi Arabia prior to the year 1352 A.H., all of that, being on the left hand side of the said line, belongs to the Kingdom of Saudi Arabia.

Everything mentioned regarding Yam, Najran al-Hadhn, Zur Wada'a and the Wa'ila people in Najran is based on His Majesty Imam Yahya's delegation to His Majesty King 'Abdulaziz of the right to decide on Yam, and the decision by His Majesty King 'Abdulaziz that all of it belongs to the Kingdom of Saudi Arabia. Because Al-Hadhn, Zur Wadi'a and the members of the Wa'ila in Najran belong to the Wa'ila, and were only included in the Kingdom of Saudi Arabia for the reason stated, neither they nor their brothers from Wa'ila will be prevented from enjoying the usual and customary relations, interaction and cooperation.

This line then extends from the end of the aforementioned boundaries between the tribes of the Kingdom of Saudi Arabia and Hamdan bin Zayd and all the other tribes of Yemen, apart from the Yam. The Yemeni Kingdom includes all the Yemeni towns and outlying areas up to the end of Yemen's borders in all directions; the Kingdom of Saudi Arabia includes all the towns and outlying areas up to the end of its borders in all directions. All points mentioned in this article, whether north, south, east or west, are to be considered in relation to the predominant flow of the frontier line in the directions mentioned. It frequently bends due to the uneven nature of (the territory) of each of the two kingdoms. The demarcation and fixing of the said line, determining tribal affiliation and specifying tribal locations in the best possible manner, shall be carried out in an amicable, fraternal and non-injurious manner, following established tribal usage and custom, by a committee consisting of an equal number of people from the two parties.

Article 5

In view of the desire of both parties for continued peace and calm, and to prevent any intimidation of these two countries, they mutually agree not to construct any fortified building within a distance of five kilometers anywhere on either side of the border.

Article 6

The two important contracting parties undertake to immediately withdraw their troops from the territory that becomes the possession of the other party, by virtue of this treaty, and to guard its inhabitants and troops against all harm.

Article 7

The two important contracting parties undertake to prevent their people from committing any harmful or hostile act against the people of the other kingdom, in any district or on any route; to prevent raiding between the Bedouins on both sides; to return, after the ratification of this treaty, and based on legal investigation, all property that has been taken; to give compensation for all damage where crimes of killing or the wounding of others have been committed, to the extent that is legally necessary; and to severely punish anyone who have committed a hostile act. This article will remain in force until another agreement has been drawn up between the two parties on the method of investigating and estimating damage and loss.

Article 8

The two parties both undertake to refrain from force in any disputes between them, and to do their utmost to settle by friendly means any disputes that may arise between them, whether caused by this treaty or the interpretation of all or any of its articles or resulting from any other cause. In the event that they are unable to agree, each one undertakes to resort to arbitration, of which the conditions and procedure are explained in the appendix attached to this treaty. This appendix will have the force and authority of the treaty, and shall be considered an integral part of it.

Article 9

The two parties undertake to prevent, with all the moral and material means at their command, the use of their territory as a base and center for any preparations for or actual hostile action against the territory of the other party. They also undertake to immediately take the following measures on receipt of a written demand from the government of the other party:

(1) If the person endeavoring to foment disturbances is a subject of the government that receives the application to take action, he should, after the matter has been legally investigated and he has been convicted, receive a punishment that will put an end to his actions and prevent their recurrence.

(2) If the person attempting to foment disturbances is a subject of the government demanding that measures be taken, he should be immediately arrested by the government that was approached and handed over to the government making the demand. The government that was asked to surrender him shall not have any right to excuse itself from carrying out this demand, but shall be bound to take adequate steps to prevent the flight of the person requested, and in the event of the requested person being able to escape, the government from whose territory he has fled shall not allow him to return to its territory, and if he is able to return, it shall arrest him and hand him over to his government.

(3) If the person endeavoring to foment disturbances is a subject of a third government, the government to which the demand is made and which finds the person in its territories, shall immediately and directly after receiving the demand from the other government take steps to expel him from its country, consider him as an undesirable and prevent him from returning there in future.

Article 10

The two important contracting parties agree not to receive anyone who has fled from the jurisdiction of his government, whether he be important or unimportant, official or nonofficial, an individual or a group. Each of the important contracting parties shall take adequate and effective administrative or military measures to prevent these fugitives from entering the borders of its country. If one of them succeeds or all of them succeed in crossing the frontier and entering its territory, it shall be bound to disarm the refugee, arrest him and hand him over to the government of the country from which he has fled. In the event of it being unable to arrest him, it shall take adequate steps to drive him out of the country that he has entered and into the country to which he belongs.

Article 11

The two important contracting parties undertake to prevent their *Amirs* (Saudi local governors), *Amils* (Yemeni local governors) and officials from having dealings in any way whatsoever, either directly or indirectly, with the subjects of the other party. They undertake to take all measures to prevent any disturbance or misunderstanding as a result of such actions.

Article 12

Each of the two contracting parties recognizes that the people of all areas accruing to the other party by virtue of this treaty are subjects of that party. Each of them undertakes not to accept as its subjects any person or persons who are subjects of the other party, except with the consent of that party. Furthermore, each party undertakes that the subjects of the parties, when in the country of the other party, shall be treated in accordance with local law.

Article 13

Each of the two contracting parties undertakes to announce a full and complete amnesty for all crimes and hostile acts that may have been committed by any person or persons who are subjects of the other party but reside in its own territory (i.e., in the territory of the party issuing the amnesty). Similarly, each one of them undertakes to issue a full, general and complete amnesty for all crimes to those of its subjects who may have gone to, or taken refuge with, or in any manner linked themselves to the other party; and for the property that they may have taken to the other party from the time when they went until their return, whatever its nature and whatever its value; and not to allow any sort of injury or punishment to or constraint upon them on account of their having taken refuge there, or for the manner in which they did so. If either party has any doubt about the occurrence of anything contrary to this undertaking, the party entertaining the doubt may request the other party to call a meeting of the representatives who signed this treaty; if it is impossible for any of them to attend, he may send another fully authorized and empowered person, well-acquainted with the localities and committed to effect a settlement between the parties and to ensure the rights of both, to investigate the matter, so that no injustice or dispute may arise. The decision of these representatives shall be considered as binding.

Article 14

Each of the two important contracting parties undertakes to return the property of those subjects whom it pardons, and to hand it over to them or their heirs on their return to their country, in accordance with the law of their country. Similarly, the important contracting parties undertake not to retain any of the goods and movable property that belong to the subjects of the other party, and not to create obstacles to their free use or their legitimate disposal.

Article 15

Each of the two important contracting parties undertakes not to have dealings with a third party, whether it be an individual, group or government, or to agree with him in any matter that may injure the interests of the other party, or that may raise problems and difficulties, or that may create a risk to its welfare, interests or existence.

Article 16

The two contracting parties, who are bound by their Islamic brotherhood and Arab origin, announce that their nation is one, that they do not wish any evil to anyone, that they are striving to promote the interest of their nation in the shade of tranquility and quiet, and that they are doing their best in everything for the good of their countries and their nation, intending no hostility toward any nation.

Article 17

In the event of any external aggression against the country of one of the two important contracting parties, the other party shall be bound to carry out the following undertakings:

(1) To adopt complete covert and overt neutrality;

(2) To give all possible moral assistance;

(3) To begin talks with the other party to discover the best way of guaranteeing the safety of the territory of that party and of preventing it from being harmed, and to refrain from any act that might be interpreted as assisting an external aggressor.

Article 18

In the event of insurrection or hostilities taking place within the country of one of the two important contracting parties, both of them mutually undertake the following:
1. To take all the necessary effective measures to prevent the aggressors or the insurgents from using their territories;
2. To prevent fugitives from taking refuge in their countries, and to hand them over or expel them if they have entered, as explained in Articles 9 and 10 above;
3. To prevent its subjects from joining the aggressors or insurgents, and to refrain from encouraging or supplying them;
4. To prevent assistance, supplies, arms or ammunition from reaching the aggressors.

Article 19

The two important contracting parties announce their desire to do everything possible to facilitate postal and telegraphic services, to increase communications between the two countries, and to facilitate the exchange of commodities, agricultural and commercial products between them; to undertake detailed negotiations on a customs agreement in order to safeguard the economic interest of their two countries by standardizing customs duties throughout the two countries, or by special regulations designed to secure the advantage of both sides. Nothing in this article shall restrict the freedom of either of the two important contracting parties in any manner until the agreement referred to has been concluded.

Article 20

Each of the two important contracting parties declares its readiness to authorize its representatives and delegates abroad, if there are such representatives, to represent the other party in any matter or at any time, whenever the other party wants this to happen. It is understood that whenever representatives of both parties are together in one place they will collaborate in order to coordinate their policy and to promote the interests of their two countries, which form one nation. It is understood that this article does not restrict the freedom of either side in any manner whatsoever regarding any of its rights. Similarly, it cannot be interpreted as limiting the freedom of either of them or compelling either of them to adopt this course.

Article 21

The provisions of the agreement signed on *shaban* 5, 1350, will be terminated on the ratification date of this treaty.

Article 22

Their Majesties, the two Kings, having regarded the common interest of both sides, shall ratify and confirm the treaty within the shortest possible time. It shall come into force from the date of exchange of the instrument of ratification, except insofar as Article 1, regarding the ending of the state of war immediately after its signature, is concerned. It shall remain in force for a period of 20 lunar years. It may be renewed or amended during the six months preceding its expiration. If not renewed or amended by that date, it shall continue to remain in force for six months after the date of the notice given by one party to the other party of his desire to amend it.

Article 23

This treaty shall be called the Treaty of Taif. Two copies of it have been drawn up in the noble Arabic language, with each of the important contracting parities being in possession of one copy.

As a witness hereof, each of the Plenipotentiaries has affixed his signatures.

Written in the city of Jeddah on *safar* 6, 1353.

(signed) Khalid ibn Abdulaziz Al-Saud

(signed) Sayyid Abdullah bin Ahmad Al-Wazir

Arbitration Covenant between the Kingdom of Saudi Arabia and the Kingdom of Yemen

Whereas their Majesties King Abdulaziz, king of the Kingdom of Saudi Arabia, and King Yahya, king of Yemen, have agreed, pursuant to Article 8 of the Treaty of Peace, Friendship and Good Understanding, known as the Treaty of Taif, signed on *safar* 6, 1353, to refer to arbitration any dispute or difference that may arise from the relations between them, their governments and countries, when all friendly representations fail to settle it, the two important contracting parties undertake to give effect to arbitration in the way indicated in the following articles:

Article 1

Each of the two contracting parties undertakes to accept the reference of a dispute to arbitration within one month of the date of receiving a demand for arbitration from the other party.

Article 2

The arbitration will be undertaken by a commission comprising an equal number of arbitrators, half of whom will be selected by each of the two parties. A chief arbitrator will be selected by mutual agreement between the two important contracting parties. If they do not agree in this respect, each of them will nominate a person, and if either party accepts the person nominated by the other party, the person in question will become the chief arbitrator. If even this cannot be agreed upon, the chief arbitrator will be chosen by ballot, on the understanding that the ballot will only be drawn by persons acceptable to both parties. The person chosen by ballot will become the head of the arbitration commission and will be entitled to settle the case. If, however, agreement cannot be reached by the people acceptable to both parties, negotiations will be carried on until the two parties agree on this point.

Article 3

The selection of the arbitration commission and its head will be completed within one month from the end of the month fixed for the reply of the party whose acceptance of arbitration was requested by the other party. The arbitration commission will meet at a place to be agreed upon, within a period not exceeding one month after the expiration of the two months provided for at the beginning of this article. The arbitration commission will give its award within a period that, in any case, should not exceed one month after the expiration of the fixed date for the meeting. The decision of the arbitration commission will be made by a majority of votes and will be considered binding on the two parties. It will be obligatory to execute the decision immediately after it was made and communicated. Each one of the two important contracting parties may appoint a person or persons to defend his case before the arbitration commission and to produce the necessary evidence and arguments.

Article 4

Expenses for the arbitrators of each party will be charged to their respective parties. Both parties will be equally responsible for the expenses of the chief arbitrator, as well as the expenses of other investigations.

Article 5

This covenant will be an integral part of the Treaty of Taif signed this day, *safar* 6, 1353, and will remain in force during the period of the treaty's validity. It will be written in Arabic, with two copies and with each of the two contracting parties being in possession of one.

Signed on *safar* 6, 1353.
(signed) Khalid Bin Abdulaziz Al Saud
(signed) Abdullah Bin Ahmed Al Wazir

Attached Side Letters

Side Letter 1

From Khalid Ibn Abdulaziz to His Excellency Seya Abdullah Al Wazir, Plenipotentiary of His Majesty Imam Yahya Hamidaddin, dated *safar* 6, 1353. (After the usual compliments)

Regarding the signature of the Treaty of Taif between you and us on behalf of Their Majesties, the rulers of the Kingdom of Saudi Arabia and the Kingdom of Yemen, I wish to confirm in this side letter that this treaty can only be considered and accepted as valid under the following conditions:

(1) That the surrender of the Idrisis, the evacuation of our mountains in the Tihamah and the release of hostages happen at once.

(2) That the contents of this treaty will be kept secret and will not be published by either party, especially the part concerning the question of the frontiers, on account of the disturbance that might result, particularly in the Tihamah. (The troops of His

Majesty King Abdulaziz shall be withdrawn in complete safety and with honor, from the beginning to the end, and any hostile action that may be committed against the troops during that period will be indemnified by His Majesty the Imam.)
Most respectfully,
(signed) Khalid Ibn Abdulaziz Al Saud

Side Letter 2

From Abdullah bin Ahmad al-Wazir to His Royal Highness the Amir Khalid, dated *safar* 6, 1353 (After the usual compliments)

I have received Your Highness' letter dated *safar* 6 and have noted Your Highness' stipulations on the entering into force of the Treaty of Taif, concluded between the two parties, namely the surrender of the Idrises, the evacuation of the mountains in the country of His Majesty King Abdulaziz, which were occupied by the troops of Imam Yahya, the release of the hostages (taken) from the people, that the treaty should be kept secret, especially the question of frontiers, until the completion of the measures we have agreed to carry out, and that the troops of His Majesty King Abdulaziz should be withdrawn in complete safety and with honor, from beginning to end, and that any hostile action committed against them during that time should be indemnified by His Majesty the Imam Yahya. I have noted all these conditions, and I am glad to inform Your Highness that we accept and agree to them, and that they will be observed on our part.

Most respectfully, (signed) Abdullah Bin Ahmad Al Wazir

Side Letter 3

From Abdullah bin Ahmad al-Wazir to His Royal Highness the Amir Khalid, dated *safar* 6, 1353. (After the usual compliments)

I have the honor to confirm, in accordance with the Treaty of Taif, which has been signed by Your Highness on behalf of His Majesty King Abdulaziz, and by me on behalf of His Majesty the King, Imam Yahya, that I undertake in the name of His Majesty Imam Yahya:

(1) The surrender of the Idrisis to His Majesty, King Abdulaziz:

The necessary measures have been taken to hand over Seyyid Hasan and Seyyid Abdulaziz bin Muhammad Al-Idrisi, who will be handed over immediately to His Highness Amir Faysal in the Tihamah, but as Seyyid Abdulwahhab Al-Idrisi is still in the 'Abadil area, the necessary steps have been taken to bring him from there so that we can obtain his surrender. In the event of him disobeying the order, I give the following undertakings in the name of His Majesty Imam Yahya:

a) The government of Imam Yahya will refuse him all moral and material assistance, and will prevent any aid or support from their country from reaching him.

b) If the government of His Majesty King Abdulaziz wants to arrest him in their territories, the government of His Majesty Imam Yahya, on its part, will implement every kind of military restriction in its power in order to prevent him from fleeing into their territories, and undertakes to arrest him, together with any person from any district or tribe in the Kingdom of Saudi Arabia who may have joined him in his activities, and surrender them unconditionally to the Government of His Majesty King Abdulaziz if they enter the districts of the Yemeni Kingdom, and prevent him, and any persons who may have joined him in his activities, from escaping abroad if they enter the territories of the Kingdom of Yemen.

(2) Those Sharifs and others who were in any way connected with the Idrisis and their activities:

If they should desire to join the Idrisis, they shall be granted the safety, protection, respect and regard due to their position by the government of His Majesty King Abdulaziz. However, if they should not desire this, they shall be expelled from the territories of Imam Yahya and shall not be allowed to remain there, and, in the event of their returning to it a second time, they shall be expelled at once and warned that if they return they will be handed over to the government of His Majesty Abdulaziz. If they should return after their expulsion, I undertake, in the name of His Majesty, Imam Yahya, to surrender them unconditionally to the government of His Majesty King Abdulaziz.

I request that Your Highness will regard this as a firm undertaking with the same value as the treaty concluded this day between us and Your Highness, may God be witness to it. I request that this be considered as confirmation of the verbal agreement reached between us in this matter.

Most respectfully

Abdullah Bin Ahmad Al Wazir

Side Letter 4

From Khalid bin Abdulaziz to Sayyid Abdullah Al Wazir, dated *safar* 6, 1353. (After the usual compliments)

I have the honor to acknowledge the receipt of your Excellency's letter, dated today, on the undertakings regarding the Idrisis and their followers that you have given in the name of His Majesty Imam Yahya. I am confident that your undertakings will be carried out with the honesty and faithfulness which we have come to expect from His Majesty Imam Yahya, and we hope that they will be carried out as early as possible.

Most respectfully, Khalid Bin Abdulaziz

Side Letter 5
From Khalid bin Abdulaziz to Sayyid Abdullah Ahmad Al Wazir, dated *safar* 6, 1353. (After the usual compliments)

With reference to the signing of the Treaty of Taif between our kingdom and that of the Yemen, I hereby confirm our agreement regarding the movement of subjects of the Kingdom of Saudi Arabia and the Kingdom of Yemen in the two countries, namely that movement at the present time shall continue as in the past, until a special agreement is drawn up between the two governments on the method of regulation of such movements, whether for pilgrimage, for trade or for any other purpose or reason. I hope to receive your reply agreeing on this issue.

Most respectfully,
Khalid Ibn Abdulaziz.

Side Letter 6
From: Abdullah Al Wazir to His Royal Highness Amir Khalid, dated *safar* 6, 1353. (After the usual compliments)

I acknowledge the receipt of Your Highness' letter, dated *safar* 6, regarding the movement of the subjects of the two parties between the two countries, and I agree with Your Highness that movement at present shall continue as in the past until a special agreement is drawn up regarding the regulation of such movements in future, and that this undertaking will be observed by our Government as it is by yours.

Most respectfully,
Abdullah Bin Ahmed Al Wazir

Appendix III
General Agreement between the Kingdom of Saudi Arabia and the Kingdom of Yemen concerning the Settlement of Matters relating to the Subjects of the two Kingdoms, 1936[3]

Article 1

a) The zone of pasture on both sides of the second part of the boundary mentioned in this treaty shall be limited to 20 kilometers.

b) Shepherds from both countries have the right to use the pasture areas and water sources on both sides of this part of the boundary in accordance with prevailing tribal traditions and customs, for a distance not exceeding 20 kilometers.

c) The two contracting parties shall hold annual meetings of consultation to determine the crossing points for the purposes of pasture according to its current condition and availability.

Article 2

Shepherds who are subjects of the Kingdom of Saudi Arabia and the Yemeni Republic shall be exempted from:

a) Regulations regarding residency and passports, and will be issued with transit passes by the competent authorities in their respective countries.

b) Taxes and duties on personal effects, food and consumer goods that they carry with them. This does not prevent either party from imposing custom duties on livestock in transit and commodities for commercial purposes.

---

3. Author's translation.

Article 3

Each of the two contracting parties has the right to impose the restrictions and regulations it deems appropriate regarding the number of vehicles accompanying shepherds crossing into its territory, as well as the type and quantity of permitted firearms, provided they are licensed by the competent authorities in the two countries and the identity of their carrier can be established.

Article 4

In the event of the outbreak of an epidemic disease afflicting livestock, each party has the right to take the necessary preventive measures and to impose restrictions on the import and export of infected animals. The relevant authorities in both countries shall cooperate to limit the spread of the epidemic as far as possible.

Article 5

Neither party to the agreement shall be allowed to deploy its armed forces at a distance of less than 20 kilometers on either side of the second part of the boundary mentioned in this treaty. The activity of any party on either side shall be restricted to mobile security patrols carrying customary weapons.

Article 6

In the event of the discovery of extractable natural wealth along the boundary extending from the (Red) Sea, exactly from the quay of R'as Al-Mu'waj north of the Radif-garad outlet, to 19 degrees North latitude and 52 degrees East meridian, the two parties to the contract shall conduct the necessary bilateral negotiations for the purpose of a joint exploitation of such resources.

Article 7

This appendix shall constitute an indivisible part of this Treaty and shall be ratified in accordance with the established procedures in the two countries.

Appendix IV
Memorandum of Understanding between the Government of the Kingdom of Saudi Arabia and the Government of the Yemeni Republic, signed in Mecca, Saudi Arabia on 26 February 1995[4]

In the Name of Allah the Merciful, the Compassionate.

A Memorandum of Understanding between the Government of the Kingdom of Saudi Arabia and the Government of the Yemeni Republic.

Desiring to further enhance and strengthen the fraternal ties between the Kingdom of Saudi Arabia and the Yemeni Republic and their two brotherly peoples, the two Parties have agreed to the following:

Article 1: The two Parties affirm their commitment to the validity and binding force of the Treaty of Taif, known as the Taif Treaty (hereafter, "the treaty"), concluded on the sixth day of the month of *safar* in the year 1353 A.H., corresponding to the twentieth of May 1934.

Article 2: The formation within thirty days of a joint committee composed of equal numbers from both parties entrusted with the task of restoring the remaining and dilapidated boundary markers in accordance with the Boundary Reports attached to the treaty, starting from the boundary point on the (Red) Sea coastline, exactly at the quay of R'as Al-Mu'waj-Shami, north of the outlet (Manfath) of Radif-Garad, located between Midi and Al-Muwassam, to the last boundary marker previously established on Jabal Al-Thar. Modern

---

4. Author's translation.

scientific means shall be used to establish the markers by contracting a specialist company chosen by the two parties to carry out its work under the supervision of the committee.

Article 3: The current committee formed by the two parties shall continue its work to determine the necessary procedures and steps, including an agreement on a mechanism for arbitration in the case of a dispute between them, that will lead to the delimitation of the remaining boundaries, starting from Jabal Al-Thar to the final point of the borders of the two countries.

Article 4: The formation of a joint committee to negotiate the maritime boundary in accordance with international law, starting from the land boundary terminus on the Red Sea referred to in Article Two.

Article 5: The formation of a high-level joint bi-national military committee to prevent coordinates from being established and military movements on the borders between the two countries.

Article 6: The formation of a joint ministerial committee to develop economic, cultural and commercial ties between the two countries and promote the spheres of cooperation between them. This committee shall commence work within thirty days from the date of the signature on this Memorandum.

Article 7: The formation of a high-level (supervising) joint committee to work for the realization of the objectives previously mentioned, and to facilitate the tasks of the said committees and remove whatever obstacles and difficulties may obstruct their work.

Article 8: The two countries reaffirm their commitment to prevent the use of their countries as a base and center to commit aggression against each other or to carry out any political, military or propaganda activity against the other.

Article 9: To maintain an appropriate and cordial atmosphere in order to ensure the success of negotiations, each party pledges to refrain from conducting any propaganda activity against the other.

Article 10: Nothing in this Memorandum contains an amendment to the Treaty of Taif and its annexures, including the boundary reports.

Article 11: Minutes of all negotiations conducted by the said committees shall be recorded in memoranda and signed by both sides.

This Memorandum has been signed in Makkah al-Mukarramah (Mecca) on Sunday, the twenty-seventh day of the blessed month of Ramadan in the year 1415 *hegira,* corresponding to February 26, 1995. It shall enter into force on the date of exchange of its instruments of ratification.

For the Government of Saudi Arabia
Special Counselor to the Custodian of the Two Holy Mosques
Ibrahim Abdullah Al-'Angry

For the Government of the Yemeni Republic
Deputy Prime Minister and Minister for Planning and Development
Abdulgader Abdulraman Bajammal

Appendix V

Text of the International Boundary Treaty signed between the Government of the Republic of Yemen and the Government of the Kingdom of Saudi Arabia in Jeddah, Saudi Arabia on June 12, 2000[5]

To strengthen the brotherly, friendly and close bonds between the fraternal peoples in the Kingdom of Saudi Arabia and the Yemeni Republic, and

Based on the ideals and principles of the Islamic faith founded on cooperation, piety and benevolence, and

Emanating from the existing fraternal ties between the leaders of the two countries, personified in the Custodian of the Two Holy Mosques, King Fahad bin Abdulaziz Al-Saud, King of the Kingdom of Saudi Arabia and his brother, His Excellency President Ali Abdullah Saleh, the President of the Yemeni Republic, may God preserve them, and characterized by friendliness, clarity and the desire to strengthen and fortify the intimate fraternal relationships between the two brotherly peoples and their determination to find a permanent solution to the land and maritime border issue between their two countries that will be acceptable to consecutive generations and will preserve at present and in the future the boundary as defined in the Treaty of Taif, signed between the two kingdoms in the year 1353h, which corresponds to 1934, and demarcated by the joint committees as indicated in the boundary reports attached to the treaty or the undefined boundary, the following has been agreed upon:

---

5. Author's translation.

Article 1

The two contracting parties confirm the Treaty of Taif and its attachments, including the boundary reports attached to it, as being valid and binding on both parties. They also confirm their commitment to the Memorandum of Understanding signed on Ramadan 27, 1415h (February 26, 1995).

Article 2

The final and permanent dividing boundary line between the kingdom of Saudi Arabia and the Yemeni Republic is defined as follows:

A) The First Part: This part starts from the coastal marker on the Red Sea (precisely at the quay of R'as Al-Mu'waj, north of the Radif-garad outlet), with the following coordinates: 16 24 14 08 degrees north latitude and 42 46 19 07 degrees east longitude, and it ends at the marker of Jabal Al-Thar with the coordinates: 44 21 58 east and 17 26 00 north. The set of coordinates of this line is shown in Appendix 1. The status of villages along this line will be decided in accordance with the stipulations of the Treaty of Taif and its attachments, including their tribal affiliation. In the event that any of the coordinates is at a location of a village or villages belonging to one party, the point of reference in establishing the status of this village or these villages will be its affiliation to one of the two parties, and when the boundary marker is placed, the course of the line shall be adjusted accordingly.

B) The Second Part is that sector of the boundary line that has not been defined. The two contracting parties have agreed to demarcate this sector in an amicable way. This sector starts at Jabal Al-Thar, whose coordinates have been defined above, and ends at the geographical point where 19 degrees north latitude intersects with 52 degrees east meridian, as indicated in detail in the set of coordinates shown in Appendix 2.

C) The Third Part is the maritime sector of the boundary line, which starts from the land terminus on the seashore, precisely at the quay of R'as Al-Mu'waj north of Radif-garad outlet, whose co-ordinates are defined above and which extends to the end of the maritime boundary between the two countries, as described in detail in the set of coordinates in Appendix 3.

Article 3

Desiring to establish markers along the boundary line, which starts at the intersection of the two countries' borders with the Sultanate of Oman, at 19 degrees north latitude and 52 degrees east meridian, and which ends at the seashore, precisely at the quay of R'as Al-Mu'waj north of Radif-garad, with the coordinates mentioned in Appendix 1, the two contracting parties will commission an international company to undertake a field survey of the whole land and maritime boundary. The specialized company carrying out the work and the joint team from the two contracting sides must adhere precisely to the distances and directions between each point and the next one, and the remaining specifications contained in the boundary reports attached to the Treaty of Taif. These stipulations are binding on both parties.

(2) The specialized international company shall undertake the preparation of detailed maps of the land boundary between the two countries.

These maps, after being approved by representatives of the Kingdom of Saudi Arabia and the Yemeni Republic, shall be recognized as official maps indicating the boundary between the two countries in detail, and shall become an indivisible part of this treaty. The two contracting parties will rely on them as official maps demarcating the border between the two countries, which will become an integral part of this treaty. The two contracting parties will sign an Agreement to cover the cost of work by the company, which is commissioned to establish markers on the land boundary between the two countries.

Article 4

The two contracting parties affirm their commitment to Article 5 in the Treaty of Taif regarding the withdrawal of any military post located at a distance less than five kilometers from the boundary line, as demarcated in the boundary reports attached to the Treaty of Taif. As for the undefined boundary line extending from Jabal Al-Thar to the intersection point at 19 degrees north latitude and 52 degrees east longitude, this shall be subject to Appendix 4, which is attached to this treaty.

Article 5

This treaty will enter into force after being ratified in accordance with the procedures followed in each of the two contracting states, and their exchange of the instruments of ratification.

    For the Yemeni Republic
    Abdulgader Abdulrahman Bajammal
    Deputy Prime Minister, Foreign Minister

    For the Kingdom of Saudi Arabia
    Saud Al-Faysal
    Minister of Foreign Affairs

Jeddah (Saudi Arabia) 10 *rabi' awal* 1421h, corresponding to June 12, 2000

Appendix 1

A set of geographical coordinates for the 1934 boundary markers, as demarcated in the 1937 joint commission reports. It is not reproduced here.

Appendix 2

A set of coordinates indicating the line from Jabal Al-Thar to the intersection of the Saudi-Yemeni-Omani border at parallels 19 degrees North 52 degrees East. It is not reproduced here.

Appendix 3

The maritime boundary between the Kingdom of Saudi Arabia and the Yemeni Republic:

1. The line begins at the land terminus point on the (Red) Sea shore, precisely at the quay of R'as Al-Mu'waj, north of the Radif-Garad outlet, with the following coordinates: 16 24 14 08 degrees North latitude and 42 46 19 0 7 degrees East longitude.

2. The line extends in a straight line parallel to the latitude until it crosses with the meridian at 42 09 00 East.

3. The line then bends in a south-westerly direction until it reaches the coordinates at 16 24 14 08 North and 42 09 00 East.

4. From there (the line) extends in a straight line parallel to the latitude in a westerly direction to the end of the maritime boundary between the two countries, to a point with the co-ordinates 16 17 24 degrees East and 41 47 00 degrees North.

NOTES

Introduction

1. The author's unpublished Ph.D. dissertation was on *The Legal Status of the Saudi-Yemeni Treaty of Taif*, Faculty of International Law, Moscow State Institute of International Relations (MGIMO), Moscow, the Russian Federation, 2000.

2. See for example, F. Gregory Gause III, *Saudi-Yemeni Relations: Domestic Structures and Foreign Influence* (New York, NY: Columbia University Press, 1990); Richard Schofield, *Negotiating the Saudi-Yemeni International Boundary*, a lecture delivered before the British Yemeni Society (March 31, 1999) at http://www.al-bab.com/bys/articles/schofield00.htm (hereafter *Negotiating the Saudi-Yemeni International Boundary*). For works generally reflecting a pro-Yemeni view on the border dispute with Saudi Arabia, see for example Muhammad Ali Al-Shihari, *Al-Matam'i Al-Su'udiyah Al-Tawassu'iyah Fi Al-Yaman* (Saudi Expansionist Designs on Yemen) (Beirut: Dar Ibn Khaldun, 1979) (hereafter "Shihari"); Muhsin Al'ayni, *Khamsoun 'Aman Fi Al-Rimal Al-Mutaharikah: Gissati M'a Bina Al-Dawlah Al-Hadithah Fi Al-Yaman* (Fifty Years in Shifting Sands: My Story of the Building of the Modern State of Yemen) (Beirut: Dal al-Nahaar, 2000); Riad Najib el-Rayyes, *Riyah Al-Janoub: Al-Yaman Wa Dawrahu Fi Al-Jazeerah Al-'Arabiyah 1990-1997* (The Winds of the South: The Role of Yemen in the Arabian Peninsula, 1990-1997) (Beirut: Riad el-Rayyes Books, 1998) (hereafter "Rayyes"). For works generally reflecting a pro-Saudi view, see for example Ahmad Abdullah Al-Ghamdi, *Gadhiyat Al-Hudud Al-Su'Udiyah Al-Yamaniyah* (The Saudi-Yemeni Border Question) (Riyadh: n.p., 1999) (hereafter "Ghamdi"); Mshari A. Al-Na'im, *Al-Hudud Al-Siyasiyah Al-Su'udiyah: Albahth 'An Al-Istigrar* (Saudi Political Boundaries: In Search of Stability) (London: Al-Saqi Books, 1999); Eed Mas'ud Al-Juhani, *Al-Hudud Wa 'Al-'Alagaat Al-Su'udiyah-al-Yamaniyah* (Saudi-Yemeni Border Relations) (Riyadh: Dar al-Ma'arif al-Su'udiyah, 1994).

Chapter 1

3. For the Arabic text of the 1926 Mecca agreement, see Ministry of Foreign Affairs (Saudi Arabia), *Majmu'at Al-Mu'ahadat, aljuza alawwal: Min 1341 Ila 1370 Hijriyah, Almuwafiq:1922 -1951* (Collection of Treaties, vol. 1: 1922-1951) (Mecca: Government Printing Office, 1375h/ 1955), 23 (hereafter

Ministry of Foreign Affairs, *Majmu'at*); for the English text, see Richard Schofield (editor) *Arabian Boundary Disputes: Saudi Arabia-Yemen, 1913-1992* vol. 20 (London: Archive Editions 1993) (hereafter Schofield, *20 Arabian Boundary Disputes*), 48-49.

4. Despatch from Sir E. Drummond, British ambassador, Rome to the Foreign Office, London, 19 April 1934, enclosure no. 1 Eastern (Arabia), no. 342, E2600/2/25 in Doreen Ingrams and Leila Ingrams (editors) *Records of Yemen: 1798-1960, vol. 8: 1933-1945* (London: Archive Editions, 1993) (hereafter Ingrams and Ingrams, *8 Records of Yemen*), 128.

5. For Imam Yahya's rejection of the 1926 Mecca Treaty, see Shihari, op. cit., 158; Boutros Boutros-Ghali, "The Anglo-Yemeni [sic] Dispute," *Revue Egyptienne de Droit International* vol. 11 (1955), 13, 27.

6. Despatch from Sir Andrew Ryan, British Minister to Saudi Arabia, Jeddah, to FO, June 7, 1934, Eastern (Arabia), no. 145 E3761/79/25, in Ingrams and Ingrams, *8 Records of Yemen*, op. cit., 170.

7. "Bayn Al-Riyadh Wa San'a," *Um Alqura* (official Saudi government gazette), October 20, 1931. For translated extracts of the Saudi refutation of the Yemeni government's geographical and historical notion of Yemen, see Schofield, *20 Arabian Boundary Disputes*, op. cit., 515.

8. Despatch from Sir E. Drummond, British ambassador, Rome to FO, April 19, 1934, enclosure no. 1 Eastern (Arabia), no. 342, E2600/2/25, in Ingrams and Ingrams, *8 Records of Yemen*, op. cit., 128.

9. Despatch from Sir E. Drummond, British ambassador, Rome to FO, April 19, 1934, enclosure no. 1 Eastern (Arabia), no. 342, E2600/2/25, Ingrams and Ingrams, *8 Records of Yemen*, op. cit., 128.

10. Ibid.

11. "Saudi Arabia: Annual Report 1933," paragraph 51 in Penelope Tuson and Anita Burdett (editors) *Records of Saudi Arabia: Primary Documents: 1902-1960*, vol. 5: 1932-1935 (London: Archive Editions, 1992), 213.

12. The text of the agreement, also known as the Abu 'Arish agreement, appears in Penelope Tuson and Emma Quick (editors), *Arabian Treaties 1600-1960* vol. 4 (London: Archive Editions, 1992) (hereafter Tuson and Quick, *4 Arabian Treaties*), 153.

13. According to the Saudi Foreign Ministry, in a telegram to the British Legation in Jeddah, on December 29, 1932 Saudi Arabia ratified the 'Aru agreement, also called Abu 'Arish after the place of the signature, and Yemen did so in the form of a telegram from the Imam to Ibn Saud on January 24, 1933. Tuson and Quick, *4 Arabian Treaties*, op. cit., 157 and 158.

14. From the Saudi point of view, the alleged agreement was reached on December 31, 1927. Under its terms, Yemen accepted the Saudi settlement proposals, whereby Najran and the country north of it belonged to Saudi Arabia, while the territory of the tribe of Wa'ilah and southwards would become part of Yemen, and the frontier in the east extending westward to the Red Sea would remain as it was. Yemen, however, denied the existence of such an agreement and, as a result, refused to ratify the 'Aru Agreement. Schofield, *20 Arabian Boundary Disputes*, op. cit., 554.

15. Schofield, *20 Arabian Boundary Disputes*, op. cit., 496.

16. Exchange of letters between the heads of the Saudi and Yemeni delegations in *Bayan 'An Al-'Ala 'Qat Bayn Al-Mamlakah Al-'Arabiyah Al'Su'udiyah wa Al-Imam Yahya Imam Yahya Hamidul-Din* (Mecca, 1934) (hereafter *Bayan*), 189.

17. For a short background of the pre-1934 history of the border dispute between the two countries, see Arnold J. Toynbee (ed.) *Survey of International Affairs 1934* (Oxford: Oxford University Press, 1935) and Clive Leatherdale, *Britain and Saudi Arabia 1925-1939: The Imperial Oasis* (London: Frank Cass Publishers, 1983).

18. Prince Khalid, son of Ibn Saud and the future king, signed on behalf of Saudi Arabia, while Abdullah ibn Ahmad-Al-Wazir, cousin of Imam Yahya, signed on behalf of Yemen. The Arabic text of the Treaty of Taif and all relevant attachments appear in Ministry of Foreign Affairs, *Majmu'at*, op. cit., 152-198. For the Arabic text, without the 1936 agreement on cross-border movement and the 1937 joint demarcation report, and with an English translation, see Ingrams and Ingrams, *8 Records of Yemen*, op. cit., 191-228. For the English text of the Treaty of Taif only, see Tuson and Quick, *4 Arabian Treaties*, op. cit., 336-45. For the English translation of the 1937 Saudi-Yemeni Joint Commission's Demarcation Report, see the "Annexure to the Taif Agreement for the Demarcation of Borders between the Kingdom of Yemen and the Kingdom of Saudi Arabia, 1937," in Schofield, *20 Arabian Boundary Disputes*, op. cit., 643-672.

19. King Ibn Saud of Saudi Arabia ratified the treaty on June 8, 1934. On June 19, 1934, the Saudi Arabian Ministry of Foreign Affairs communicated to the British Legation in Jeddah "the receipt of an official communiqué from the Yemen Foreign Minister to the effect that His Majesty Imam Yahya, King of Yemen, has this day...approved the Treaty of Taif...and has affixed his gracious signature on the instrument of ratification." Tuson and Quick, *4 Arabian Treaties*, op. cit., 325 and Shihari, op. cit., 270, note 248. Al-Shihari added that the Imam wrote the following note after his signature of ratification: "this is the first agreement and treaty between us and our brother, His Majesty, King Abdulaziz bin 'Abulrahman." Shihari, op. cit., 310. The Imam's note apparently implied his non-recognition of the 1926 Mecca Treaty and the 1931 Al'Aru (Abu 'Arish) Agreement. However, Article 2 pertaining to territorial cession in the Treaty of Taif was clearly based on the settlement in the 1926 Mecca agreement, and Article 23 expressly abrogated the 1931 agreement.

20. Despatch from the British Legation, Jeddah, to FO, London, 18 July 1934, no. 209 E Eastern (Arabia) E4626/79/25, in Ingrams and Ingrams, *8 Records of Yemen*, op. cit., 187.

21. *Um Alqura*, June 23, 1934.

22. Text of the "General Agreement between the Kingdom of Saudi Arabia and the Kingdom of Yemen concerning the Settlement of Matters relating to the Subjects of the Two Countries," in Ministry of Foreign Affairs, *Majmu'at*, op. cit., 194-198.

23. Treaty of Taif, Article 1.

24. Al-'Aayidh, the *de facto* ruling family of the autonomous region of the northern highland Asir Al-Surat, which extends to the eastern hinterland of Najran, was nominally under the authority of the Idrisi emirate, before falling under Saudi rule in terms of an agreement between the Idrisi and the Saudi ruler in 1920. Bayan, op. cit., document 54, 177-8; Shihari, op. cit., 99, 104.

25. The British government's Arabic experts correctly established that the Arabic word *hudud* (*had* singular) denotes a line, not a specified area like a frontier. To emphasize the linear nature of *hudud*, the Treaty of Taif frequently preceded the term with the word *khat* (line). See Doreen Ingrams and Leila Ingrams (editors, 1993) *Records of Yemen: 1798-1960, vol. 14: 1957-1958* (London: Archive Editions, 1993) (hereafter Ingrams and Ingrams, *14 Records of Yemen*).

26. Treaty of Taif, Art. 4. In addition, Article 5 required that the two sides refrain from constructing any fortified building "within a distance of 5 kilometers" on either side of the boundary line.

27. Treaty of Taif, Art. 4.

28. For the text of the 1937 joint commission boundary demarcation report, see "Annexure To The Taif Agreement For The Demarcation Of Borders Between The Kingdom Of Yemen And The Kingdom Of Saudi Arabia, 1937" in Schofield, *20 Arabian Boundary Disputes*, op. cit., 643-672; also in Ministry of Foreign Affairs, *Majmu'at*, op. cit., 166-193.

29. The Saudi view of the boundary line from Jabal Al-Thar to Radm Al-Amir was represented by the 1936 Line, the so-called Philby Line, based exclusively on tribal allegiance and drawn by the British explorer H. St. John Philby, a close confidant of Ibn Saud, who carried out an expedition in the area in 1936, purportedly on behalf of Saudi Arabia. See H. St. J.B. Philby, *Sheba's Daughters: being a Record of Travel in Southern Arabia* (London: Methuen and Co. Ltd., 1939), 251, 59, 671 and 431-2. See also Philby's view on the eastern border limits of the "Imamate of Yemen" in "Summary of Statements made by Mr. Philby about his Expedition to Shabwa and beyond" to the British Minister in Jeddah on February 18, 1937, Enclosure No. 16 in Schofield, *20 Arabian Boundary Disputes*, op. cit., 675-8. The Imam of Yemen protested to Saudi Arabia that Mr. Philby, "accompanied by an armed Saudi guard (had) entered Yemen territory at Jawf and Marib." The Saudi government, although it "disclaimed" responsibility for Mr. Philby's mission, insisted that the area visited by the explorer did not form "part of Jawf and Marib." Report from the British Minister in Jeddah, Sir R. Bullard, to the FO, London, 28 February 1937, "Saudi Arabia – Annual Report, 1936" in Penelope Tuson and Anita Burdett (editors) *Records of Saudi Arabia: Primary documents: 1902-1960, vol. 6: 1935-37* (London: Archive Editions, 1992) (hereafter Tuson and Burdett, *6 Records of Saudi Arabia*), 356 and 370-2.

30. On the process of establishing boundaries through stages of "allocation," "delimitation" and "demarcation," see Surya P. Sharma, *Delimitation of Land & Sea Boundaries Between Neighboring Countries* (Lancer's Book, 1989), 11-12; J.R.V. Prescott, *Political Frontiers and Boundaries* (London: Allen and Unwin, 1987), 69-77 and Georg Ress, "The Delimitation and Demarcation of Frontiers in International Treaties and Maps," *Thesaurus Acroasium* XIV (1985) 395, 407-18, 431-37.

31. Treaty of Taif, Art. 12.

32. The term "modify" in the text of the Article appears as a more accurate translation of the Arabic original word *ta'dil*. See Richard Schofield and Gerald Blake (editors) *Arabian Boundaries: Primary Documents 1853-1957: Saudi Arabia-Imamate of Yemen, 1931-1957* vol. 4 (London: Archive Editions, 1988), 400.

33. Treaty of Taif, Arts. 7, 9, 10 and 18.

34. Treaty of Taif, Art. 9.

35. Treaty of Taif, Art. 9.

36. Treaty of Taif, Art. 10.

37. Treaty of Taif, Art. 8 and Annexure: Covenant of Arbitration, Art. 2 in Schofield, *20 Arabian Boundary Disputes*, op. cit., 98-99.

38. Treaty of Taif, Covenant of Arbitration, Art. 3.

39. See text of the Letters in Schofield, *20 Arabian Boundary Disputes*, op. cit., 100-102, Ministry of Foreign Affairs, *Majmu'at*, op. cit., 164-66; Ingrams and Ingrams, *8 Records of Yemen*, op. cit., 226-7.

40. Letter no. 5 and letter no. 6, both dated *safar* 6, 1353h (May 20, 1934) in Ministry of Foreign Affairs, *Majmu'at*, op. cit., 165; Ingrams and Ingrams, *8 Records of Yemen*, op. cit., 226-7.

41. Letter no. 5 and letter no. 6, both dated *safar* 6, 1353h (May 20, 1934), in Ministry of Foreign Affairs, *Majmu'at*, op. cit., 165; Ingrams and Ingrams, *8 Records of Yemen*, op. cit., 226-7.

42. Text of the General Agreement between the Kingdom of Saudi Arabia and the Kingdom of Yemen Concerning the Settlement of Matters relating to the Subjects of the two Kingdoms. Annexure to the Treaty of Taif, Ministry of Foreign Affairs, *Majmu'at*, op. cit., 194-198.

43. Treaty of Taif, Art. 4. The article provides a tribal rationale for such privileges. It states that the tribes of Yam, Najran al-Hadhn, Zur Wada'a and the Wa'ila section inhabiting the Najran area originally belonged to Yemen. They were only included in the Kingdom of Saudi Arabia as a result of Imam Yahya's delegation of the power to decide their nationality to the Saudi king. The latter judged that they all belonged to Saudi Arabia, with the proviso that

the al-Hadhn, Zur Wadi'a and Wa'ila would still enjoy the customary relations, interaction and cooperation.

44. *Um Alqura*, March 20, 1953, 1. The Saudi government arranged for the text of the communiqué to be published simultaneously in the other capitals of Arab states where Saudi Arabia maintained diplomatic representation, such as Cairo, Damascus and Amman. See the *Hawl Al-Alam* weekly, Amman (Jordan), March 21, 1953, 16.

45. *Daily Telegraph* (London), July 13, 1960. Yemeni sources also reported the Saudi notification, made in 1959. The notification explained that the fact that the Asir and Najran actually formed part of Saudi Arabia "did not need legal texts" for support, i.e. the Treaty of Taif. See Shihari, op. cit., 17.

46. Despatch from the British Legation, Taiz, Yemen, September 4, 1960, no. 10343/3/60 in Ingrams and Ingrams, *14 Records of Yemen*, op. cit., 64.

47. Ibid.

48. Ibid.

49. Ibid.

50. Ibid.

51. For a background on Saudi-Yemeni political relations from the 1962 revolution to the late 1980's, see for example Gause, *Saudi-Yemeni Relations*, op. cit.

52. In 1966, at the height of the Yemeni civil war, and following the Saudi government's restriction of entry and residency with respect to Yemeni nationals, the Republican Council and the Council of Ministers, the highest ruling organs in the new revolutionary government, issued a joint formal statement that in effect declared the Treaty of Taif to be null and void. It reaffirmed Yemen's determination to "recover by force if necessary the Yemeni territories in the north and north-west, including the regions of Najran, Jizan and Asir that Saudi Arabia had acquired by force of arms, in spite of the fact that they are geographically and historically part of the territory of Yemen. *Al-Ahram* daily (Egypt), May 5, 1966, cited in Jibran Shamiyah, *Lubnan, al-yaman, ittihad al-janoub al-'arabi: sijjil al-ara hawl al-wagai'i al-siyasiyah fi al-bilad al-arabiyah: al-yaman-ayyar 1966* (Lebanon, Yemen, the Federation of South Arabia: Record Of Views On Political Events In Arab Countries: Yemen-May (Beirut: Dar Albhath wa Alnashr,

1966), 11. Significantly, although the statement implicitly denounced the Treaty of Taif, it did not attempt to expressly invoke any of the alleged Saudi transgressions as a ground for terminating the treaty in whole or in part, possibly because Yemen regarded it as being void *ab initio*. The Yemeni government's statement came after the Egyptian President Nasser, who maintained a strong military presence in Yemen, declared during the May Day speech of the same year: "We will take Jizan and Najran, which originally are Yemeni but conquered by the Saudis...The Yemenis may demand their return and Egyptians will fight side by side with the Yemenis for this goal." *Al-Ahram*, May 2, 1966, cited in ibid., 7.

53. Statement by the Qadhi Abdulrahman Al-Iryani, member of the Republican Council, during an official visit to Egypt. *Al-Ahram*, May 13, 1966, cited in ibid., 20. The subsequent trilateral Saudi-Egyptian-Yemeni Taif accord and Jeddah agreement signed in August of the same year failed to end the Yemeni civil war that involved these three states. Ibid., 2-8 and Schofield, *20 Arabian Disputes*, op. cit., 697-8.

54. The high-level bilateral talks held in the Saudi capital in March 1973 coincided with the imminent expiration of the second extension of the treaty of Taif. The Saudi side was led by King Faysal of Saudi Arabia who, in addition to being head of state, also held the portfolios of prime minister and foreign minister, and Mr. Omar Saqqaf, under-secretary at the foreign affairs ministry. The Yemeni delegation was headed by the Qadhi Abdullah Al-Hajri, Member of the ruling Council of the Presidency and Prime Minister of the Arab Republic of Yemen (North Yemen), and included Mr. Muhammad Ahmad Nu'man, the Yemeni foreign minister. See the text of the Joint Communiqué in *Um Alqura*, March 23, 1973, 1, 8.

55. *Um Alqura*, March 23, 1973, 1, 8. In fact, two months before the communiqué, the Yemeni President himself, Qadhi Abdulrahman al-Iryani, had made a statement acknowledging that the Treaty of Taif had the same legal effect. He said "We have declared on the morning of September 26 (the 1962 revolution) our commitment to all agreements and international conventions concluded between Yemen and other countries, and at the forefront, of course, was the Treaty of Taif." Interview with the Lebanese weekly magazine, *Al-Hawdith*, January 19, 1973, cited in Shihari, op. cit., 17.

56. Unlike the Yemeni President's statement of January 1973, the joint communiqué of March caused widespread criticism and condemnation in Yemen, despite the fact that the head of the Yemeni delegation had been "empowered" by the

President to agree to the content of the communiqué. Shihari, op. cit., 13, 16. The Yemeni government later declared that the communiqué was without any legal effect, since the paragraph in question had been made without authorization, and since it had not been ratified by "freely elected constitutional institutions representing the Yemeni people." Shihari, op. cit., 18.

57. The Hamza Line was originally suggested to the British government by Saudi Arabia on April 3, 1935. Despatch from Sir A. Ryan, Jeddah, to Sir John Simon, London (E 2281/77/91) (No. 84.), No. 42, Jeddah, April 6, 1935, in Schofield, *20 Arabian Boundary Disputes*, op. cit., 127.

58. The 1955 Saudi Line came in the form of a reply dated October 18, 1955, stating the Saudi rejection of Britain's unilaterally declared line of August 4, 1955, and making a territorial counter-claim. Paragraph 4 of the Saudi letter, for the first time, gave details of the territory claimed by Saudi Arabia west of the point where the 1935 Hamza Line, the basis of the 1955 line, crossed the Anglo-Ottoman Violet Line of 1914. Schofield, *20 Arabian Boundary Disputes*, op. cit., 205.

59. The Violet Line refers to the line that was defined in the 1914 Anglo-Ottoman Convention, signed on March 9, 1914, but never ratified. It demarcated the sphere of influence in southern Arabia, running north-eastwards into the Empty Quarter. Neither Saudi Arabia nor Yemen ever accepted it. Moreover, the British government's own Foreign Office legal advisor seriously questioned the legality of the line under international law. Schofield, *20 Arabian Boundary Disputes*, op. cit., 813.

60. The British government's communication of a note to the Saudi Government of Britain's minimum territorial claim in Arabia (Riyadh Line), 25 November 1935, Enclosure 1 in No. 66, handed to the Saudi deputy foreign minister, Fuad Bey Hamza at Riyadh on November 25, 1035, by British Minister Sir Andrew Ryan. Schofield, *20 Arabian Boundary Disputes*, op. cit., 127-9.

61. The British government's unilateral declaration of the 1955 line came in a Note on August 4, 1955 from the British Embassy in Jeddah to the Saudi Ministry for Foreign Affairs, describing, inter alia, the frontier between the Aden Protectorate and Saudi Arabia. Schofield, *20 Arabian Boundary Disputes*, op. cit., 206-7.

62. For the overlapping Saudi-Yemeni territorial claims in this sector, see the maps in Schofield, *20 Arabian Boundaries*, op. cit., 226-7 and 847, also at http://www.al-bab.com/bys/articles/border2.htm, and in Richard Schofield, *Negotiating the Saudi-Yemeni International Boundary*, op. cit.

63. Abduljalil Marhoun, "Niza'at Al-Hudud Fi Shibh Al-Jazeerah Al-'Arabiyah" (Border Dispute in the Arabian Peninsula) *Shu'un Awsatiyah* vol. 47, 60. Yemen accused the British authorities of handing over the Yemeni desert town of Sharorah to Saudi Arabia in the early 1960's, who continued to slice off territory from the territory in South Yemen, culminating in the occupation of Al-Wadi'ah in 1969 and later of Alkharkhair. Shihari, op. cit., 12.

64. The Yemeni government had formally registered their protests against the Saudi-Omani border negotiations that resulted in the agreement of 1990. The Yemeni government claimed that these negotiations involved territory that they claimed as part of South Yemen, *Al-Hayat*, May 20, 1992. During its protest the Yemeni government explained that Saudi Arabia had no direct border with Oman, since all territory north of Oman were claimed to be Yemeni, based on its doctrine of "historical rights."

65. Both South and North Yemen governments had committed themselves in the 1972 Cairo Accord not to enter into border negotiations or conclude separate border agreements with Saudi Arabia as long as the two Yemens remained two separate states. Interview with the Yemeni foreign minister, Da'irat Al-Tagah, August 11, 1992. Shortly before the formal merger of the two Yemens, a Saudi delegation to South Yemen failed to secure a separate border agreement. *Alyawn Alsabi*, July 14, 1990 at http://www.nic.gov.ye/SITE%20CONTAINTS/presedency/itrvews/1990/s039.html (visited October 15, 2001). According to the Yemeni president Saleh, in an interview with the *New York Times*, the visit at the time by prince Saud Al-Faysal of Saudi Arabia to Aden intended to persuade the South Yemen government by monetary inducement to prevent the unification of the two Yemens, or at least to agree to sign a separate Saudi-South Yemen border agreement. *New York Times*, October 29, 1990, Arabic text of the interview at http://www.nic.gov.ye/SITE%20CONTAINTS/presedency/itrvews/1990/s068.html.

Chapter 2

1. The first statement presented by the government of the unified Yemeni Republic to the newly assembled parliament declared Yemen's readiness to commence negotiations on its border issues with Saudi Arabia and Oman, based on the parties accepting "the rules and principles of international law guaranteeing the parties legal and historic rights." Text of the Government Statement dated June, 16, 1990, as well as the inaugural speech of the Yemeni president on May 26, 1990, repeating the initiative, on the official internet website of the Yemeni Presidential office at www.nic.gov.ye/SITE%20CONTAINTS/presedency/itrvews/1990/s003.htm.

2. Within months after unification, Yemen commenced border negotiations with Oman, which culminated in the signing of a formal agreement in October 1992, and in 1998-99 with Eritrea, to settle the issue through third party arbitration. This left Saudi Arabia, Somalia and Djibouti as the only neighboring states left to conclude maritime border agreements with Yemen.

3. Nathaniel Kern, "Saudi-Yemeni Border Dispute," *Petroleum Politics* (June 1992), 32.

4. Treaty of Taif, Articles 15 and 17. Article 15 prohibited the two contracting states from dealing with or entering into an agreement with a third party in any matter that might be to the disadvantage of the interests and existence of the other party. Article 17 stipulated that, in the event of an external threat of aggression against one of the contracting parties, the other was required to adopt a benevolent neutrality, providing "all possible moral support" and refraining "from any act which might be interpreted as assistance" to the external aggressor. It is possible to argue that, by officially invoking the two articles, or for that matter any other provisions of the treaty, as a ground for its decision to revoke the special exemptions, Saudi Arabia would at least implicitly acknowledge them as legal obligations in terms of the Taif Treaty.

5. Kern, op. cit., 32. In an interview with the *New York Times*, the Yemeni president demanded that the Saudi government "rescind its decisions taken against the sons of our people."

6. In an interview with the *New York Times*, the Yemeni president stated that the Treaty of Taif was "an agreement signed in 1934 between the Imam and King Abdulaziz to be renewed every twenty years, but which the revolutionary government of Yemen has not yet agreed to renew or discuss." He further

demanded that the Saudi government "rescind its decisions taken against the sons of our people." *New York Times*, October 29, 1990, op. cit.

7. Kern, op. cit., 32.

8. In April 1992, the Yemeni government protested to Riyadh about the maneuvers of Saudi troops staging military exercises for several days near the disputed border with Yemen. Schofield, *20 Arabian Boundary Disputes*, op. cit., 235. Yemen accused Saudi Arabia of mobilizing its armed forces in areas adjacent to the Red Sea and the Haradh area, and of renewing its warnings to British, American and French companies to cease oil exploration operations in Yemen, not only under the pretext of the existing territorial dispute in Yemen, but also aimed at preventing the country from "benefiting from its economic resources and wealth, and to consequently weaken and control it." "Saudi Forces Said Massed on Border." *Al-Jumhuriyah*, an Iraqi government daily, Baghdad, April 30, 1992, cited in Schofield, *20 Arabian Boundary Disputes*, op. cit., 236.

9. On May 14, 1992, during a visit to Riyadh, Shaykh Abdullah Bin Hussain Al-Ahmar, an influential Yemeni tribal leader with good ties to Saudi Arabia, spoke of Saudi Arabia's readiness to negotiate with his country to settle their border dispute peacefully. "Saudi Arabia said to want better ties with Yemen," Schofield, *20 Arabian Boundary Disputes*, op. cit., 237. In response to Saudi overtures, the Yemeni foreign ministry issued an official statement expressing Yemen's "desire and eagerness" to commence talks on the border issue with Saudi Arabia through direct bilateral official channels. "Yemeni Foreign Ministry Welcomes Saudi Statement On Border Dispute." Yemeni Republic Radio, Sana'a, 31 May 31, 1992, cited in Schofield, *20 Arabian Boundary Disputes*, op. cit., 248.

10. In addition to, and perhaps because of, its traditional strategic alliance with Saudi Arabia, the US government openly supported and welcomed the unification of Yemen in 1990, and opposed the southern Yemeni secessionists supported by Saudi Arabia during the 1994 civil war. In an interview in early 1995, the Yemeni president expressed his government's appreciation for strong US support, despite Saudi reservations, of the unification of North and South Yemen in 1990, and its equally strong rejection of the failed Saudi-supported southern Yemeni attempt at secession. Interview of the Yemeni president with the Lebanese daily, *Assafir*, April 2, 1995, text of the interview at http://www.nic.gov.ye/SITE%20CONTAINTS/presedency/itrvews/1995/s036.html.

11. On May 14, 1992, the US ambassador to Saudi Arabia, Mr. Charles Freeman, stated that the US government "preferred to see all the states in the region find a peaceful solution to their border disputes." Saudi Press Agency, 14 May 14, 1992 in Schofield, *20 Arabian Boundary Disputes*, op. cit., 237. A senior Yemeni official said in Sana'a that the US government had informed Yemen that Saudi government officials were "ready to negotiate with their Yemeni counterparts in a bid to peacefully settle the conflict." Ibid. On June 1, Yemeni President Saleh received a reply from US President George Bush, who asserted the US "concern for resolving border problems between Yemen and Saudi Arabia peacefully and by having recourse to dialogue, understanding. and negotiations." "US Support for Resolving Border Dispute Noted," in ibid., 257.

12. The Yemeni side was headed by Abdulaziz al-Dali, Minister of State for Foreign Affairs, while the Saudi delegation was led by the then education minister, Abdulaziz al-Khuwaytir, Yemeni Republic Radio, Sana 1700 GMT, 20 July 1992, cited in Schofield, *20 Arabian Boundary Disputes*, op. cit., 267.

13. Public statement issued by the Yemeni foreign ministry, "Yemeni Foreign Ministry Welcomes Saudi Statement On Border Dispute," Yemeni Republic Radio, Sana'a, May 31, 1992, cited in Schofield, *20 Arabian Boundary Disputes*, op. cit., 248.

14. In an interview with a London-based Arabic daily, the Yemeni president Ali Saleh asserted that "I do not believe that there is anyone in the Arab homeland who does not know what our…historical and legal rights are." *Alquds Alarabi*, May 28, 1992, 4, also at http://www.nic.gov.ye/SITE%20CONTAINTS/presedency/itrvews/1992/s30.html. For Yemen's official "political" map of "Greater Yemen," see *Al-kharitah al-siyasiyah l'il al-jumhuriyah al-yamaniyah* (Political Map of the Yemeni Republic), the Yemeni President's office at the National Information Center (NIC) (Sana'a) on NIC's official Arabic language website, http://www.nic.gov.ye/SITE/20%CONTAINTS/geography/maps/mm.JPG (last visited March 2, 2002). For the historical map, see *Al-kharitah al-tabi'iyah l'il al-yaman* (Natural Map of the Yemeni Republic), ibid. at http://www.nic.gov.ye/SITE%CONTAINTS/aboutyemen/history/MAPS/M.htm (last visited March 2, 2002). For published sources, see for example Hussain Ali Al-Waysi, *Al-Yaman Al-Kubra: Dirasat Jughrafiyah, Gulugiyah wa Tarikhiyah*, vol. I, (2nd edition, 1991), 14, 133-6; Abdullah Ahmad Al-Thawr, *Hathi-Hiya Al-Yamen* (Cairo: Almadani Press, 1969); Hussain A. Al-Hubaishi, *Al-Yaman wa Albahr Alahmar: Almawdh'i wa Almakan* (Beirut: n. p. 1992), 32-33. Mr. Al-Hubaishi was

Yemen's senior legal advisor in the Saudi-Yemeni border negotiations leading to the Treaty of Jeddah.

15. The treaty established Ibn Saud as an Ottoman *mutassarif* (local governor) of the *sanjak* (local province) of Najd in central Arabia, then under Ottoman suzerainty. By virtue of the 1913 and 1914 Anglo-Ottoman Conventions, his rule did not extend in the east to the coast of the Gulf or to the south. For the text of the Saudi-Ottoman agreement of 1914, see Schofield, *20 Arabian Boundary Disputes*, op. cit., 21-24.

16. The 1913 and 1914 Anglo-Ottoman Conventions established that Turkish suzerainty did not extend east and south of the Violet Line, declared to be a British "sphere of influence." For more information on the so-called Violet Line of the 1914 Anglo-Ottoman Convention, see Schofield, *20 Arabian Boundary Disputes*, op. cit., 9-18, 849.

17. Yemen adopted the same British argument in its claim against Saudi Arabia. As a successor state to the Ottoman empire, Ibn Saud could not legally claim territory south of the Violet Line, since the 1914 Convention excluded Turkey's suzerainty south of it. However, there were fundamental problems with Yemen's adopted position. First, Yemen and Saudi Arabia had both repeatedly and publicly rejected the 1914 Violet Line as null and void. Secondly, while Saudi Arabia might be a successor state to Turkey, the convention did not indicate to whom the territory south of the line belonged. Even the British Government recognized that Turkey's acknowledgment of the fact that the territory was in the British "sphere of influence" would not under the prevailing international law prevent that territory from being *res nullius* and thus open to acquisition after 1914 by Saudi Arabia or any other neighboring country, including Yemen. Saudi Arabia had acquired the territory by establishing a sovereign title through occupation, and under the same principle it might "legitimately acquire more of the territory, if it is not occupied by or under the effective authority of any other State by the same means." Memorandum on "Ibn Saud's Claims in Respect of the South-Eastern Frontiers of Saudi Arabia," June 30, 1940 in Schofield, *20 Arabian Boundary Disputes*, op. cit., 849. Moreover, as far back as 1934 the British Government's own Legal Advisor at the Foreign Office stated categorically that both the 1914 Violet Line, and by implication the 1955 Riyadh or Independent Line derived from it, contravened the principles of international law. See the text of the opinion of the Legal Advisor in "Minute by Mr. W. E. Beckett," August 29,

1934 in Schofield, *20 Arabian Boundary Disputes*, op. cit., 856-858. It was primarily because of the legal "danger" presented by the Saudi claim to the territory that the British government refused in the 1950's to submit this area to arbitration. The same area subsequently became the subject of the Saudi-Yemeni dispute, before the implementation of "certain measures" aimed at establishing "effective administration in the area concerned." Minutes by the Eastern Department, Colonial Office, July 22, 1953 in Schofield, *20 Arabian Boundary Disputes*, op. cit., 883.

18. The line adopted by Yemen after 1990 represented the maximum Yemeni demands, as shown in the South Yemeni government map of 1972 and North Yemen's map in 1967. See Ghamdi, op. cit., 74, 79.

19. The Treaty of Taif had been formally renewed only once upon the expiration date of its first duration, which, according to the Arabic calendar, was due late in 1953. The renewal was in the form of an exchange of notes in March 1953 between King Ibn Saud and Imam Ahmad, which extended it for another 20 years. Text of the note in *Um Alqura*, March 20, 1953.

20. The Yemeni President accused Saudi Arabia of "slicing (off) a large part" of Yemen, as a result of its systematic and continuous violation of the Yemeni border "since 1934," "especially in the northern and eastern region as well as along the borders of Al-Jawf, Hadhramout and Mahrah governorates." Presidential Press Conference with Representatives of the French and Arab News Agencies," Paris, January 17, 1995, at http://www.nic.gov.ye/SITE%20CONTAINTS/presedency/itrvews/1995/s007.html.

21. For the Saudi refutation of the Yemeni argument about a historical Greater Yemen, see the "geographic and historical annex (in Arabic)" in Bayan, op. cit.

22. In an interview with a Saudi government daily, the Yemeni deputy premier and Foreign Minister appeared to state that the two sides had already signed a non-prejudicial agreement by September 1999, an apparent Saudi concession to Yemen's long-standing demand. From the context of his statement, such an agreement would not be applicable to the 1934 Treaty of Taif, an apparent Yemeni concession to the Saudis. *Alriyadh*, September 25, 1999, 40.

23. "Yemen Lacking 'Seriousness' on Border Issue," Saudi Press Agency, May 28, 1992, quoted in Schofield, *20 Arabian Boundary Disputes*, op. cit., 246.

24. The 1984-86 line appeared south of the modified Hamza line of 1955 and represented "Saudi maximum demands" in the disputed most eastern section

of the 1934 line, as shown in the 1983 map of the "Arabian Peninsula," published by the Saudi Ministry of Petroleum and Minerals, Ghamdi, op. cit., 74.

25. For the overlapping Saudi-Yemeni territorial claims in this sector of the disputed border, see the map "border 2" at http://www.al-bab.com/bys/articles/border2.htm in Richard Schofield, *Negotiating the Saudi-Yemeni International Boundary*, op. cit. and Schofield, *20 Arabian Boundaries*, op. cit., 226-7 and 847.

26. Ghamdi, op. cit., 77.

27. See the comments by the Yemeni president about the Saudi concentration of troops on the border area, "Presidential Press Conference with Representatives of the French and Arab News Agencies," Paris, January 17, 1995 at http://www.nic.gov.ye/SITE%20CONTAINTS/presedency/itrvews/1995/s007.html; *Alsharq Alawsat*, January 17, 1995; Brian Whitaker, "Crisis over the border," *Middle East International*, January 29, 1995 at http://www. al-bab.com/yemen/artic/mei10.htm.

28. El-Rayyes, *Riyah Al-Janoub*, op. cit., 153; the influential Yemeni armed forces official weekly, *Sitta-Wa-Ishreen Septembar*, July 20, 2000, 23.

29. Arabic text of the MOU in i.e. *Al-Riyadh*, February 27, 1995. Unofficial English translation at http://www.al-bab.com/yemen/pol/mou.htm (last visited July 1, 2000). Mr. Ibrahim Al-'Angari, special counsel to King Fahad, was empowered to sign for Saudi Arabia, while Mr. Abdulgader Bajammal, then deputy prime minister, signed for Yemen.

30. *I.C.J. Reports 1994*, Case Summaries: Case Concerning the Territorial Dispute (Libyan Arab Jamahiriya/Chad, Judgment of 3 February 1994, paragraphs 25-26, 52,72-73,74-75 at the International Court of Justice official website, http://www.icj-cij.org/icjwww/idecisions/isummaries/idtsummary940203.htm. The full text of the Judgment is obtainable from http://www.icj-cij.org/icjwww/icases/idt/idt_ijudgments/idt_ijudgment_19940203.pdf.

31. *ICJ Reports 1978*, The Aegean Sea Continental Shelf Case (Greece v. Turkey) (Jurisdiction), Judgment of 19 December 1978. The Court stated that it "knows of no rule of international law which might preclude a joint communiqué from constituting an international agreement." paragraph 96, 39; also at http://www.icj-cij.org/icjwww/idecisions/isummaries/igtsummary781219.htm.

32. ICJ, Judgment on Jurisdiction Case between Qatar and Bahrain Concerning Maritime and Territorial Questions, July 1, 1994, *ICJ Reports 1994*, 126-127,

cited in *ILM* (xxxiv, no. 5, September 1995), 1211, also at http://www. icj-cij.org/icjwww/idocket/iqb/iqbframe.htm (visited September 19, 2000). ICJ, Case Concerning Maritime Delimitation and Territorial Questions Between Qatar and Bahrain (Qatar v. Bahrain) Jurisdiction and Admissibility, paragraphs 23, 25 and 41 at http://icj-cij.org/icjwww/idocket/iqb/iqbframe.htm (visited September 19, 2000).

33. During a visit to Saudi Arabia and soon after the signing of the MOU, the Yemeni President made a point during a press conference of explaining that Yemen's formal confirmation of the Treaty of Taif emanated primarily from "all the exemptions the treaty brings in terms of labor, cross-border movement…and other benefits, and no one can evade this treaty which will establish the basis of future relations between the Yemen and the Kingdom." Text of "Presidential answers in the press conference held in Jeddah, June 7, 1995" at http://www.nic.gov.ye/SITE%20CONTAINTS/presedency/itrvews/1995/s058.html. In an interview with the BBC Radio Arabic Service, July 9, 1995, the president said that the Treaty of Taif accorded "special privileges" to Yemenis as far as cross-border movement and residency in Saudi Arabia were concerned. Text of the interview at http://www.nic.gov.ye/SITE%20CONTAINTS/presedency/itrvews/1995/s060.html.

34. Interview with the Yemeni President, *Assafir*, April 2, 1995, op. cit.

35. Yemen previously insisted that the 1934 line stopped near the Jabal Al-Thar and vehemently rejected Saudi arguments that the line, though still not demarcated in this section, ran in an easterly direction well beyond Jabal Al-thar to the Radm al-amir, where the borders of Yemen, Saudi Arabia and the British Aden Protectorate (and its successor South Yemen) would intersect.

36. Under conventional and customary law, the text of a treaty must be legally interpreted in a way that is rational, gives meaning to each of its provisions and does not render them meaningless or ineffective. See L.F. Oppenheim (ed. H. Lauterpacht) *International Law* (London: Longman, 1955), 955. See also the ICJ Reports, Anglo-Iranian Oil Co. (Jurisdiction), 1953 (July 22), 92, 105.

37. Brian Whitaker, "Border Deal Nearer," *Middle East International*, September 26, 1997 at http://www.al-bab.com/yemen/artic/mei27.htm (last visited December 2000).

38. The Como agreement was confirmed by senior Yemeni and Saudi officials. See the statement by the Yemeni President, *Sitta-wa-Ishreen-Sebtambar*, December 2, 1999, 7; interview with the Yemeni Foreign Minister, *Okaz*

(Saudi daily), July 9, 2000, 23; press conference by Prince Naef, the Saudi Minister of the Interior "Detailing Yemeni Aggressions And Border Movements, Prince Nayef Ibn Abdulaziz: We Did Not Start To Open Fire And Acted In Self-Defense, *Ain Al-Yaqeen*, July 22, 1998 at http://www.ain-al-yaqeen.com/issues/19980722/feat4en.htm. See also "Al-amir Nayef yuwadhih al-haga'ig fi mu'tamar sahafi: thalath arba' jazirat al-duwaimah sau'di, wa tawjiduna fiha mashru'" (In A Press Conference, Prince Nayef Clarifies Facts In Response To Yemeni President' Statements: Three Quarters Of The Duwaimah Island Belongs To Us And Our Presence On it is Legitimate), *Aljazeerah*, July 22, 1998 at http://www.al-jazirah.com/aarchive.htm (visited March 20, 2001).

39. Brian Whitaker, "Border Deal Nearer," *Middle East International*, September 26, 1997 at http://www.al-bab.com/yemen/artic/mei27.htm (last visited December 2000).

40. Interview with the Yemeni President, *Sitta-Wa-Ishreen Septembar*, February 24, 2000, 3. See also another interview with the Lebanese LBC TV, a transcript of which was published in *Alayyam* (Yemeni weekly), May 26, 1999, 6.

41. *Sitta-Wa-Ishreen Septambar*, July 20, 2000, 23.

42. Yemen's traditional notion of historic Yemen also included all of modern-day Oman and beyond. This nation had officially formed the basis of its territorial claim against both Oman and Saudi Arabia. However, Yemen had abandoned the use of the notion of ancient rights in negotiating and signing the 1992 border agreement with Oman, and could as a result no longer sustain the same argument in its negotiation with Saudi Arabia. The Yemeni President publicly acknowledged that the provisions of the Yemeni-Omani border agreement was based on "neither historical facts nor the imposition of a *fait accompli*". Text of "Presidential answers in the press conference held in Jeddah, June 7, 1995 at <http://www.nic.gov.ye/SITE%20CONTAINTS/presedency/itrvews/1995/s058.html. He thus proposed a similar approach for the Yemeni-Saudi conflict based on a "compromise settlement that will not be based on absolute historic title nor on *fait accompli*." Interview with *Al-Hayat*, June 16, 1995. The Yemeni President's proposal was a restatement of a similar position expressed in 1992 by the Yemeni Foreign Minister, Mr. Abdulkarim Al-Iryani, who insisted however that Yemen "did not recognize the Taif [treaty] or at least did not want to accept it as a basis for border settlement." He nevertheless indicated that his government would prefer an

agreement with the Saudis "like that reached with Oman, based on neither Taif nor historical or previous agreement or *fait accompli*." Interview with *Sheehan* (Jordanian weekly), June 13-19, 1992, 14. The Oman–Yemen border agreement was signed on October 1, 1992, *Middle East Survey*, vol. 37 no. 1, October 4, 1993, A8.

43. See for example John C. Wilkinson, *Arabia's Frontiers: The Story of Britain's Boundary Drawing in the Desert* (New York: I.B. Tauris, 1991), 159-64. Wilkinson, for example, wrote that the 1934 Anglo-Yemeni treaty did not mention the 1914 line because "it was clear that the Imam would not formally recognize any boundary line and would certainly not tolerate any reference to the 1914 Convention." Ibid., 162. Indeed, both Yemen and Saudi Arabia had for a long time rejected the 1914 Violet and 1955 British Line as invalid under international law. The Saudi government had rejected the lines during its dispute in the 1950's with the British Gulf protectorate of Abu Dhabi over the Buraimi oasis region, before it relented under the 1974 border agreement with the UAE and the 1990 agreement with Oman. Likewise, Yemen had also rejected them as a possible basis for defining its border with Oman and Saudi Arabia, since they would contravene its historic argument. Yemen then abandoned this position when it signed the subsequent border agreements with Oman and Saudi Arabia.

44. A British government's official memorandum on the geographical coordinates and course of the 1955 line, for example, expressly indicated by name that Al-Kharkhair and Sharorah, towns long claimed by Yemen, were "absolutely" on the Saudi side of the 1955 Riyadh Line. See Richard Schofield and Gerald Blake (editors) *Arabian Boundaries: Primary Documents 1853-1959*, vol. 29 (London: Archive Editions, 1990), 516.

45. For the British government's awareness of the weakness of its legal position on the 1914 and 1955 Lines, see "Memorandum on Ibn Saud's Claims in Respect of the South-Eastern Frontiers of Saudi Arabia," June 30, 1940 in Schofield, *20 Arabian Boundary Disputes*, op. cit., 849, "Minute by Mr. W. E. Beckett" (Foreign Office Legal Advisor), August 29, 1934, ibid, 856- 858 and "Minutes" by Eastern Department, Colonial Office, July 22, 1953, ibid., 883.

46. The border agreement between Saudi Arabia and Oman was signed on March 21, 1990 and the instruments of ratification exchanged on May 21, 1991. *Middle East International*, May 30, 1991. Interestingly, some official Saudi maps, including the 1984-1986 maps published under the auspices of the Saudi Ministry of Petroleum and Minerals and by the Defense Ministry's

Military Survey Department, show a Saudi-Omani boundary line strikingly similar to the one subsequently agreed upon in the 1990 border agreement. See for example, *Atlas Al-Mamlakah Al-'Arabiyah Al-Sau'Diyah* (1999); As'ad Abduh, *Mu'ajam Asma Al-Amakin Fi Al-Mamlakah Al-'Arabiyah Al-Sau'diyah Al-Maktubah 'Ala Kharitat Jazirat Al-'Arab Magas 1:500000* (Jeddah: Madani Publishing, 1996). The names of geographical locations were based on two US government charts, *Arabian Peninsula: Official Standard Names, approved by the US Board on Geographic Names*, prepared in the Office of the Geographer of the US Department of State and published by the Central Intelligence Agency, Washington, DC (July 1961) and *Saudi Arabia: Official Standard Names, approved by the US Board on Geographic Names* and prepared by the US Defense Mapping Agency Topographic Center, Washington, DC (March 1978). See Abduh, op. cit., 7.

47. In the 1948 'Abr agreement, Saudi Arabia recognized the tribes of Al-Sei'ar, Al-Karb, Al-'Awamir and Al-Manahil as part of the British Aden territory, while the British government recognized the Yam, Gahtan and Dawasir as Saudis. For the text of the agreement, see the documentary record (King Abdulaziz Public Library), *Mawsu'at Tarikh Al-Malik 'Abdulaziz al-Dublumasi* (Encyclopaedia of the Diplomatic History of King Abdulaziz), (Riyadh, 1999), 433-8.

48. Ibid.

49. Interview with the Yemeni President, *Sitta-wa-Ishreen-Sebtambar*, February 24, 2000, 3 and "Transcripts of President Ali Abdullah Saleh's Interview With Lebanese LBC TV," *Alayyam*, May 26, 1999, 6. The dispute over the location of the two points led to the cancellation of a planned visit by the Yemeni Prime Minister to Saudi Arabia. *Alsharq Al-Awsat*, October 29, 1999, 4.

50. "Transcripts of President Ali Abdullah Saleh's Interview With Lebanese LBC TV," op. cit.; statement by the Yemeni Prime Minister reported in *Alsharq Al-Awsat*, November 29, 1999, 4.

51. Ibid.

52. Ibid. The Saudi Arabian argument as to the location of Jabal Al-Thar appeared to be motivated by security. The Saudis feared that Yemeni control of Jabal Al-Thar would put the Saudi city of Najran at the mercy of potential Yemeni

artillery. Saudi Arabia had apparently agreed to a Yemeni proposal for a demilitarized zone in the area, which Article 5 of the Treaty of Taif as well as the subsequent Jeddah Treaty had in any case already stipulated for.

53. Press conference by the Saudi Minister of the Interior, *Ain Al-Yaqeen*, July 22, 1998, op. cit.

54. The Yemeni President's interview with *Sitta-wa-Ishreen-Sebtambar*, February 24, 2000, 3.

55. "Transcripts of President Ali Abdullah Saleh's Interview With Lebanese LBC TV," op. cit.

56. "Yemen Follows Treaty," Middle East News Agency (MENA) Cairo, July 17, 1998 (FBIS-NES-98-197).

57. Text of the official Saudi statement in *Okaz*, July 18, 1998, 1.

58. Brian Whitaker, "Border row with the Saudis," *Middle East International*, July 31, 1998 at www.al-bab.com/yemen/artic/me138.htm.

59. Text of the declaration signed on July 29, 1998 in the Saudi newspaper, *Okaz*, 30 July 1998 and the Yemeni newspaper, *Althawrah*, (Yemen government daily) 30 July 1998. For the English text of the protocol, see "Kingdom, Yemen Sign Protocol," *Riyadh Daily*, July 30, 1998, 1.

60. *Sitta-Wa-Ishreen-Septembar*, December 14, 2000, 5.

61. Interview of the Yemeni President, with *Alquds Alarabi*, as reported in *Sitta-Wa-Ishreen-Septembar*, January 1, 1999, 3.

62. Yemeni President's "Inaugural statement at the symposium for peaceful settlement of disputes," *Sitta-Wa-Ishreen-Septambar*, December 2, 1999, 7.

63. Interview with the Yemeni Foreign Minister, *Sitta-Wa-Ishreen-Septambar*, November 19, 1999, 5.

64. "Transcript: Press Conference with Ambassador Edward S. Walker Assistant Secretary of State for Near Eastern Affairs," US Embassy, Sana'a, Yemen, February 14, 2000. Distributed by the Office of International Information Programs, US Department of State, at http://www.usinfo.state.gov (visited June 30, 2000).

65. Interview with the Yemeni Foreign Minister, *Sitta-Wa-Ishreen-Septambar*, February 24, 2000, 2.

66. Interview of the Yemeni President with *Alquds Alarabi*, reprinted in *Sitta-Wa-Ishreen-Septambar*, February 24, 2000, 3.

67. "Interview Of the Week: Reactions to the Treaty," *Yemen Times*, June 26-July 2, 2000 at http://www.yementimes.com/00/iss26/intrview.htm.

68. Statement and press conference by the US Under-Secretary of State for Near Eastern Affairs, Sana'a, Yemen, May 24, 2000. *Sitta-Wa-Ishreen-Septambar*, May 25, 2000, 2.

Chapter 3

1. Text of the joint communiqué at the conclusion of the short but intensive talks. *Okaz*, June 13, 2000, 2.

2. For news reports of the signing of the Treaty of Jeddah, see *Okaz*, June 13, 2000, 1; *Althawrah*, June 14, 2000, 1.

3. For a complete text of the ratified Treaty of Jeddah, see *Algumhuryah*, June 27, 2000, 1, with "an official map" of the new boundary line; *Aljazeerah*, June 27, 2000, 16; *Umm Al-Qura*, July 7, 2000, 1-4; *Sitta-Wa-Ishreen-Septambar*, June 22, 2000, 8-9. Unofficial English translations appear in *The Yemen Times*, June 26-July 2, 2000, op. cit.; Yemen Gateway http://www.al-bab.com/yemen/pol/int5/htm (visited 23 September 2000) ; *Middle East Economic Survey* (MEES) vol. 43, no. 27 (June 25-29, 2000) http://www.mees.com/back_issues/v43n27/index.html (visited February 16, 2001); Saudi Press Agency (spa), a very poor and unreliable translation on 26 June 2000: political/royal decree) http:/www.spa.gov.sa/html/spa_a_news.asp (visited on June 26, 2000), reprinted (along with maps) in the *Riyadh Daily*, 27 June 2000, 1, 3. The text of the treaty that was published in the Saudi and Yemeni papers was accompanied by the same map, showing the final maritime and land boundary line and significantly described, in the Yemeni media only, as "an official map" of the new Saudi-Yemeni border.

4. The Foreign Ministers of Saudi Arabia and Yemen formally exchanged the instruments of ratification in Sana'a, the Yemeni capital, on July 4, 2000. *Al-Gumhuryah*, July 5, 2000, 1.

5. On July 28, the Yemeni and Saudi Permanent Representatives at the UN met the UN Secretary General to register a "joint letter" on behalf of their respective governments, signifying their formal joint deposition with the UN Secretariat of a copy of the treaty, its annexures and instruments with ratification, *Alriyadh*, July 29, 2000, 1, 6 at http://server1.alriyadh.com.sa/29-07-2000/page1.html#2. It is not clear whether the two state parties also included copies of the Treaty of Taif along with all its own annexures, as they should have done, since the latter legally constitutes an integral, indivisible part of the new treaty.

6. On August 9, 2000, Yemeni and Saudi representatives officially lodged a copy of the treaty, its annexures and instruments of ratification with the League Secretariat in Cairo. Yemen News Agency (saba), August 9, 2000 at http://www.sabanews.gov.ye (visited 9 August 2000).

7. *Al-Thawrah*, 13 June 2000, 1 and *Okaz*, June 13, 2000, 1.

8. Treaty of Jeddah, the Preamble.

9. Treaty of Jeddah, Art. 2.

10. Treaty of Jeddah, Art. 1.

11. Treaty of Jeddah, Art. 2.

12. Treaty of Jeddah, Art. 2(a); Treaty of Taif, Art. 4.

13. Treaty of Jeddah, Art. 2(a).

14. Treaty of Jeddah, Art. 2 (a).

15. Treaty of Jeddah, Art.3(1).

16. Treaty of Jeddah, Art 2(b).

17. Treaty of Jeddah, Art 2(c). Although the Tribunal denied Yemen's request with respect to the island, it later came under full Yemeni sovereignty, in accordance with the terms of the Treaty of Jeddah.

18. Treaty of Jeddah, Art. 3.

19. Treaty of Jeddah, Art. 4 and Treaty of Taif, Art. 5.

20. Treaty of Jeddah, paragraph 5 of Annexure 4. Paragraph 7 defined Annexure 4 as an "indivisible part" of the Treaty of Jeddah.

21. Treaty of Jeddah, paragraph 5 of Annexure 4.

22. Treaty of Jeddah, Annexure 4, paragraph 1(a)(b)(c), paragraphs 3 and 4.

23. Treaty of Jeddah, paragraph 6 of Annexure 4. No reference was made to possible common maritime resources.

24. See the statement issued by the joint commission, headed by the two ministers of the interior of the two states and entrusted with the task of implementing the provisions of the treaty. *Sitta-Wa-Ishreen-Septambar*, July 27, 2000, 1-2.

25. Ibid.

26. Yemeni parliamentary resolution ratifying the treaty and quoted in Alray, June 27, 2000, 2 and in an interview with the Yemeni president, *Al-Sharq Al-Awsat*, July 16, 2000, 10.

27. The new territorial gain had added four new major "oil blocks," as well as increased the area of some of the existing 69 blocks with promising oil, gas and mineral reserves covering the land and Red Sea maritime area. Interview with the Yemeni Minister of Oil and Minerals, *Sitta-Wa-Ishreen-Septambar*, July 12, 2001, 11, and July 27, 2000, 3; *Al-Sharq Al-Awsat*, July 26, 2000, 11.

28. Statement by Yemeni Colonel A. Atif, member of the Yemeni-Saudi Joint Military Committee and member of the Saudi-Yemeni Boundary Markers Restoration Joint Committee, *Sitta-Wa-Ishreen-Septambar*, July 20, 2000, 23.

29. Yemeni parliamentary resolution ratifying the treaty, quoted in *Alray* (Yemeni weekly), June 27, 2000, 2; *Al-Sharq Al-Awsat*, June 25, 2000, 4; an interview with the Yemeni President, *Al-Sharq Al-Awsat*, July 16, 2000, 10.

30. However, under the relevant provisions on demilitarized zones in the Treaty of Jeddah, the Saudi military bases, out of which these villages grew and on which they largely depended for their existence, would have to be dismantled. This could possibly precipitate the depopulation process and eventual abandonment of the area.

31. This area appeared to form part of the new block no. 58, *Sitta-Wa-Ishreen-Septambar*, July 27, 2000, 3.

32. Official communiqué issued by the Saudi-Yemeni joint military committee following its meeting in Aden on 8 January 2001. *Sitta-Wa-Ishreen-Septambar*, January 11, 2001, 1; *Alriyadh*, January 12, 2001, 1; statement by Saudi Defense Minister, *Alriyadh*, December 14, 2000, 7. Saudi withdrawal from this sector was reportedly completed during the following April 2001.

33. The Red Sea land terminus point, the finishing point of the 1934 line, had under the Treaty of Jeddah become the starting point of the entire land boundary line, extending eastward and terminating at the intersection of the Saudi, Yemeni and Omani borders.

34. According to the Yemeni Foreign Minister, the Saudi Crown Prince Abdullah was instrumental in "deciding the maritime point" in favor of Yemen, despite apparent strong protest from the Saudi side and an interview with the Yemeni Foreign Minister, Mr. Abdulgader Bajammal. *Okaz*, July 9, 2000, 1 and 21.

35. For official maps showing the official Yemeni location of the land terminus point, visit the Yemeni government *khara'it tafsiyliyah* (Detailed maps), coastal map no. E38-c1 at <http://www.nic.gov.ye/SITE%20CONTAINTS/geography/maps/SADAHMAP1.htm> (last visited March 2, 2002). See also Al-Hubaishi, *Al-Yaman wa Albahr Alahmar*, op. cit., 402, chart no. 6 at 432 and chart 7 at 433. For the Saudi maps, see for example *Atlas Al-Mamlakah Al-'Arabiyah Al-Sau'diyah*, op. cit., map no. 23, 241; Abduh, *Mu'ajam Asma*, op. cit., 9 and the enclosed maps, numbers 216-220.

36. In an interview with a Saudi daily, the Yemeni Foreign Minister, Mr. A. Bajammal, a senior member of the Yemeni negotiating team, stated that Yemen had succeeded during treaty negotiations in its demand to delimit the contested maritime line by "drawing it in a certain way to make it advantageous to Yemen in a big way because Yemen needed free access for its ships and fishermen" to the open sea. Text of the interview in *Okaz*, July 9, 2000, 21. Although Saudi Arabia, unlike Yemen, appeared to have maintained a periodic and largely military presence on the Dhu-Hirab island as late as 1998, Yemen alleged that it had reached an agreement with Saudi Arabia in the mid-1980s under which the latter had withdrawn its forces from the island.

37. The 1974 border agreement between Saudi Arabia and the United Arab Emirates was partly based on the so-called Blue and Violet Lines of the

Anglo-Ottoman Conventions of 1913 and 1914 respectively, which Saudi Arabia had hitherto rejected. Under its terms, Saudi Arabia not only abandoned its actual control of the Buraimi Oasis until 1955, and its long claim to the area, which is less than 100 kilometers off the coast of the Gulf of Oman on the Indian Ocean, but also pulled back inland for hundreds of kilometres, apparently in exchange for a narrow outlet on the northern Gulf, where Saudi Arabia already had a long shoreline of about 500 kilometers.

38. During the Saudi-Omani border negotiations, Oman refused to grant Saudi Arabia a direct territorial corridor to the Indian Ocean or oil and gas pipeline transit rights. Under the terms of the border agreement signed in 1990, Saudi Arabia abandoned its Hamza Line claim and accepted the 1955 British Line emanating from the 1914 Violet Line, in the process conceding more than 90 thousand square kilometers. Under the deal, points on the original Saudi boundary claim less than 30 kilometers off the coast of the Indian Ocean were pushed back inland for more than 250 kilometers. Saudi Arabia had apparently gained nothing in return for its terms of territorial concession, except perhaps a possible Omani pledge not to oppose a future Saudi-Yemeni agreement that involves granting Saudi Arabia some form of territorial corridor to the Indian Ocean via the coastal Mahrah-Dhufar region, then a disputed area wedged between the ideological enemies Oman and the former South Yemen. However, in 1992, soon after the unification of Yemen and despite Saudi protest, Oman and Yemen signed a border agreement in which the disputed region was divided between them.

39. Yemen and Eritrea had settled their maritime boundary through arbitration. For the first phase in 1998, see the "Permanent Court of Arbitration (PCA): Eritrea-Yemen Arbitration (First Stage: Territorial Sovereignty and Scope of Dispute", October 9, 1998, text of decision, 40 *ILM* 900 (2001); also at http:llwww.pca-cpa.org./ER-YEAwardTOC.htm, visited on 28 December 1998 and September 18, 2000 (hereafter referred to as "1998 Eritrea/Yemen"). For the second phase in 1999, see "Permanent Court of Arbitration (PCA): Eritrea-Yemen Arbitration (Second Stage: Maritime Delimitation), December 17, 1999, *ILM* vol. 40 (2001), 983; see also the text of the Award in PCA "Eritrea-Yemen Award Phase II: Maritime Delimitation," at http://www.pca-cpa.org/ERYE2TOC.htm (hereafter "1999 Eritrea/Yemen Award"). Before the Tribunal decision, the Eritrean government had rejected previous Saudi approaches to enter into bilateral negotiation, partly due to Saudi claims over part of the north-eastern Zula block, which was awarded by Eritrea to an oil exploration company in the Red Sea. However, after the

Tribunal decision and conclusion of the Saudi-Yemeni treaty, Eritrea approached both Saudi Arabia and Yemen to settle the issue through the conclusion of a tripartite agreement by the year 2002. Interview with the Eritrean Minister of Foreign Affairs, *Sitta-Wa-Ishreen-Septambar*, October 10, 2001, 3 and an interview with the Yemeni Foreign Minister, *Al-Sharq Al-Awsat*, April 16, 2001, 3.

Chapter 4

1. Despatch no. 19 (1037/1) from M.B. Jacomb, Taiz, Yemen, to FO, London, 5 August 1952, in Ingrams and Ingrams, *14 Records of Yemen*, op. cit., 749.

2. However, it is important to note that, according to the public records consulted, no Yemeni government and for that matter no Saudi government had communicated any formal notification to this effect in terms of article 22 of the treaty or any other relevant clause of conventional law, neither to the Saudi government nor other relevant regional or international bodies like the UN or the League of Arab States.

3. Articles 47-72 of the 1969 Vienna Convention on the Law of Treaties (hereinafter VCT), Document A/CONF.39/11/Add.2, United Nations, *Treaty Series*, vol. 1155, Chapter XXIII: Law of Treaties, at 331; text of VCT, also at http://www.un.org/law/ilc/texts/treaties.htm.

4. Marhoun, *Niza'at al-hudud fi shibh al-jazeerah al-'arabiyah*, op. cit., 60. There was also Yemen's allegation, denied by Saudi Arabia, of Saudi detention during the war of Mr. Al-Wazir, the Yemeni negotiating representative, and subsequent coercion to move him to co-sign the 1934 treaty. Shihari, op. cit., 271.

5. Kern, op. cit., 30.

6. VCT, art. 51.

7. Gerhard von Glahn, *Law Among Nations: An Introduction to Public International Law* (New York: Macmillan, 1986), op. cit., 508.

8. Despatch no. 194 (1837/17/536) from Andrew Ryan (Jeddah) to John Simon, FO, London, 19 June 1934, in Ingrams and Ingrams, *8 Records of Yemen*, op. cit., 184, 182.

9. Shihari, op. cit., 230-1.

10. Charter of the UN, adopted on June 26, 1945, Article 1, Paragraph 1, Charter of the United Nations and the Statute of the International Court of Justice (1987).

11. Mavrommatis Palestine Concessions Case, Judgment, 1924, PCIJ, series A. no. 2.

12. *ICJ Reports*, Judgment, 2 February 1973, Fisheries Jurisdiction (UK v. Iceland), (Jurisdiction of the Court), also at http://www.icj-cij.org/icjwww/idecisions/isummaries/iaisummary730202.htm.

13. For more details on the topic, see for example Elias, "Doctrine of Intertemporal Law," *AJIL* vol. 74, 285.

14. Prior to the First War, the states' right to wage war was considered an inalienable part of their sovereignty, subject only to international rules concerning their conduct while prosecuting the war (*jus in bello*). The Hague Peace Conferences of 1899 and 1907, in which the Convention for the Pacific Settlement of International Disputes was signed, were the first serious international (European) attempts to curtail the rights of states to resort to war. The CPSID, in turn, established the Permanent Court of Arbitration, and states were urged to submit their disputes for peaceful settlements there. Yutaka Kawasaki, "Was the 1910 Annexation Treaty Between Korea and Japan Concluded Legally?," *E Law – Murdoch University Electronic Journal of Law*, vol. 3, no. 2 (July 1996), 2-5 at http://www.murdoch.edu.au/elaw/issues/v3n2/kawasaki.html (visited March 17, 2002) (visited October 10, 1999).

15. The General Treaty for the Renunciation of War as an Instrument of National Policy, adopted on August 27, 1928, text in *League of Nations Treaty Series* vol. 94, 57. See also C.D. Wallace, "Kellogg-Briand Pact (1928)," in R. Bernhardt (ed.) *Encyclopedia of Public International Law* vol. 3 (1982), 235-9.

16. Arts. 12-15 of the Covenant of the League of Nations, adopted on June 28, 1919.

17. Art. 1 of the Kellogg-Briand Pact, op. cit.

18. The Saudi accession came in a diplomatic note from the US government sent in reply to an invitation to join the Pact and delivered by the US Legation in Jeddah. Texts of the reply and the subsequent Royal Decree announcing the

accession of Saudi Arabia to the Kellogg-Briand Pact appeared in *Maju'at*, op. cit., 98. No records consulted thus far have shown that Yemen joined the Kellogg-Briand Pact.

19. J.G. Starke, *Introduction to International Law* (London: Butterworths, 1989), 535, cited in Kawasaki, op. cit., 3, 4.

20. Ibid., 1.

21. Glahn, op. cit., 508.

22. Despatch no. 194 (1837/17/536) from Andrew Ryan (Jeddah) to John Simon, FO, London, 19 June 1934, in Ingrams and Ingrams, *8 Records of Yemen*, op. cit., 184.

23. Bayan, op. cit., 2-3.

24. Letter from the head of the Saudi negotiation team to Abdullah al-Wazir, head of the Yemeni negotiation team, (Arabic month of) *dhu-al-qi'dah* 23, 1353h; document no. 161 in Bayan, op. cit., 189.

25. Instructions from Ibn Saud to his negotiating delegation at Abha, in Asir, final session, *dhu-al-qi'dah* 1352h, ibid.

26. In the Yemeni view, by inserting the fixed duration Article 22, Yemen had not "totally abandoned" the Asir and Najran, whose ownership became merely "suspended." Under the article Yemen maintained its right to seek "at the appropriate time" the amendment of the treaty, whereby the two provinces returned to Yemen. Shihari, op. cit., 16.

27. Kern, op. cit., 31.

28. Glahn, op. cit., 513.

29. Interview with Mr. Abdulkarim al-Iryani, Yemeni Deputy Prime Minister and Foreign Minister. *Sheehan* (a weekly newspaper in Amman, Jordan), June 13-19, 1992, 14.

30. L.F. Oppenheim, (H. Lauterpacht, ed.) *International Law*, vol. II (London: Longman, 1953), 946.

31. *Yearbook of the International Law Commission* (1963), 211.

32. *Yearbook of the International Law Commission II* (1966), 247.

33. The "1936 General Agreement between the Kingdom of Saudi Arabia and the Kingdom of Yemen Concerning the Settlement of Matters Relating to the Subjects of the Two Kingdoms," attached to the Treaty of Taif. Text in Ministry of Foreign Affairs, *Majmu'at*, op. cit., 194-198.

34. Kern, op. cit., 32; Marhoun, *Niza'at al-hudud fi shibh al-jazeerah al-'arabiyah*, op. cit., 60.

35. Ibid.

36. The article provided a tribally-based rationale for such privileges. It states that the tribes of Yam, Najran al-Hadhn, Zur Wada'a and the Wa'ila section inhabiting the Najran area originally belonged to Yemen. They were only included in the Kingdom of Saudi Arabia as a result of the Imam Yahya's delegation of the power to decide their nationality to the Saudi king, His Majesty King 'Abdulaziz. The latter decided that all of them belonged to the Kingdom of Saudi Arabia, so that the Al-Hadhn, Zur Wadi'a and the Wa'ila could enjoy the usual and customary relations, interaction and cooperation.

37. Text of the letter, dated 6 *safar* 1353h (20 May 1934) in i.e. Ministry of Foreign Affairs, *Majmu'at*, op. cit., 165.

38. Peter Malanczuk, *Akehurst's Modern Introduction to International Law*, (London: Routledge, 1999), 135.

39. Ghamdi, op. cit., 64.

40. Attached letter no. 1, in Ministry of Foreign Affairs, *Majmu'at*, op. cit., 204.

41. Additionally, Article 8 of the Treaty of Taif explicitly provided that the annexed Covenant of Arbitration has "the same force and power as the treaty does this treaty and constitutes an integral part of it."

42. Kern, op. cit., 32.

43. VCT, Art. 62.

44. Ian Brownlie, *Principles of Public International Law* (Oxford: Clarendon Press, 1973), 598. A recent example of the application of this rule would be the grounds on which the 1977 Trade Agreement between the German Democratic Republic (GDR) and the Republic of the Philippines were terminated. As a result of the German unification in 1990, the GDR proposed the termination of the trade agreement. The foreign affairs ministry of the GDR invoked Article 62 of the VCT regarding a fundamental change of

circumstances as a ground for termination. In response, the Filipino foreign ministry agreed that the abolition of the German Democratic Republic constituted a fundamental change of circumstances as contemplated in the Article, and the agreement was subsequently terminated. Lotilla, *Asian Yearbook Of International Law 1991*, op. cit., 177.

45. *Daily Telegraph* (London), July 13, 1960; Shihari, op. cit., 17. However, one would have expected Saudi Arabia to invoke Articles 15 and 17 of the Treaty of Taif as a legal ground to suspend termination of the non-territorial clauses while keeping the territorial clauses legally intact as executed provisions. These articles prohibit both contracting state parties from unilaterally joining any third party alliance perceived by either party as posing a threat to its interests.

46. *Daily Telegraph* (London), 13 July 1960. Other Yemeni sources put the year as 1959. Shihari, op. cit., 280.

47. Despatch from the British Legation, Taiz, Yemen, September 4, 1960, no. 10343/3/60 in Ingrams and Ingrams, *8 Records of Yemen*, op. cit., 64. However, other Yemeni Foreign Ministry officials contradicted their colleague's assertion and indicated instead that Saudi Arabia only wanted to amend the treaty provisions relating to the "employment of Yemenis within the Kingdom of Saudi Arabia" by subjecting them to the same regulations that applied to other nationals from Arab League countries. The apparently confused Yemeni comments on Saudi action stemmed in part from the seemingly contradictory official Saudi announcements issued on 10 July, 14 July and 9 August by Prince Faysal, the Saudi Crown Prince, Prime Minister and Foreign Minister. The announcements stated that Yemeni nationals working in Saudi Arabia would henceforth be subject to the same employment regulations as other Arab League nationals. However, Articles 15 and 17 of the Treaty of Taif prohibit both contracting state parties from unilaterally joining any third party alliance perceived by either party as posing a threat to its interests. One would have expected Saudi Arabia to invoke these articles as a legal ground to suspend termination of the non-territorial clauses, while keeping the territorial clauses legally intact as executed provisions.

48. Ibid.

49. Brownlie, op. cit., 599.

50. As, for example, in the case of the termination by mutual consent of the 1977 GDR-Filipino Trade Agreement, *Asian Yearbook Of International Law 1991*,

op. cit., 177, or the Czechoslovak-U.S. Treaty of Naturalization on August 20, 1997.

51. Text of Agreement Unifying the Yemen Arab Republic and the People's Democratic Republic of Yemen, thereby Establishing the Republic of Yemen, signed on April 22, 1990, *ILM* vol. 30 (1991), 820.

52. The legal sanctity of this important principle of customary law has been enhanced further during the aftermath of the unification of Germany, the dissolution of the USSR and Yugoslavia. Member states of the European Community and other east European countries, particularly Poland and the former Czechoslovakia, both of which have common borders with Germany, made their diplomatic recognition of the new unified German state conditional upon the latter's formal pledge to be bound by the doctrine. The EC, currently the European Union, officially adopted a common position in the form of guidelines on the process of recognition of these new states that emerged as a result of German unification and the dissolution of the USSR and Yugoslavia. This required their commitment to respect, inter alia, the provisions of the UN Charter and "the inviolability of all frontiers which can only be changed by peaceful means and by common agreement." See Danilo Türk, "Annex 1: Declaration on "Guidelines on the Recognition of New States in Eastern Europe and in the Soviet Union (16 December 1991)," *EJIL* vol. 4, no. 1 (1993), 72 at http://www.ejil.org/journal/Vol4/No1/index.html (visited May 12, 2001).

53. Akehurst, op. cit., 268. This adherence by the new state was in accordance with the relevant clauses in the VCS on treaties, though neither of the two former Yemeni states, nor the emergent one, became party to either the VCT or VCS. A similar contemporary example would be the unification of Germany, which came into being soon after the Yemeni union on 3 October 1990, when the German Democratic Republic (East Germany) was integrated with the Federal Republic of Germany (West Germany) and, as a result, ceased to exist. Article 35 of the unification treaty stipulates that its provisions "are without prejudice to the international treaties concluded by the Federal Republic of Germany or the German Democratic Republic with third parties." Jean-Paul Jacqué, "German Unification and the European Community," *EJIL* vol. 2 no.1 (1991), 1-17 at http://www.ejil.org/journal/Vol2/No1/index.html (visited May 12, 2001).

54. The 1926 Mecca Treaty, as previously mentioned, formally put the Idrisi territory under Saudi "protection," a situation that continued until the end of

1930, when the Idrisi ruler was forced to relinquish control of internal affairs as well. Schofield, *20 Arabian Boundary Disputes*, op. cit., 470. On September 23, 1932, shortly after the crushing of an anti-Saudi rebellion there, the whole emirate legally ceased to exist and formally became the "southern province" of the newly renamed Kingdom of Saudi Arabia. See i.e. Fuad Hamza, *Galb Jazeerat Al'Arab* (The Heart of Arabia) (Cairo: 1937), 321.

55. For the text of the Idrisi-British treaty of Sabia, signed on April 30, 1915, and the "supplementary agreement" signed on January 22, 1917, which recognized the Farasan Islands as an integral part of the Idrisi territory that came under British protection under the provisions of the 1915 agreement, see Tuson and Quick, *4 Arabian Treaties*, op. cit., 177-179.

56. The Anglo-Najdi treaty, called the Darin or Uqair agreement, was signed on December 26, 1915, a few months after the conclusion of the Anglo-Idrisi agreement. Like the latter, it placed Ibn Saud's territory in central Arabia under *de jure* British protection, with full control over his territory and the conduct of his foreign relations. For the text of the treaty, see Schofield, 20 *Arabian Boundary Disputes*, op. cit., at 35-6. It was superceded in May 1927 by the officially named Treaty of Jeddah, which formally granted independence to Saudi Arabia but kept intact some important capitulatory provisions of the 1915 treaty pertaining to, inter alia, restriction on certain aspects of Saudi foreign relations and granting exclusive rights to British Muslim subjects. For the text of the 1927 treaty, see Tuson and Quick, *4 Arabian Treaties*, op. cit., 101-108.

57. From a strictly legal point of view, one may raise a question concerning the precise current status of the 1927 British-Saudi Treaty of Jeddah under international law, and its potential legal implications on the position of not only the 1926 Mecca agreement, but also the 1934 Treaty of Taif and the 2000 Treaty of Jeddah that Saudi Arabia had signed with Yemen. On 14 October 1943, upon receipt of an official Saudi government request, the British government agreed through a formal Exchange of Notes to an amendment effecting an "indefinite" prolongation of the 1927 treaty. See Penelope Tuson and Anita Burdett (editors) *Records of Saudi Arabia: Primary Documents: 1902-1960 vol. 7, 1938-1946* (London: Arabic Editions, 1992), 313-318 (hereafter *7 Records of Saudi Arabia*). There appears to be no existing record showing that the two parties had sought to terminate the treaty together or unilaterally. Thus, it is not clear whether the legal force of the 1927 treaty ceased to exist under international law on the ground that its

provisions had long fallen into disuse and were thus legally inoperable, or if it still remains valid, especially in light of the fact that Saudi Arabia, apparently pursuant to certain clauses granting privileged rights to British Muslim nationals, in 1999 officially accorded Great Britain the unique diplomatic privilege of being the only Western power to maintain a consulate in the Muslim holy city of Mecca, in light of the fact that the British Muslim population was far smaller than that of the United States, Russian Federation or France. For the Anglo-Saudi agreement to open a British consulate in Mecca, see for example *The Guardian* (UK), November 5, 1999 at www.guardianunlimited.co.uk/Archive/Article/0,4273,3926088,00.html (visited January 23, 2001).

58. Despatch from Sir Andrew Ryan, Jeddah, to FO, June 7, 1934, Eastern (Arabia), no. 145 E3761/79/25, in Ingrams and Ingrams, *8 Records of Yemen*, op. cit., 170. For the Imam's views on Asir and Najran, see for example Schofield, *20 Arabian Boundaries Disputes*, op. cit., 505.

59. A.N. Talalyev, "Unequal Treaties as a mode of prolonging the colonial dependence of the new States of Asia and Africa." *Sovietskii Ezhegodnik Mezhdynarodnogo Prava* (1961), 169-170, cited in Nozari, op. cit., 118.

60. For the 1930 resolution of the Idrisi local assembly that handed over internal control of the emirate to Ibn Saud, and the subsequent rebellion in 1931-1932 against Saudi rule, see i.e. Shihari, op. cit., 162, 165; Schofield, *20 Arabian Boundary Disputes*, op. cit., 422, 472, 509.

61. Art. 2, Treaty of Taif.

62. See the relevant section in Chapter Four on "Implications of the Eritrea-Yemen Arbitration Award of 1998" on Yemen's Historical Claim Argument Against Saudi Arabia.

63. Art. 2, Treaty of Taif. The Al-'Aayidh, the ruling dynasty of the northern highland Asir were nominally under the suzerainty of the Idrisi. Under a 1920 agreement, the latter relinquished the territory to Ibn Saud, then Sultan of Najd. For the background and text of the agreement, see Schofield, *20 Arabian Boundary Disputes*, op. cit., 38-44; Bayan, doc. No. 54, 177-8; Shihari, op. cit., 104.

64. For the Idrisi's 1915 agreement with Britain, see Wahba, *Jazeerat Al-Arab fi Al-Qarn Al-Ishreen*, op. cit., 320-1; Shihari, op. cit., 104.

65. Despatch from Sir E. Drummond, British ambassador, Rome to FO, 19 April 1934, enclosure no. 1 Eastern (Arabia), no. 342. E2600/2/25, in Ingrams and Ingrams, *8 Records of Yemen*, op. cit., 128.

66. Ibid. and Schofield, *20 Arabian Boundary Disputes*, op. cit., 529.

67. Despatch from Sir John Simon (London) to Sir R. Graham (Rome), October 13, 1933 in Schofield, *20 Arabian Boundaries*, op. cit., 509.

68. Despatch from Sir E. Drummond, British ambassador, Rome to FO, 19 April 1934, enclosure no. 1 Eastern (Arabia), no. 342. E2600/2/25, in Ingrams and Ingrams, *8 Records of Yemen*, op. cit., 128 and Schofield, *20 Arabian Boundary Disputes*, op. cit., 529.

69. For the Yemeni government's insistence on "historical and legal rights," as a basis for border negotiations with Saudi Arabia, see the statements by Yemen's President and other senior officials. Presidential press conference, Sana'a, May 24, 1990 at http://www.nic.gov.ye/SITE%20CONTAINTS/ presedency/itrvews/1992/s29.html; *Alyawm Al-Sabi*, July 14, 1990 at http://www.nic.gov.ye/SITE%20CONTAINTS/presedency/itrvews/1990/s03 9.html; presidential interviews with French TV, 21 September 1990, at http://www.nic.gov.ye/SITE%20CONTAINTS/presedency/itrvews/1990/s05 5.html; *Alquds Alarabi* newspaper (London) 28 May 1992, p. 4; *Alwasat* (London) magazine, June 7, 1992 at http://www.nic.gov.ye/SITE%20 CONTAINTS/presedency/itrvews/1992/s32.html; with British TV, May 1, 1992 at http://www.nic.gov.ye/SITE%20CONTAINTS/presedency/itrvews/ 1992/s27.html; French and Arab news agencies, Paris, January 17, 1995 at http://www.nic.gov.ye/SITE%20CONTAINTS/presedency/itrvews/1995/s00 7.html. The Yemeni Foreign Minister, Mr. Al-Iryani, demanded the "return," not only of the Saudi southern administrative provinces of Jizan, Asir and Najran, which were ceded under the Treaty of Taif, but also territory that extended to include the "very large geographical expanse of al-Rub' al-Khali (Empty Quarter) that pushes northward the border of Yemen to reach the heart of Saudi Arabia as it is currently located." See the interview with the Jordanian weekly *Sheehan*, 13-19 June 1992, 14. For the official "natural" and "political" Yemeni maps of "Greater Yemen," visit the official website (Arabic version) of the Yemeni government agency, National Information Center, at http://www.nic.gov.ye/SITE/20%CONTAINTS/geography/maps/ mm.JPG (last visited March 2, 2002); for the historical "natural map of Yemen as delineated by al-Hamadani" see http://www.nic.gov.ye/SITE% CONTAINTS/aboutyemen/history/MAPS/M.htm (last visited March 2,

2002). For published books in Arabic, see Al-Waysi, *Al-yaman al-kubra*, op.cit., 14, 133-6, Al-Thawr, *Hathi-hiya al-yaman*, op. cit., 14, 22-8.

70. *Alquds Alarabi*, 28 May 1992, 4.

71. The Treaty (of Taif) abandoned for ever the slogan the Imam had adopted before the signing of the Treaty and used against Britain, Ibn Saudi, the Idrisi and Italy, which called for a "Yemen for the Yemenis" and the realization of the "Yemeni unity" of the territories, which he considered to be historically Yemeni. Shihari, op. cit., 17.

72. Interview with the then Foreign Minister, Mr. Abdulkarim Al-Iryani, in *Sheehan*, 13-19 June 1992, 14.

73. The Yemeni Foreign Minister stated that "the groundwork" of the Yemeni-Omani border negotiations, which were continuing at the time, was aimed at producing a boundary line based on neither historical claim nor *fait accompli*." Ibid.

74. In 1995, after the signing of the MOU, the Yemeni President, during a visit to Saudi Arabia, stated that Yemen would welcome a solution to the border issue based on "neither absolute historic title nor on fait accompli." Interview with *Al-Hayat*, June 16, 1995 at http://www.nic.gov.ye/SITE%20 CONTAINTS/presedency/itrvews/1995/s062.html. In an earlier press conference held in Jeddah, he suggested the Yemeni-Oman border agreement as a model for a Saudi-Yemeni border treaty, since in the case of the former both historical rights and accomplished facts were taken into consideration. Press conference, Jeddah, June 7, 1995 at http://www.nic.gov.ye/SITE%20CONTAINTS/presedency/itrvews/1995/s058.html.

75. For the Eritrean and Yemeni historical arguments, see Chapter IV:"Historic Title and Other Historical Considerations," *1998 Eritrea-Yemen Award*, op. cit., paragraphs 116-120, 24.

76. Ibid., para. 447, 80.

77. Quoted in ibid.

78. Ibid., 79.

79. Ibid.

80. Ibid.

81. Ibid., 80.

82. Ibid. It is possible here that the Tribunal's rejection of the two doctrines was preceded and perhaps influenced by the ICJ's rejection of similar Libyan arguments in a territorial dispute with Chad. See ICJ (Judgment) 1994, Territorial Dispute (Libyan Arab Jamahiriyah v. Chad), op. cit., 27. It is also worth noting that Lord Jennings was the presiding judge in both judicial and arbitral processes.

83. 1998 Eritrea-Yemen Arbitration Award, par. 446 at 80.

84. Ibid.

85. W. Michael Reisman, "The Government of the State of Eritrea and the Government of the Republic of Yemen: Award on Sovereignty over Disputed Islands in the Red Sea." *AJIL* vol. 93 (1999), 670.

86. *1998 Eritrea/Yemen Award*, paragraph 122 at 25 (italics added).

87. Ibid.

88. Ibid. A strongly pro-Yemeni writer appeared to implicitly support this view, though perhaps inadvertently. Shihari, op. cit., 14, 89.

89. In deciding the northern end of the maritime boundary, the 1999 Eritrea/Yemen Tribunal observed that the area might prejudice other boundary disputes with neighboring countries, i.e. Saudi Arabia, after it acknowledged receipt of a formal Saudi note to the Registrar of the Tribunal on August 31, 1997, pointing out that Saudi Arabian boundaries with Yemen were disputed, reserving its position with respect to its claim in the area, and suggesting that the Tribunal should restrict its decisions to areas "that do not extend north of the latitude of the most northern point on Jabal Al-Tayr island." While Eritrea stated that it had "no objection" to the Saudi Arabian proposal, the Yemeni government, for its part, expressed its wish to extend the northern sector to its utmost limit, i.e. to the latitude of 16N, in order to include, inter alia, the Jabal al-Tayr island. See "Permanent Court of Arbitration (PCA)," Eritrea-Yemen Arbitration (Second Stage: Maritime Delimitation, December 17, 1999, text of decision *ILM* vol. 408 (2001) 47, paragraph 44. See also the text of the Award in PCA, "Eritrea-Yemen Award Phase II: Maritime Delimitation," at http://www.pca-cpa.org/ERYE2TOC.htm (hereafter "1999 Eritrea/Yemen Award").

90. Reisman, op. cit., 681.

91. Island of Palmas (US v. Netherlands), 2 R.I.A.A. 1929, 829.

92. *ICJ Reports*, 1953, Minquiers and Ecrehos (UK v. France), Judgment of November 17, 1953, 47, also at http://www.icj-cij.org/icjwww/idecisions/isummaries/ifuksummary531117.htm.

93. Memorandum by the Foreign Office Research Department, Minutes by Mr. W. E. Beckett, FO Legal Advisor, "The Claims of Ibn Saud against His Majesty's Government," August 29, 1934, Schofield, *20 Arabian Boundary Disputes*, 858.

94. Reisman, op. cit., 681. In terms of geography, demographic structure and parties to the dispute, the case of the Western Sahara of North Africa, initially involving Mauritania, Morocco and Algeria, was similar in many ways to the vast area of the dispute covering the southern fringes of the vast Empty Quarter between Saudi Arabia, Yemen, Oman and United Arab Emirates. See ICJ, Western Sahara, Advisory Opinion of October 16, 1975, at http://www.icj-cij.org/icjwww/idecisions/isummaries/isasummary751016.htm.

95. The disputed eastern sector covered most of the vast area adjacent to the southern edges of the vast Empty Quarter and inhabited by nomadic tribesmen who, in terms of physical appearance, religious affiliation, dialects, customs and social interaction, have more affinity with their kindred desert tribesmen roaming the southern frontier of Saudi Arabia and less with the settled, village-based and predominantly Zadyi tribesmen of highland Yemen.

96. In 1994, for example, the Yemeni government rejected proposals for holding a plebiscite in the disputed border region with Saudi Arabia. The then Foreign Minister Abdulkarim al-Iryani said "our dispute with Saudi Arabia is over land, not people." "Saudi Arabia–Yemen: Diplomatic Relations Deteriorate," *Alquds Alarabi*, June 5, 1997, in International Boundaries Research Unit, May 6, 1997 (FBIS-NES-97-156) at http://www-ibru.dur.ac.uk/cgi-bin/data.pl (visited December 20, 2000). In addition, Yemen was perhaps also aware of the possibility that significant numbers of the local population, motivated by potential economic and financial benefits, would opt for the other party.

97. In the 'Abr agreement, Saudi Arabia recognized as part of the British Aden territory the tribes of Al-Sei'ar, Al-Karb, Al-'Awamir and Al-Manahil, while the British government recognized the Yam, Ghahtan and Dawasir as Saudis. For the text of the 'Abr agreement, see the documentary record

(King Abdulaziz Public Library) *Mawsu'at tarikh al-malik 'abdulaziz al-dublumasi* (Encyclopaedia of the Diplomatic History of King Abdulaziz) Riyadh, 1999, 433-8.

98. Ibid.

99. "International Court of Justice (ICJ): Case Concerning Maritime Delimitation and Territorial Questions Between Qatar and Bahrain (Qatar v. Bahrain) (March 16, 2001) *ILM* vol. 40 (2001), 847. For the full text of the decision, see also ICJ, 2001, Case Concerning Maritime Delimitation and Territorial Questions between Qatar and Bahrain (Qatar v. Bahrain), Merits, March 16 at http://www.icj-cij.org/icjwww/idocket/iqb/iqbframe.htm; a summary of the Judgment of 16 March 2001 at http://www.icj-cij.org/icjwww/ipresscom/ipress2001/ipresscom2001-9bis_qb_20010316.htm.

100. Statement by the Saudi Foreign Minister, Saud Al-Faysal, *Al-Hayat*, December 8, 1998, 1, 6, *Sitta-Wa-Ishreen Septembar*, December 10, 1998, 2.

101. Brian Whitaker, "Crisis over the border," *Middle East International*, January 19, 1995 at http://www.al-bab.com/ycmcn/artic/mei10.htm. Brian Whitaker, "Border row with the Saudis," *Middle East International*, July 31, 1998 at www.al-bab.com/yemen/artic/mei38.htm; Brian Whitaker, "Tensions with the Saudis," *Middle East International*, December 19, 1997 at www.al-bab.com/yemen/artic/mei29.htm; *Alquds Alarabi*, August 4, 1997; *Albayan* (UAE daily) October 10, 1998, 1.

102. "Ali Saleh Announced Commitment To Amicable Solution With Saudi Arabia," Yemen, Politics, December 15, 1998 at http://www.arabicnews.comlansub/Daily/Day/00091520.htm; the Yemeni president later declared emphatically that "we will not resort to arbitration so long as there is a political will," *Al-Hayat*, September 27, 1999, 2; the then Yemen Foreign Minister, Mr. Bajammal also declared that "neither Yemen nor Saudi Arabia want to resort to international arbitration to settle their border dispute." *Alsiyasah* (Kuwaiti daily), December 8, 1998. He later explained that Yemen did not prefer a resolution through arbitration because it would "not guarantee the benefits accrued from" a settlement by amicable bilateral conciliation. *Al-Sharq Al-Awsat*, September 25, 1999, 3; *Alriyadh*, September 25, 1999, 40.

103. Statement by Saudi Foreign Minister made in February 19, 1999, Yemen, Politics, February 19, 1999 at www.Arabic new.comlansub/Daily/Day/0009.htm.

Chapter 5

1. Article 2(1)(a) of the VCT.

2. The definition was adopted from the Draft Article in the *International Law Commission International Yearbook*, II, op. cit., 645; Brownlie, op. cit., 583.

3. Article 4 of the VCT.

4. Article 38 of the ICJ.

5. Article 6 of the VCT.

6. I.M. Sinclair, the Vienna Convention on the Law of Treaties, (1973), 27 cited in Louis Henkin, Richard C. Pugh et al., *International Law: Cases and Materials* (St. Paul, MN: West Publishing 6, 1980), 596.

7. Preamble of the Treaty of Taif.

8. Ibid.

9. Neither Yemen nor Saudi Arabia was a member of the League of Nations. When approached by these Arab states in the early 1930's, Great Britain, then the dominant member of the League, repeatedly discouraged both states in formal communication from submitting applications for membership. Saudi Arabia would appear to be entitled to automatic membership in the League by virtue of being a successor state of the former Kingdom of Hejaz, a founding member of the League. Nevertheless, the British government, in terms of the provisions on a semi-protectorate of the 1927 Treaty of Jeddah with Saudi Arabia, rejected the Saudi approaches for formal admission, ostensibly due to the practice of slavery and despite the absence of anti-slavery provisions in the Covenant and the fact that Abyssinia, a state with slavery, was a member of the League.

10. Article 18 of the League of Nations.

11. Article 102 (20), UN Charter.

12. For more detailed discussions and guidelines concerning the topic of "Reservations to treaties", see, for example, the work of the 50th session in 1998, in the International Law Commission Report 1998, Chapter XI "Reservations to Treaties," where it considered the third report of the Special Rapporteur regarding the definition of reservations (and interpretative declarations). The Commission adopted seven draft guidelines on the

definition of reservations, the object of reservations, instances in which reservations may be formulated, reservations with a territorial scope, reservations formulated when notifying a territorial application, reservations formulated jointly and the relationship between definitions and the admissibility of reservations. The work report of the fiftieth session of the International Law Commission was issued in UN document A/53/10, 1998.

13. Letter no. 1, Schofield, *20 Arabian Boundary Disputes*, op. cit., 100.

14. See for example Article 19 of the Covenant of the League of Nations; Articles 14, 108 and 109 of the UN Charter, and Articles 39-41 of the VCT. Most publicists assert that in general there is no real distinction between "modification," "amendment" and "revision" of the treaty. Brownlie, op. cit., 603.

15. Ibid.

16. Art. 8, Treaty of Taif.

17. Under the Gregorian calendar, the signing of the 1995 MOU approximated the expiration date of the *de facto* second extension of the Treaty of Taif in March 1973, upon the expiration of the 20 years duration of the first formal extension signed in 1953, leading to the assumption that both states appeared to accept at least tacitly that the March 1973 Joint Communiqué and 1995 MOU as constituting a second and third extension agreements of the Treaty of Taif under the force of its article 22.

18. Arts. 39, 41 and 42 of the VCT.

19. See for example Arts. 39, 41 and 42 of the VCT.

20. *Okaz*, June 14, 17.

21. Article 31(3) of the VCT.

22. Articles 31-33 of the VCT lay down the general rules dealing with the interpretation of the provisions of treaties.

23. For a more recent study of international and U.S. developments regarding the theory and practice of treaty interpretation, see Detlev F. Vagts, "Treaty Interpretation and the New American Ways of Law Reading," *European Journal of International Law* vol. 4, no. 4 (1993), pp. 472-506.

24. Paragraph 3(a) of Article 31 of the VCT.

25. *International Yearbook*, International Law Commission, II, op. cit., 645 and Brownlie, op. cit., 583.

26. *I.C.J. Reports,* 1978, The Aegean Sea Continental Shelf Case (Greece v. Turkey), (Jurisdiction of the Court), Judgment of December 19, 1978, 36; also at http://www.icj-cij.org/icjwww/idecisions/isummaries/igtsummary 781219.htm.

27. See the "Judgment on Jurisdiction Case between Qatar and Bahrain concerning maritime and territorial questions," July 1, 1994, paragraphs 126-127, 34 ILM (September 1995), 1211; see also "Case Concerning Maritime Delimitation And Territorial Questions Between Qatar And Bahrain (Qatar v. Bahrain) Jurisdiction And Admissibility," July 1, 1994 at http://www.icj-cij.org/icjwww/idocket/iqb/iqbframe.htm.

28. Gyorgy Haraszti, *Some Fundamental Problems of the Law of Treaties* (Budapest: Akademiai Kiado, 1973), 265-6.

29. *ICJ Reports*, 1962, Case Concerning the Temple of Preah Vihear (Thailand v. Cambodia), (Merits), Judgment of 15 June 1962, 61; also at http://www.icj-cij.org/icjwww/idecisions/isummaries/ictsummary620615.htm.

30. Telegram from Sir Andrew Ryan, the British minister in Jeddah to Sir John Simon, the Foreign Office, London, 29 December 1933, Schofield, *20 Arabian Boundary Disputes*, op. cit., 548.

31. Sir Andrew Ryan to Sir John Simon, "Saudi Arabia: Annual Report 1933," Penelope Tuson and Anita Burdett, no. 129, April 28, 1934, paragraph 46, 12 in *Records of Saudi Arabia: Primary Documents 1902-1960*, Vol. 5 1932-1935 (editors 1992), 212.

32. The 1997 Como agreement could not be included among agreements preceding the 2000 Jeddah treaty, since its contents, whether verbal or in written form, has not yet been officially revealed to the public by either party.

33. ICJ (Judgment) 1994, Territorial Dispute (Libyan Arab Jamahiriyah v. Chad) op. cit., 27.

34. Brownlie, op. cit., 163-4.

35. Ibid., 164.

36. Article 45, VCT.

37. Temple of Preah Vihear, Merits, op. cit., 33.

38. Brownlie, op. cit., 165.

39. P.C.I.J., 1933, Legal Status of Eastern Greenland (Norway v. Denmark), Judgment, Ser. A/B, no. 53, 68-9, cited in Brownlie, 165.

40. ICJ, 2001, Case Concerning Maritime Delimitation and Territorial Questions between Qatar and Bahrain (Qatar v. Bahrain), Merits, op. cit., Separate opinion of Judge Al-Khasawneh, paragraphs 1, 13.

41. Ibid. Another example of reaffirming this principle would be the collective decision of member states of the European Community taken in the aftermath of the unification of Germany, the dissolution of the USSR and Yugoslavia, to make their diplomatic recognition of the new unified German state conditional upon the latter's formal pledge to respect its present frontiers with Poland and the former Czechoslovakia established under post 1945 peace treaties. See Türk, "Annex 1: Declaration on the 'Guidelines on the Recognition of New States in Eastern Europe and in the Soviet Union (16 December 1991)," op. cit., 72.

42. *Um Alqura*, February 21, 1936.

43. See the text of the Saudi-Iraqi Arab Brotherhood and Alliance Treaty, signed on April 2, 1936, and the text of the formal Yemeni note of accession containing relevant articles of the treaty, dated 26 August 1937, in Ministry of Foreign Affairs, *Majmu'at*, 222-224 and 241-44 respectively. It is noticeable that the official published Saudi Arabian records of the treaty texts only refer to the Treaty of Taif and its arbitration covenant in article 2 of the Treaty. This is the version included in the formal Yemeni note of accession. No similar reference is made in the bilateral Iraqi-Saudi text of the treaty, where article 2 merely calls for an arbitration "protocol" to be concluded shortly after the signing of the treaty, in an apparent allusion to the expected Yemeni accession that the two signatories formally invited to join.

44. UN Report by the Secretary General to the Security Council on Developments Concerning Yemen, 29 April 1963, UN Document s/5298; UN, Second Report of the Secretary-General to the Security Council on Developments Relating to Yemen, 27 May 1963, Document S/5321. In a UN-prepared map, annexed to the report, the location of the demilitarized zone, along "the demarcated Saudi Arabia-Yemen border" appears to correspond to that of the 1934 Treaty of Taif boundary. However, it also carried the caption: "The

boundaries shown on this map do not imply official endorsement or acceptance by the United Nations." Map No. 1477.1 (United Nations) October 1963; see also UN, "Exchange of Letters Constituting Agreement relating to Privileges, Immunities and Facilities for the Observation Operation (UNYOM) along the Saudi Arabian-Yemen Border" established pursuant to Security Council resolution, New York, June, 1963.

45. The North Yemen government had rejected British and American proposals to bring about UN disengagement and demilitarization on the Yemen–British Aden frontier similar to the Saudi-Yemeni UNYOM, since this "connotes acceptance of some frontier line" that Yemen would never agree to. "Memorandum of Conversation/1/," Washington, no. 44, April 27, 1964, National Archives and Records Administration, RG 59, Central Files 1964-66, Pol 19 Aden. Secret, Foreign Relations of the United States, 1964-1968, Volume XXI, Near East Region, Arabian Peninsula, Department of State, Washington, DC.

46. Haraszti, op. cit., 236.

47. Ibid., 235.

48. Article 54 of the VCT.

49. Ibid.

50. *Okaz*, June 14, 2000, 17.

51. ICJ Reports 1994, Territorial Dispute Between Libyan Arab Jamahiriya and Chad (Judgment), op. cit., 6.

52. Ibid., paragraph 52, p. 25-6.

53. Ibid., paragraphs 74-75, 38-40.

54. ICJ Reports 1962, the Temple of Preah Vinear (Merits; Judgment), op. cit., 340.

55. ICJ Reports 1978, Aegean Sea Continental Shelf, Judgment, op. cit., 3, 36.

56. Brownlie, op. cit., 611.

57. Ibid., 265.

58. Ibid.

59. Arie E. David, *The Strategy of Treaty Termination: Lawful Breaches and Retaliations* (New Haven, CT: Yale University Press, 1975), 14.

60. Brownlie, op. cit., 308.

61. Other executed provisions pertaining to repatriation of war prisoners and withdrawal of troops, for example, had also been duly executed.

62. Art. 1, the Treaty of Taif.

63. Haraszti, op. cit., 265.

64. Brownlie, op. cit., 599.

65. Article 62(2)(a), VCT.

66. Oppenheim, *International Law*, I, op. cit., 227.

67. Ibid., 938.

68. Haraszti, op. cit., 401, 403.

Chapter 6

1. The Saudi government, clearly taken aback by the extent of Yemeni public and media reaction to the signing of the treaty, declared that it "interpreted the celebration in a positive light as an expression of the happiness of our Yemeni brothers with the agreement." Statement by the Saudi Minister of the Interior in a press conference held a few days after the signing of the Treaty of Jeddah, *Alriyadh*, 18 June 2000.

2. Following the signing of the Treaty of Jeddah, an analysis appeared in the influential Saudi government *Okaz* daily, which read in part: "the Treaty of Jeddah is nothing more than an implementation of the preamble of the Treaty of Taif calling for a fixing of the boundary between the two countries. The Treaty of Jeddah is the practical and legal outcome of the text of the preamble of the Treaty of Taif, which called for the parties to settle in a friendly manner any dispute that may arise between them." *Okaz*, June 24, 2000, 22.

3. As reported in a Saudi newspaper, "highly placed" Yemeni officials had to "apologize" to the Saudi government following the latter's "formal protest

expressing its dismay over the 'premature leaking of the provisions' of the treaty" and "Yemeni media reports of an 'allegation' that Saudi Arabia would under the treaty 'return' substantial land and sea territory to Yemen." *Al-Sharq Al-Awsat*, June 25, 2000, 4.

4. Political opposition groups, like the Nasserite People's Unionist Party, who in the past had traditionally rejected the whole Treaty of Taif, had now changed course and became one its most ardent proponents. A leading member of the party stated that his party concurred with the Yemeni Prime Minister's characterization of the treaty as "a legend that became reality" and indicated that his party wholeheartedly supported the treaty, first, because of its affirmation of the Treaty of Taif, and second, "the area of the (present) State of Yemen has, as from June 12, 2000 (date of the treaty signature), somewhat exceeded half of Yemen's region, "namely that comprising the territory of a historical Greater Yemen. Ali Saif Hassan, "Border Agreement: Why is It a Legend?" *Yemen Times*, July 31-August 7, 2000 at http://www.yementimes.com/00/iss31/ln.htm.

5. Statement by the Minister of Parliamentary and Legal Affairs published in *Sitta-Wa-Ishreen Septembar*, 15 June 2000, 2; see also *Al-Sharq Al-Awsat*, July 1, 2000, 12.

6. Statement by Ahmad Sufan, Yemeni Minister for Planning and Development, quoted in *Sitta-Wa-Ishreen Septembar*, July 20, 2000, 7; also *Aljazeerah*, July 25, 2000, 36.

7. Statement by Mr. Ali Abdullah Buhleeg, head of the Yemeni parliament's Committee of Constitutional and Legal Affairs, quoted in *Sitta-Wa-Ishreen Septembar*, July 20, 2000, 7.

8. A speech during the debate by Deputy Abdullah al-Udainy of the governing parliamentary coalition of the Reform Congregation party, as reported in the party's newspaper, *Alsahwah* (a Yemeni opposition party weekly), 29 June 2000, 1-2.

9. Ibid.

10. Parliamentary Law no. 16 for the Year 2000, ratifying the Treaty of Jeddah. The law followed the report and recommendations of the committee formed for this purpose, quoted in *Alray* (a Yemeni opposition party weekly) June 27, 2000, 1-2, *Alsahwah*, 29 June 29, 2000, 1-2.

11. An interview held in Riyadh with the Editor-in-Chief of the Yemeni weekly, *Sitta-Wa-Ishreen Septembar*, August 10, 2000, 10-11 and published simultaneously in other Saudi newspapers, including *Okaz*, 12-13.

12. The Saudi employer sponsorship law was formally repealed in early 2001, soon after and in large part as a consequence of the ratification of the Treaty of Jeddah.

13. Despatch from the British Legation, Taiz, Yemen, September 4, 1960, no. 10343/3/60, in Ingrams and Ingrams, *14 Records of Yemen*, op. cit., 64.

14. Ibid.

15. Ibid.

16. Kern, op. cit., 32.

17. Ibid.

18. Although clearly motivated by Yemen's declared intention in 1960 to join the union of Egypt and Syrian, which Saudi Arabia perceived to be an anti-Saudi tripartite alliance, and by its perception of Yemen's hostile attitude towards the 1990 Iraqi invasion of Kuwait, the Saudi government inexplicably did not attempt to invoke articles 15 and 17 of the Treaty of Taif as a ground for its decision. The first article prohibited either party from entering into a third party alliance deemed to be injurious to the interests and existence of the other party, while the other stipulated that, in the event of an external threat of aggression against one of the contracting parties the other was required to support it or at least adopt a benevolent neutrality. It is possible, however, to invoke the Treaty of Taif as a ground for its decision to repeal what would appear to be, at least implicitly, as a Saudi acknowledgment that these privileges are mandated by the terms of the treaty as a legal obligation.

19. In a symposium discussing the Treaty of Jeddah and held in Sana'a, government officials, opposition groups and academics who participated in it generally agreed that "those Yemeni expelled (by Saudi Arabia in 1990) must be allowed to return, the Saudi employer's sponsorship law abrogated because it does not exist in the Treaty of Taif and steps taken regarding travel entry exemptions for Yemeni." *Sitta-Wa-Ishreen Septambar*, June 15, 2000, 11.

20. *Sitta-Wa-Ishreen Septambar*, August 2, 2001, 1. This was by no means the first time the Yemeni government had publicly expressed its dissatisfaction with Saudi Arabia regarding the implementation of so-called special privileges provisions since the conclusion of the Treaty of Jeddah. In September 2000, two months after the signing ceremony, the then Yemeni Minister of Interior protested that "despite talks on this subject and Saudi understanding of this matter, we have not seen any tangible result and we are looking forward to see concrete action in this regard." *Sitta-Wa-Ishreen Septambar*, September 14, 2000, 11.

21. In an apparent partial acquiescence to the Yemeni request, the Saudi ministry of the interior issued a statement to indefinitely "postpone" its decision to indigenize (Saudiize) the economically powerful gold and jewelry market traditionally dominated by Yemenis. *Alriyadh*, August 23, 2001, 10.

22. Interview with the Yemeni President in the program of the Qatar-based Aljazeera TV, "bila hudud," as transcribed in *Sitta-Wa-Ishreen Septambar*, September 6, 2001, 5. Three months later, the GCC held its twenty-second annual summit in Muscat, Oman and took the first formal step towards admitting Yemen as a full member in the regional body by giving it in effect an associate membership status to participate in the GCC's collective work on important labor, social and health issues. Excerpts from the text of the GCC 22nd Summit final communiqué in *Al-Hayat*, January 1, 2002, 4.

23. "The 1936 General Agreement between the Kingdom of Saudi Arabia and the Kingdom of Yemen Concerning the Settlement of Matters relating to the Subjects of the two Kingdoms," annexed to the Treaty of Taif. Ministry of Foreign Affairs, *Majmu'at*, op. cit., 194-198 (hereafter the "1936 General Agreement").

24. Saudi and Yemeni officials have repeatedly denied the existence of secret annexures or agreements related to the content of the Treaty of Jeddah. See for example the Yemeni President's denial of the existence of any "secret protocols, written or unwritten agreements or any deals." Interview with *Almajallah* (Saudi weekly magazine), July 23-9, 2000, 21; statement by the Saudi Minister of the Interior in a press conference that "there is no secret provisions." *Alriyadh*, 18 June 2000, 8; *Al-Eqtisadiah*, June 18, 2000, 6. However, when depositing copies of the ratified Treaty of Jeddah with the UN and Arab League, the two parties did not, as they perhaps should have done, include copies of the 1995 MOU and especially the Treaty of Taif and its annexures as an integral part of the body of the Treaty of Jeddah. Article

102(1) of the UN Charter required member states to register agreements between them with the UN. Although secret or non-registered treaties are not necessarily deemed non-binding, they could not be invoked under article 102(2) before any organ of the UN, i.e. the ICJ. In practice, however, non-registered agreements creating future rights and obligations have commonly been invoked by member states before international judicial and arbitral bodies.

25. The article provided a tribal rationale for such privileges. It states that the tribes of Yam, Najran al-Hadhn, Zur Wada'a and the Wa'ila section inhabiting the Najran area originally belonged to Yemen and were only included in the Kingdom of Saudi Arabia as a result of the Imam Yahya's delegation to the Saudi King of the power to decide their nationality. His Majesty King 'Abdulaziz decided that all of them belong to the Kingdom of Saudi Arabia, which allowed the al-Hadhn, Zur Wadi'a and the Wa'ila to enjoy the usual and customary relations, interaction and cooperation.

26. Letter no. 5, Treaty of Taif.

27. 1936 General Agreement.

28. Article 7 (1) of the 1936 General Agreement, 196.

29. Article 7 (3), ibid., 197.

30. Art. 12 of the Treaty of Taif.

31. Ghamdi, op. cit., 64.

32. Yemen also rejected the Saudi assertion that Saudi border posts were located in territory where most of the inhabitants were Saudi nationals. It accused Saudi Arabia of using its economic leverage to sustain its territorial claim, by granting many Yemeni subjects who inhabited the border area to accept Saudi citizenship, including members of tribes and villages defined as Yemen under the Treaty of Taif. For example, Shaykh bin Shaj'I, currently a fierce opponent of the Treaty of Jeddah, was a strong ally of Saudi Arabia until 1986, enjoying regular benefits that included additional monetary stipends that granted him and many of his Yemeni tribesmen Saudi nationality. Interview with Shaykh bin Shaj'i, *Yemen Times*, August 28-September 3, 2000 at http://www.yementimes.com/00/iss34/intrview.htm#1 (visited 2 September 2000); also *Yemen Times*, March 11-17, 2002 at http://www.yementimes.com/02/iss11/front.htm#3.

33. Tribal opposition to the Treaty of Jeddah manifested in early 2001 in sporadic armed attacks on Saudi and Yemeni border posts and military patrols. This motivated the two sides to establish a joint border regulatory authority not stipulated for in the Treaty of Jeddah. In its first meeting in May 2001, the joint border regulatory authority "strongly recommended the necessity of formulating an annex" to the Treaty of Jeddah, in order to "activate security cooperation particularly in relation to the border issue." This was mainly the result of existing and possible future tribal opposition in the central and western common border sectors to the implementation of the Treaty of Jeddah. *Alwatan* (Saudi daily), May 18, 2001, 3.

34. The two sides later agreed to establish several border-crossing points. The agreed crossing points are two existing ones: between Altiwal (Saudi Arabia) and Haradh (Yemen) near the Red Sea coast, between 'Alma-alkhadhra (Saudi Arabia) and Albaq'a (Yemen) in the Najran-Jabal Al-Thar area, and a new one, between Al Wadi'ah (Saudi Arabia) and Al'abr (Yemen) in the middle sector. See the text of the joint communiqué and press statements at the conclusion of the third meeting of the joint treaty implementation commission held in Riyadh at the end of October 2000. *Aljazeerah*, October 30, 2000, 4; *Sitta-Wa-Ishreen Septembar*, October 25, 2001, 2. Yemen appears to have different names and locations as well as numbers for the border-crossing points, which the Yemeni President named as follows: "the land crossing points between Yemen and Saudi Arabia are Jizan-Haradh, Khamis-mushait-'Albin, Albaq'a-Najran and Al Wadi'ah-Al'abr." Interview with the Yemeni President, *Sitta-Wa-Ishreen Septembar*, September 6, 2001, 5. Significantly, there was no reference to the establishment of official cross-border points along the length of the eastern sector of the common boundary covering almost the whole northern border of the former South Yemen, whereas Saudi Arabia alone maintained an unofficial border post at Al Kharkhair long claimed by Yemen before the Treaty of Jeddah. However, in February 2002, the Yemeni President announced a policy of resettling a large section of the Yemeni tribal population along the common Saudi-Yemen border area, particularly in the eastern sector, and asked the Saudi government to agree to establish an official border-crossing point in the al-Kharkhair area.

35. *Sitta-Wa-Ishreen Septembar*, July 27, 2000, 1 and 2.

36. Initially, the Saudi government appeared to regard the Treaty of Jeddah as having an exclusively territorial bearing and no linkage to special exemptions regarding trade and labor that were unrelated to boundaries. Immediately

after the signing of the treaty, the Saudi Minister of the Interior asserted that "the issue of Yemeni labor has, in fact, no relation with the boundary treaty." *Okaz*, 13 June 2000, 4; in a subsequent official press conference held a few days later, he repeated his assertion, stating that "the treaty is restricted to maritime and land boundary and the subject of exemption to Yemeni workers is not part of it." *Alriyadh*, June 18, 2000, 8; *Al-Eqtisadiah*, June 18, 2000, 6.

37. Interview with *Sitta-Wa-Ishreen Septembar*, 10 August 2000, 10-11, *Okaz*, 12-13.

38. Quoted in *Sitta-Wa-Ishreen Septembar*, 27 July 2000, 2.

39. Press conference on July 4, 2000, on the occasion of the formal exchange of the Treaty of Jeddah's ratification instruments, held in Sana'a. *Al-Gumhuryah*, 5 July 2000, 1.

40. See *Al-Eqtisadiah*, December 14, 2000, 1, 2; *Al-Gumhuryah*, December 14, 2000, 1 and 2.

41. *Sitta-Wa-Ishreen Septembar*, December 7, 2000, 1; interview with the Yemeni Prime Minister, *Alwatan*, December 9, 2000, 4; interview with the Yemeni Foreign Minister, *Alwatan*, January 9, 2001, 17; *Alsharq Alawsat*, June 25, 2000, 4.

42. Interview with the Saudi Chairman of the Joint Preparatory Committee for the second SYCC meeting, *Alwatan*, June 20, 2001, 19.

43. According to the Yemeni Ministry of Finance, the Saudi decision to "reschedule" the Yemeni debt had reduced it by 80% and extended the date of due repayment of the remainder to a further 40 years. *Alwatan*, February 26, 2001, 1.

44. As already mentioned, the Yemeni parliamentary approval of the Treaty of Jeddah was linked to Saudi implementation of several conditions that included, inter alia, Saudi financing of important highway projects. Early on, the Yemeni Foreign Minister appeared to interpret the text of the parliamentary "recommendations" in this regard to mean that Saudi Arabia would be required to "link by road the border areas between Jabal Al-Thar to the border cross point with the Sultanate of Oman." *Alsharq Alawsat*, June 25, 2000, 4. Two-thirds of the Saudi loan granted in the context of the Treaty of Jeddah was targeted specifically at the "roads sector," including finance for the strategic "unity" Safir-Hadhramout-Tarim-Thamud highway, linking

for the first time the far ends of western and eastern parts of Yemen by paved highway. *Sitta-Wa-Ishreen Septembar*, June 10, 1999, 12.

45. A subsequent meeting of the Yemeni-Saudi Coordination Council was held on 20-22 June 2001, during which the two sides concluded further agreements intended to ultimately lead to "full partnership." Text of joint communiqué of the June meeting in *Okaz*, June 23, 2001, 6. The Ministers of Labor had already signed an agreement to "facilitate the procedures for Yemeni labor to enter the Saudi market," currently estimated by the Yemeni and Saudi sides at close to one million. *Alsharq Alawsat*, April 19, 2001, 4.

46. *Alriyadh*, August 23, 2001, 10.

47. *Sitta-Wa-Ishreen Septembar*, October 25, 2001, 1; *Aljazeerah*, October 26, 2001, 1.

48. *Sitta-Wa-Ishreen Septembar*, August 2, 2001, 1.

Chapter 7

1. Art. 12, Treaty of Taif.

2. Previously, Yemen had strongly rejected the option of a plebiscite to be held in the disputed regions, saying, in the words of the then Foreign Minister, Abdulkarim Al-Iryani; "our dispute with Saudi Arabia is over land, not people." *Alquds Alarabi*, 5 June 1997, op. cit.

3. The Saudi Minister of the Interior denied the existence of any "ambiguity" in the Treaty of Jeddah regarding the affiliation of border tribes and villages along the Treaty of Taif's boundary line. BBC Arabic News, 10 July 2000 at http://news.bbc.co.uk/hi/arabic/news, visited 10 July 2000.

4. The tribal territory of the Wa'ilah, as claimed by its paramount Shaykh bin Shaj'I, extends for more than 200 kilometers in length from the western coastal plains of the Red Sea to Wadi Altifah in the eastern hinterland, east of the Jabal Al-Thar, i.e. along the entire length of the 1934 treaty boundary line. Interview with Shaykh Muhammad bin Shaj'i, *Yemen Times*, August 28-September 3, 2000 at http://www.yementimes.com/00/iss34/intrview.htm#1 visited 2 September 2000.

NOTES

5. The powerful Dahm tribe, along with the Dhu Heen, Bani Nawf and Hamadan tribes, inhabiting Wadi Alyatmah in Yemeni al-Gawf province near the Yemeni-Saudi border, declared their rejection of the Jeddah treaty because it would, in their view, concede part of their tribal territory to Saudi Arabia. This led to frequent armed clashes between them and both Yemeni and Saudi forces in the area. See "Tensions Mount In Al-Gawf," *Yemen Times*, July 31-August 7, 2000 at http://www.yementimes.com/00/iss31/ln.htm; "Dahm Tribe Rejects the Jeddah Border Treaty and Threatens Demarcation Companies," *Yemen Times*, April 30-May 6, 2001, at http://www.yementimes.com/00/iss18.

6. "More Reactions to the Border Treaty," *Yemen Times*, July 3-9, 2000 at http://www.yementimes.com/00/iss26/treaty.htm (visited July 13, 2000).

7. Shaykh Bin Shaj'i, of the northern Yemeni tribe of Wa'ilah, declared that his tribe and the neighboring Saudi tribe of Yam "have a 241-year old document demarcating borders between our tribe and Yam tribe…even before the formation of the Kingdom of Saudi Arabia, and the Republic of Yemen." Both tribes, he insisted, reject the provisions of the Treaty of Jeddah pertaining to their tribal boundary and vowed that they will not "stay idle" when the demarcation company begins its work. "Sheik Bin Shaji' Threatens to Thwart any Demarcation Attempts." *Yemen Times*, June 26-July 2, 2000 at www.yemetimes.com/00/iss26/intrview.htm (visited June 27, 2000). In addition to genealogical links, both the Saudi tribe of Yam and the Yemeni tribe Wa'ilah are predominantly adherents of the minority Ismaeli religious sect, and when the former led an uprising in April 2000 in the Saudi city of Najran, they sought refuge with their co-religionists on the Yemeni side, which led to armed clashes between the pursuing Saudi forces and Yemeni border tribes. *Alwahdawi*, April 25, 2000, 1 and 9.

8. Ibid.

9. Both the Yemeni and Saudi governments, at least in public, appeared to dismiss as empty boasts the threats by Yemeni tribes, especially by Shaykh bin Shaj'i's tribe of Wa'ilah, to thwart the re-demarcation work of the 1934 line. The Yemeni President, for one, dismissed them as "tribal bubbles of no consequence and some tribal leaders attempting to obtain money from from Saudi Arabia through blackmail." *Alriyadh*, June 22, 2001, 3; *Okaz*, June 22, 2001, 1 and 2. Also see statements made by senior Saudi officials, including the Saudi Defense Minister, in *Alriyadh*, December 14, 2000, 7 and *Alwatan*, June 20, 2001, 19.

10. Alray, July 25, 2000, 1; "New Saudi-Yemeni Border Demarcation Challenges Arise," *Yemen Times*, May 14-May 20, 2001 at http://www.yementimes.com/01/iss20/. One incident involved an armed attack by members of some Yemeni border tribes on the land motorcade of a senior member of the Saudi ruling royal family, upon his return home from a visit to Yemen, *Alwatan*, October 30, 2000, 7.

11. In April 2001, Saudi Arabia admitted that there was fierce tribal opposition that manifested in attacks by Yemeni tribal elements on Saudi border patrols at the Alwisah, Alshifa and Sadis posts in the Najran area. The problem was further compound by the continued presence, contrary to the terms of the treaty, of Yemeni heavy armory, which was later withdrawn along the common border. See a press conference statement by the Saudi Minister of the Interior at the conclusion of one of the periodic meetings of the Saudi-Yemeni joint commission, held in April 2001 in Riyadh. *Aljazeerah*, April 5, 2001, 3. It was partly due to tribal threats that, during the previous session held in Sana'a in January, the two parties failed to sign, as originally scheduled, the demarcation contract awarded to the German survey company, Hansa Luftbild. See the text of the joint communiqué of the joint commission meeting held on 20-21 January 2001. *Aljazeerah*, January 22, 2001, 4.

12. "New Saudi-Yemeni Border Demarcation Challenges Arise," *Yemen Times*, May 14-May 20, 2001 at http://www.yementimes.com/01/iss20. Anticipating the mounting difficulties posed by the Yemeni tribes regarding the new demarcation of the 1934 line, the two countries decided to double the original two-year implementation period for the demarcation process, and, more importantly, to commence the demarcation process for this politically sensitive border sector only after the completion of the demarcation of the other two sparsely-populated eastern and maritime sectors. *Aljazeerah*, April 5, 2001, 3 and *Sitta-wa-Ishreen-Sebtambar*, April 5, 2001, 1. In April 2001, after a delay of more than four months due to violent tribal opposition and a dispute over Saudi troops' withdrawal from central and eastern areas and cross-border installations, the two countries formally signed the agreement to demarcate an almost 1500 km-long boundary line of rugged mountain and harsh desert. On October 6, 2001, the company officially commenced its work and declared its intention to complete its entire work by the year 2005. *Alwatan*, October 7, 2001, 6.

13. It seems as if the Yemeni Deputy Prime Minister and Foreign Minister who was the principal Yemeni negotiator of the Treaty of Jeddah anticipated such an eventuality. He acknowledged the problem of having to resolve the issue.

What was "in 1934 a small town of no more than 5 huts, whose population belonged at that time to either the Yemeni or the Saudi side, has now expanded greatly both in geographic scope and population reaching in some cases one million." Interview with *Okaz*, part 2, 9 July 2000, 21. According to past and current demographic standards in the region, it takes only a few shepherds to build their small huts or tents around a watering hole to constitute an established tribal settlement or village.

14. For a survey of the status of the boundary pillars until at least the early 1950's, see H. St. J.B. Philby, *Arabian Highlands* (New York, NY: Cornell University Press, 1952).

15. The Yemeni Foreign Minister stated categorically that from "the text of the treaty it is clear that a village becomes part of Saudi Arabia or Yemen on the basis of the allocation of the tribe (inhabiting such a village) to either (state) party in the Treaty of Taif and its annexures." *Alsharq Alawsat*, July 7, 2000, 1 and 4.

16. *Alwahdawi* (Yemeni opposition party weekly), December 14, 1999, 1 and 9.

17. The Saudi "citizenship" documents granted to some Yemeni border villagers and tribesmen, who also retained their original Yemeni citizenship, were known locally as "Sultan's citizenship," a reference to prince Sultan, the Saudi Deputy Prime Minister and Minister of Defense on whose orders they were issued. The validity of such documents may substantially and procedurally be in violation of Saudi Arabia's own nationality law which, inter alia, expressly prohibits acquisition of dual citizenship.

18. Interview with Shaykh bin Shaj'i, *Yemen Times*, August 28-September 3, 2000, op. cit. In early 2001, Sheik bin Shaj'i appealed to the Yemeni President to renounce the treaty and restated his tribe's determination to thwart its implementation. See the text of the letter, dated February 17, 2001, in "Bin Shaji' Appeals to President Saleh." *Yemen Times*, February 19-25, 2001, 1 at www-yementimes-com-01-iss08-front-htm#3. In January 2002, the tribe of Wa'ilah carried out its threat when an affiliated sub-tribe blew up the first demarcation boundary marks in the Alyatma area of Najran, only days after they had been installed by the German survey company, forcing the latter to suspend operations there. See "Tribesmen Blew-up Border Demarcations Marks," *Yemen Times*, 4-21 January 2002 and 21-27 January 2002, at http://www.yementimes.com/02/iss4/ln.htm#6. In early March 2002, the Shaykh himself was fatally injured in a car accident in his tribal home area of Kitaf Albag'a and later pronounced dead in a Saudi hospital across

the border in the city of Najran. *Sitta-Wa-Ishreen Septembar*, March 7, 2002. Many sources linked his death "in mysterious circumstances" to his avowed opposition to the Treaty of Jeddah. See *Yemen Times*, March 11-17, 2002 at http://www.yementimes.com/02/iss11/front.htm#3 and *Alquds Alarabi*, March 8, 2002, 1.

19. The Treaty of Jeddah does not expressly prohibit the building of new villages on the disputed border area, especially in view of the locally accepted fact that the mere installation of a few huts on a watering hole inhabited by few shepherds would constitute a permanent settlement. "Jeddah Treaty 2000 Did Injustice to Yemen," *Yemen Times*, July 17-July 21, 2000 at http://www.yementimes.com/00/iss29/l&d.htm.

20. Current Yemeni treaty-making procedures involving legislative, judicial and executive processes are embodied in articles 1, 6, 61, 91, 92, 95, 118 and 135 of the Yemeni constitution of 1994. For the Arabic text of the Yemeni constitution, see http://www.nic.gov.ye/SITE20%20CONTAINTS/politics/legislations%and%20laws/dustoor.htm (visited 17 September 2000); for the English text, see http://www.al-bab.com/yemen/gov/con94.htm (visited 16 July 2000). As shall been seen later, the constitution was amended in 2001 so that treaties will henceforth be ratified by the elected national Council of Deputies in a joint session with the newly-established second chamber, Council of *Shura* (consultation), which is composed of members appointed by presidential decree.

21. Remarks by Mr. Tahir Ali Saif, member of the ad hoc committee on the Treaty of Jeddah in the Yemeni Council of Deputies. "Reactions to the Treaty," *Yemen Times*, July 17-21, 2000 at http://www.yementimes.com/ 00/iss29/l&d.htm.

22. Relevant articles 1, 156 and 159 of the Yemeni constitution of 1994, op. cit.

23. Text of the President's letter to the speaker and members of the Yemeni Council of Deputies, which indicates in detail the articles of the 1994 constitution that should be amended, as approved by parliament in principle pending the final vote in a national referendum. *Sitta-Wa-Ishreen Septambar*, August 24, 2000, 1, 3.

24. Ibid. On November 19, 2000, the Yemeni Council of Deputies approved the proposed amendments. *Sitta-Wa-Ishreen Septambar*, December 21, 2000, 1. After a majority vote in a national referendum held on February 20, 2001, the constitutional amendments became part of the newly-amended Yemeni

constitution of 2001. For an unofficial English translation of the new constitution, visit http://www.nic.gov.ye/English%20site/SITE%20CONTAINTS/Constitution%20%20-Laws/THE%20CONSTITUTION.htm.

25. *Asshura* (Yemeni political party weekly), November 19, 2000, 4.

26. Shihari, op. cit., 18.

27. Text of King Fahad's public statement, announcing the promulgation of the first written Saudi constitution. See i.e. *Umm Al-Qura*, March 6, 1992.

28. Enacted by Royal Decree no. A/90, 27/08/1412h, March 1, 1992, with the official Arabic text in *Umm Al-Qura*, March 6, 1992; also at http://www.saudiksa.com/gov1_a.htm; unofficial English translation at http://www.uni-wuerzburg.de/law/sa00000_.html (visited 28 October 1998).

29. Art. 44 of the Saudi constitution, op. cit.

30. Under the Saudi constitution, the King is constitutionally invested with legislative, judicial and executive powers and has the sole power to approve, ratify or otherwise terminate or suspend by royal decree international agreements. For provisions in the Saudi constitution directly relevant to procedures regarding the making of treaties, see articles 70 and 81. Article 70 of the Saudi constitution states that "International treaties, agreements, regulations and concessions are approved and amended by Royal decree." Article 81 stipulates that "the implementation of this (constitution) will not prejudice the treaties and agreements signed by the Kingdom of Saudi Arabia with international bodies and organizations. Ibid.

31. Enacted by Royal Decree no. A/91, 27/08/1412h, March 1, 1992, with the official Arabic text in *Umm Al-Qura*, March 6, 1992. The English text of the laws promulgating the consultative council are at http://www.uni-wuerzburg.de/law/sa01000_.html (visited October 21, 1998).

32. For the Saudi government's official view on the religious basis and legal status of the Saudi Consultative Council, i.e. parliament, see the text of the lecture by its Speaker on the Islamic shura council in *Alriyadh*, January 24, 2001, 34.

33. Unlike the case in the Yemeni parliament, the vote in the Saudi consultative council approving the Treaty of Jeddah was far from unanimous, since there were "some" members who were "against the treaty as a whole," according to a statement by a former member of the Saudi council who wholeheartedly

voted in favor of the treaty. See the interview with Hashim A. Hashim, past member of the council and current Editor-in-Chief of the *Okaz* daily, *Sitta-Wa-Ishreen Septambar*, June 21, 2001, 16.

34. *Okaz*, June 20, 2000, 4; *Alriyadh*, June 20, 2000, 1.

35. *Okaz*, June 20, 2000, 1.

36. The constitutional procedures that the Treaty of Jeddah went through are outlined in the text of the royal decree of ratification issued on 26 June 2000, the same date as Yemen's ratification, and published in the official gazette, *Um Alqura*, Friday, 7 July 2000, 1-4 and in *Aljazeerah*, June 27, 2000.

37. Art. 22, Treaty of Taif.

38. Art. 54 of the VCT provides the principal category sanctioned by international law for the denunciation of the treaty by either party "in conformity with" its own provisions, i.e. a fixed duration clause. The Treaty of Taif and the Treaty of Jeddah, separately and together, are subject to the terms of the 1969 VCT as customary rather than conventional law. Neither country is a party to the convention yet. Moreover, the Treaty of Taif would be subject to the VCT only if it is presumed that the Taif Treaty had been legally integrated with the Treaty of Jeddah, since the terms of the 1969 VCT cannot be applied retroactively as conventional law to treaties concluded before the date of its entry into force in 1980, like the Treaty of Taif, which predates even the 1945 UN Charter.

39. Ibid.

40. Oppenheim, *International Law* I, op. cit., 938; David, *The Strategy of Treaty Termination*, op. cit., 14; the 1969 Vienna Convention of the Law of Treaties. Article 62(2)(a) at http://www.un.org/law/ilc/texts/treaties.htm; I.C.J. Reports, 1994, Case Summaries: Case Concerning the Territorial Dispute (Libyan Arab Jamahiriya/Chad, Judgment of 3 February 1994, paragraphs 25-26, 38-40, 52, 72-5, at http://icj-cij.org/icjwww/idecesions/summaries/idtsummary 940203.htm.

41. Article 65 of the VCT.

42. Art. 8, Treaty of Taif and Art 7, the 1995 MOU. The covenant of arbitration annexed to the 1934 Treaty of Taif is archaic and does not meet the modern standard of proper international arbitration. Its incorporation without

modification into the Treaty of Jeddah constituted one of the latter's many and obvious legal shortcomings.

43. Covenant of Arbitration, Art.1, Treaty of Taif.

44. The Yemeni government position in this regard was stated by the President as follows: Yemen would "insist on the submission to arbitration" of the entire Saudi-Yemeni border. He elaborated: "the settlement of the boundary issue constituted one indivisible unit subject to no separation, either in respect to the content of the Treaty of Taif or the remaining undefined boundary extending from Jabal Al-Thar to the intersection with Oman. In the event of arbitration, Yemen would insist on the submission to arbitration of the whole question of the boundary along the entire Saudi-Yemeni border." Interview with the Yemeni President, *Alquds-Alarabi*, January 28, 1999, reprinted in *Sitta-Wa-Ishreen Septambar*, January 28, 1999, 3.

45. The traditional Saudi attitude to arbitration as a method of settling its border dispute with Yemen was expressed in a press statement by the Saudi Minister of the Interior during a visit to Yemen in 1999, in which he said: "the issue of arbitration with regard to the Treaty of Taif…is not, in reality, subject to negotiation. We in the kingdom of Saudi Arabia are not inclined at all to arbitration. The depth of our ties and the element of our mutual understanding will not lead to arbitration. If the subject of arbitration is put before us and becomes inevitable, we in the kingdom will say we do not need it and we do not want it. However, if our Yemeni brethren saw things differently we will not oppose what they want or desire." *Alsharq Alawsat*, November 24, 1998, 4.

46. VCT, article 65.

47. VCT, article 67.

48. A case in point, discussed earlier, would be the reported formal Saudi communication in 1960 and the revoking of a note declaring its intention to terminate the Treaty of Taif on the basis of a fundamental change of circumstances.

49. VCT, article 66.

50. Chris L. Rozakis, *The Concept of Jus Cogens in the Law of Treaties* (Oxford: North Holland Publishing Co., 1976), 167.

51. ICJ 1995, Case concerning maritime delimitation and territorial questions between Qatar and Bahrain (Qatar v. Bahrain), jurisdiction and admissibility, February 15, 1995, 6 at http://www.icj-cij.org/icjwww/idocket/iqb/iqbframe.htm.

52. ICJ Reports, 1960-1966, South West Africa (Ethiopia v. South Africa; Liberia v. South Africa) (1960-1966), Judgment of December 21, 1962, Preliminary Objections, 1962, 319.

53. P.C.I.J., 1924 Mavrommatis Palestine Concessions, Judgment, Ser. A. no. 2, 564-69.

54. ICJ Reports, 1962, South West Africa, Preliminary Objections, op. cit., 327.

55. VCT, Article 65 (3); Rozakis, op. cit., 165.

56. 1995 MOU, Arts. 7 and 8. See similar provisions in Arts. 7, 9, 10 and 18 of the Treaty of Taif.

57. Art. 9, Treaty of Taif.

58. Ibid.

59. Art. 10, Treaty of Taif. Yemen and Saudi Arabia have traditionally accused each other of actively intervening in their internal affairs, for example by granting asylum to political dissident groups. See, for example, a statement by the Saudi Minister of the Interior to the Kuwaiti newspaper, *Al-Ra'ty Ala'am*, March 2, 2000, accusing Yemen of providing a safe-haven and passports to a Saudi opposition group, and Yemeni government allegations of Saudi Arabia being "responsible for perpetuating disturbances, kidnappings and killings" inside Yemen, *Yemen Times*, August 21-27, 2000 at http://www.yementimes.com/00/iss34/ln.htm. One immediate result of the conclusion of the Treaty of Jeddah was the declaration by some prominent Yemeni opposition groups supported by Saudi Arabia to "suspend" their political activity in conformity with the provisions of the treaty. However, it remains to be seen how long the observance would last.

60. In October 2000, the Saudi Minister of the Interior reiterated his government's commitment to the controversial provisions on asylum and extradition at a press conference after the conclusion of the third session of the joint commission for the implementation of the Treaty of Jeddah. *Aljazeerah*, October 30, 2000, 4; *Alriyadh*, October 30, 2000, 10. Subsequently, all political opposition groups and individuals previously financed by or

originating from Saudi Arabia ceased their activities to prevent being extradited to Yemen, as actually occurred in some cases. The subject of extradition of "criminals" was also at the top of the official agenda discussed at the framework of the 6th meeting of the joint Saudi-Yemeni committee for the implementation of the Treaty of Jeddah, held in Sana'a in October 2001. After the meeting, a Saudi daily reported that Yemen had agreed to extradite 21 "terrorists" who had previously crossed into Yemen from Saudi territory. *Alwatan*, October 26, 2001, 1; "Yemen extradites 21 suspected terrorists to Saudi Arabia: report," October 27, 2001, Riyadh, Agence France Press (AFP) at http://www.zawya.com/Story.cfm?id=685866817&Section=Countries &page =Yemen&channel (visited October 31, 2001). It is worth noting that in all the security agreements Saudi Arabia had so far signed with regional Arab and Muslim states, it insisted that "criminal" activity be defined to cover all forms of violent and non-violent activity by political opponents and opposition groups directed against the regime or any member of the ruling family. It was for this reason that Kuwait, for example, constrained by its own constitution, could not ratify the GCC collective security agreement initiated by Saudi Arabia. Thus, the relevant provisions had to be omitted before the Iranian parliament agreed to ratify a similar accord.

61. Yemeni Law No. 25 of 1990 on the Press and Publications signed on 27 December 1990, full English text of the law at http://www.al-bab.com/yemen/gov/off4.htm (visited 15 July 2000). Indeed, the anti-asylum provisions would seem to be in violation of the relevant articles in both the Saudi and Yemeni constitutions, which guarantee this principle.

62. Oppenheim, II, op. cit., 946.

63. Rozakis, op. cit., 167.

Chapter 8

64. According to a senior member of the opposition Nasserite Party, under the Treaty of Jeddah the territory of the state of Yemen was expanded to cover more than half of the area allegedly constituting the land of greater Yemen. Ali Saif Hassan "Border Agreement: Why is It a Legend?" *Yemen Times*, July 31-August 7, 2000 at http://www.yementimes.com/00/iss31/ln.htm.

65. *Alquds Alarabi*, June 24-25, 2000, 3. In addition, the two sides "agreed in principle" to expunge their respective "school textbooks" of any "information that may affect the special relations" between the two countries, meaning the

teaching of the sensitive subjects of geography and recent political history of their respective countries. *Alriyadh*, April 25, 2001, 15; *Sitta-Wa-Ishreen Septambar*, October 25, 2001, 11.

66. The land area gained by Yemen in the eastern sector is approximately three times the size of Lebanon, but it is still less than one-third of the almost one hundred thousand square kilometers the Saudis had ceded to Oman under the 1990 border treaty, which in turn was less than half of the area they ceded to the UAE under the 1974 agreement.

67. Some of the existing examples referred to by the Saudi military official are the 1949 "leasing" agreement with Egypt of the strategic Tiran and Sanafir islands in the Gulf of Aqaba, the 1965 border agreement with Jordan, the 1968 maritime agreement with Iran, the 1974 agreement with the UAE, the 1981 border agreement with Iraq, the 1990 agreement with Oman, as well as the agreements with Yemen and Kuwait in 2000.

68. This established pattern of Saudi conduct in dealing with issues involving a territorial dispute is acknowledged by senior Saudi officials. Commenting on Saudi territorial concessions to Yemen under the Treaty of Jeddah, the Saudi Minister of the Interior explained in a press statement that it was in line with traditional Saudi policy to "cede Saudi territory out of consideration of the circumstances of brethren states." *Alriyadh*, June 18, 2000, 8. In 1999, at the height of Saudi-Yemeni tension over the border, the Chief of Staff of the Saudi Armed Forces declared in a rare but authorized public statement that "it is known that Saudi Arabia follows a special method in settling border issues with other neighboring states. She gives and grants more territory than would be expected from her, which is evident from the living and existing examples, and Yemen will not be an exception to this rule." Press statement by the Saudi Chief of Staff, *Al-Sharq Al-Awsat*, December 5, 1999, 4.

69. After the signing of the Treaty of Jeddah and the maritime agreement with Kuwait a few weeks later, the Saudi government declared, erroneously, that it had now legally settled all its border issues with neighboring states. In fact, Saudi Arabia had yet to conclude maritime agreements with Eritrea, the Sudan and most importantly, with Egypt, especially with respect to the Gulf of Aqaba area, where a muted, but potentially serious dispute existed between them concerning the legal ownership of the strategically and economically important Tiran and Sanafir islands. According to Saudi Arabia, these islands were "leased" to Egypt under a 1949 agreement, but retained their Saudi sovereignty. Egypt, which maintained effective control

over them, except for periods of Israeli occupation in 1956 and 1967-1982, appears to regard the islands as sovereign Egyptian territory, which falls within its territorial waters in terms of a 1991 law on sea territory and officially forms a part of an administrative unit of the Governorate of South Sinai.

70. In addition to the simmering maritime dispute with Egypt, there is the potential dispute with Jordan over the present Jordanian-Israeli exploitation of the eastern coastal area of the Gulf of Aqaba, which, according to the 1965 border agreement, should be jointly exploited by Saudi Arabia and Jordan alone. There also is a potential dispute with the UAE, which protested against Saudi Arabia's unilateral deposition of the 1974 agreement with the UN in 1995, on the grounds that Saudi Arabia failed to implement some of its provisions. English text of the agreement in the *Middle East Economic Survey* (MEES), June 19, 1995. The Omani government also protested against the Saudi registration of the 1974 Saudi-UAE agreement with the UN, which encroached on Omani territory and was concluded without its knowledge, according to the government. Official maps published by Oman, the UAE and Qatar still do not show the Saudi land corridor to the Gulf gained under the 1974 agreement with the UAE. The agreement with Iraq in 1991 formally terminated all border agreements it had signed with Saudi Arabia since 1968, including the 1981 boundary agreement. *MEES* vol. 28, number 29, 52; Paul Stevens, "Pipelines or Pipe Dreams? Lessons From the History of Arab Transit Pipelines." *Middle East Journal* vol. 54 (Winter 2000), 231.

71. For a typical exposition of the Saudi government's basic view that the two complementary treaties are essentially territorial in nature, see *Okaz*, 24 June 2000, 21. This was expressed in an analysis published in the influential government daily, *Okaz*, soon after the signing of the Treaty of Jeddah: "the Treaty of Jeddah is nothing but an answer to what the preamble of the Treaty of Taif called for, i.e. the necessity to work and fix the borders between the two countries. The Treaty of Jeddah is the legal and practical outcome of what the Treaty of Taif called for." *Okaz*, 24 June 2000, 21. Shortly after the signing of the treaty, the Saudi Minister of the Interior stated in a press conference that the new treaty was not legally linked to the issue of (Yemeni) labor. *Alriyadh*, June 18, 2000, 8; *Al-Eqtisidiah*, June 18, 2000, 6; also *Okaz*, 13 June 2000, 4. As discussed in this study, the initial Saudi stand regarding

the non-territorial scope of the treaty seemed to change very soon after it appeared to contradict the Yemeni interpretation.

72. See, for example, a comment by the Chairman of the Committee of Constitutional and Legal Affairs in the Yemeni parliament. Quoted in *Sittawa-Ishreen-Sebtambar*, July 20, 2000, 7; also in *Aljazeerah*, July 25, 2000, 36.

73. Article 2 (1) (a) of the VCT defines a treaty as "an international agreement concluded between States in written form and governed by international law, whether embodied in a single instrument or in two or more related instruments and whatever its particular destination." The definition was adopted from the Draft Article of International Law Commission. See *International Yearbook*, International Law Commission, II, 645, cited in Brownlie, op. cit., 583.

74. The announcement of the signing of the Treaty of Jeddah took most observers following Saudi-Yemeni relations by surprise. Yemen claimed that the treaty was the result of continuous negotiations as far back as 1982. However, Yemeni officials involved in negotiating and formulating the treaty concurred with their Saudi counterparts that the decision to conclude a formal agreement was taken in late May 2000, during the visit of the Saudi Crown Prince Abdullah to Yemen to celebrate the 20th anniversary of the unification of Yemen. During this visit, the Saudi ruler essentially accepted the remaining Yemeni demands with regard to the location of the 1934 line, and demands regarding some islands in the Red Sea. Interview with the Yemeni President, *Alsharq Alawsat*, July 16, 2000, 4; interview with the Yemeni Deputy Premier and Foreign Minister, *Okaz*, July 8, 2000, 23 and July 9, 2000, 21. Senior Saudi officials publicly prided themselves that the whole process of negotiating and signing the treaty took less than 24 hours after the arrival of the Yemeni delegation at Jeddah, Saudi Arabia on June 11, 2000. Prince Sultan, the Saudi Deputy Prime Minister and Defense Minister was the senior official long responsible for the "Yemeni file," and was, next to the Crown Prince, the principal architect of the Treaty of Jeddah. In a speech to Arab ambassadors in Malaysia in October 2000, he said that once Crown Prince Abdullah had made the decision to negotiate and sign the treaty, the whole process of negotiation, formulation and signature of the treaty took less than twenty-four hours after the arrival of the Yemeni delegation on June 11. This took place during a visit to Yemen in late May 2000 to participate in the festivities celebrating the 20th anniversary of unification; "we sat for 24 hours and came out with an agreement covering sea, air and land." He attributed the decades-long delay to "the problem of

self-serving officials, but once we met face to face we settled the whole issue in one session lasting from sunset to noon the next day." *Alriyadh*, October 29, 2000, 8.

75. An example of the errors tainting the Treaty of Jeddah would be Annexure 2 and paragraph 6 of Annexure 4 of the official Arabic copy, published in both Saudi Arabia and Yemen. In these annexures the starting point of the land boundary line is located at the intersection of parallel 19 East with 52 North meridian, whereas the reverse should be the case (i.e. 19 North 52 East) and with the central Jabal Al-Thar at 17 East 44 North instead of 17 North 44 East. Under these erroneous coordinates, the starting point of the land boundary line would be located at a point far to the north of Yemen's maximum claim line at parallel 23 North, somewhere in northern Europe, surely not the presumed intention of the contracting parties.

76. Examples of the conclusion of an exclusively territorial boundary with bilateral agreements are the Yemen-Oman agreement of 1992 and the Saudi border agreements with Jordan, Iran, Qatar, the UAE, Kuwait and Iraq. The Iraq-Saudi boundary, signed on December 26, 1981, had two protocols on bilateral border relations as attachments, while Article 8 expressly cancelled by name all previous border-related agreements between the two countries. For the text of the agreement, see "Iraq-Saudi Arabia Boundary as agreed at Baghdad on 26 December 1981 in the International Frontier Treaty between the Kingdom of Saudi Arabia and the Republic of Iraq, with supporting documents as deposited with the United Nations by Saudi Arabia on 1 June 1991." (Office of the Geographer, US State Department) *Geographic Notes* vol. 2, no. 2 (Summer 1992), 11-12. The text of the treaty and the two protocols were reprinted in Richard Schofield (ed.) *Arabian Boundaries Disputes vol. 6: Saudi Arabia-Iraq 1922-1991* (London: Archive Editions, 1992), 793-810. However, both countries kept the content of the agreement and its protocols secret, until Saudi Arabia unilaterally deposited a copy at the UN Secretariat on June 1, 1991. The Saudi action was prompted by the Iraqi Revolutionary Command Council's decree no. 23 of January 21, 1991, which abrogated all bilateral treaties and agreements with Saudi Arabia concluded since 17 June 1968, the date of the ruling Baath party's accession to power in Baghdad. The decree cited Saudi Arabia's "violation of many of the agreements and treaties" concluded with Iraq after joining the UN-sanctioned war efforts to evict it from Kuwait in 1991. *MEES* vol. 28, no. 29, 52; Paul Stevens, "Pipelines or Pipe Dreams? Lessons From the History of Arab Transit Pipelines." *Middle East Journal* vol. 54 (Winter 2000), 231.

77. The Saudi delegation had an apparent aversion to the English term "protocol," a word that is also Arabized for use in Arabic legal terminology. Mr. Bajammal, the Yemeni Foreign Minister, claimed that during the negotiations of the 1995 MOU the Saudi delegation, composed of the same persons who later negotiated the Treaty of Jeddah, rejected Yemen's suggestion to use "protocol" as an alternative name for the MOU. A Saudi delegate, Mr. Abdulaziz al-Khuwaiter, a cabinet minister and a close confidant of King Fahad, explained that the term had a Jewish connotation, as in "the Protocols of the Elders of Zion," and should not be included. Interview with the Yemeni Foreign Minister, *Okaz*, 8 July 2000, 21. Nevertheless, Saudi Arabia is already a party to many bilateral and multilateral "protocols," including several signed by Mr. Al-Khuwaiter himself on behalf of his government.

78. Art. 21, Treaty of Taif.

79. This was a commentary on the Treaty of Jeddah by the Iranian journalist, Amir Taheri, after a visit to Yemen following the signing of the treaty. *Alsharq Alawsat*, July 20, 2000, 10.

80. *Alquds Alarabi*, June 24-25, 2000, 3. See also a subsequent commentary by a former Yemeni diplomat on Saudi-Yemeni relations in the aftermath of the treaty. *Alquds Alarabi*, February 2, 2002 at http://195.138.228.147/alquds/articles/data/2002/02/02-12/e90.htm.

BIBLIOGRAPHY

Documents

The Covenant of the League of Nations (including Amendments adopted in December 1924) (1924) at http://www.yale.edu/lawweb/avalon/leagcov.htm.

The General Treaty for the Renunciation of War as an Instrument of National Policy (Kellogg-Briand Pact), *League of Nations Treaty Series* no. 94 (1928).

Charter of the United Nations and the Statute of the International Court of Justice (New York: Office of Public Information, United Nations, 1987).

Charter of the United Nations, Statute and Rules of Court and Other Documents, ICJ Act and Documents No. 4 (1945) (The Hague: 1978).

United Nations. Report by the Secretary General to the Security Council on Development Concerning Yemen, 29 April 1963, United Nations Documents/ 5298.

United Nations. Second Report by the Secretary-General to the Security Council on developments relating to Yemen, 27 May 1963, Document S/5321, including Map No. 1477.1.

United Nations. Exchange of Letters Constituting Agreement relating to Privileges, Immunities and Facilities for the Observation Operation along the Saudi Arabian-Yemen Border (UNYOM) established pursuant to Security Council resolution (United Nations: New York, June, 1963).

Yearbook of the International Law Commission I (1963).

Yearbook of the International Law Commission II (1966).

Text of the Vienna Convention on the Law of Treaties, Document A/CONF. 39/11/Add.2, United Nations, *Treaty Series* vol. 1155, Chapter XXIII, Law of Treaties (1969) at http://www.un.org/law/ilc/texts/treaties. htm.

Text of the Vienna Convention on the Succession of States with regard to Treaties, Vienna, 23 August 1978, UN Document A/CONF.80/31 of August 22, 1978, as corrected by A/CONF.80/31/Corr.2 of October 27, 1978.

International Law Commission Report 1998, UN Document No. A/53/10 (1998).

Reports of Judicial and Arbitral Bodies

Permanent Court of International Justice (PCIJ). Mavrommatis Palestine Concessions Case, Judgment, 1924, Series A. no. 2 (1924).

Permanent Court of International Justice. Legal Status of Eastern Greenland (Norway v. Denmark), Judgment 1933, PCIJ, Ser. A/B, no. 53 (1933).

International Court of Justice. Anglo-Iranian Oil Co. Case (United Kingdom v. Iran) (1951-1952), Judgment of 22 July 1952, Preliminary Objection, at http://www.icjcij.org/icjwww/idecisions/isummaries/iukisummary520722.htm (1952).

ICJ Reports. Minquiers and Ecrehos (UK v. France), Judgment of 17 November 1953 at http://www.icjcij.org/icjwww/idecisions/isummaries/ifuksummary 531117.htm.

ICJ Reports. Case concerning the Temple of Preah Vihear (Thailand v. Cambodia), (MERITS), Judgment of 15 June 1962 at http://www.icjcij.org/icjwww/idecisions/isummaries/ictsummary620615.htm.

ICJ Reports. South West Africa (Ethiopia v. South Africa; Liberia v. South Africa) (1960-1966), Judgment of December 21, 1962, Preliminary Objections (1962).

ICJ Reports. Fisheries Jurisdiction (UK v. Iceland), (Jurisdiction of the Court), Judgment of 2 February 1973 at http://www.icjcij.org/icjwww/idecisions/isummaries/iaisummary730202.htm.

ICJ Reports. Western Sahara, Advisory Opinion of October 16, 1975 at http://www.icjcij.org/icjwww/idecisions/isummaries/isasummary751016.htm.

ICJ Reports. The Aegean Sea Continental Shelf Case (Greece versus Turkey) (Jurisdiction), Judgment of 19 December 1978 at http://www.icjcij.org/icjwww/idecisions/isummaries/igtsummary781219.htm.

ICJ Reports. Case Summaries: Case Concerning the Territorial Dispute (Libyan Arab Jamahiriya/Chad, Judgment of 3 February 1994 at http://www.icjcij.org/icjwww/idecisions/isummaries/idtsummary940203.htm. Full text of the Judgment at http://www.icj-cij.org/icjwww/icases/idt/idt_ijudgments/idt_ijudgment_19940203.pdf.

ICJ. "Judgment on Jurisdiction Case between Qatar and Bahrain Concerning Maritime and Territorial Questions, July 1, 1994." *ILM* vol. 34 (1995).

ICJ. Case Concerning Maritime Delimitation and Territorial Questions Between Qatar and Bahrain (Qatar v. Bahrain) Jurisdiction and Admissibility, July 1, 1994 at http://icj-cij.org/icjwww/idocket/iqb/iqbframe.htm.

ICJ. Case Concerning Maritime Delimitation and Territorial Questions between Qatar and Bahrain (Qatar v. Bahrain), Merits, March 16, 2001. Text of full judgment at http://www.icj-cij.org/icjwww/idocket/iqb/iqbframe.htm; text of the Summary of the Judgment of 16 March 2001 at http://www.icjcij.org/icjwww/ipresscom/ipress2001/ipresscom2001-09bis_qb_20010316.htm; see also "International Court of Justice (ICJ): Case concerning Maritime Delimitation and Territorial Questions Between Qatar and Bahrain (Qatar v. Bahrain)" (March 16, 2001) *ILM* vol. 40 (2001).

ICJ Reports. Case Concerning Maritime Delimitation and Territorial Questions between Qatar and Bahrain (Qatar v. Bahrain), Jurisdiction and Admissibility, Judgment of 15 February 1995, General List no. 87, Geneva at http://www.icjcij.org/icjwww/idocket/iqb/iqbframe.htm; see also "International Court of Justice: Judgment on Jurisdiction and Admissibility in the Case Concerning Maritime Delimitation and Territorial Questions Between Qatar and Bahrain (Qatar v. Bahrain)," Judgment of 15 February 1995, *ILM* vol. 34 (1995).

PCA. "Permanent Court of Arbitration (PCA): Eritrea-Yemen Arbitration (First Stage: Territorial Sovereignty and Scope of the Dispute)," October 9, 1998. Text of the decision, *ILM* vol. 40 (2001); also at http://www.pca-cpa.org./ER-YEAwardTOC.htm.

PCA. "Permanent Court of Arbitration (PCA): Eritrea-Yemen Arbitration (Second Stage: Maritime Delimitation)," December 17, 1999, *ILM* vol. 40 (2001); also at http://www.pca-cpa.org/ERYE2TOC.htm.

RIAA. Island of Palmas (US v. Netherlands), 2 Reports of International Arbitration Awards (1929).

Books

Abduh, As'ad S. *Muajam Asma Al-Amakin Fi Al-Mamlakah Al-'Arabiyah Al-Sau'diyah Al-Maktubah 'Ala Kharitat Jazirat Al-'Arab Magas 1:500000* (Dictionary of Names of Places in the Kingdom of Saudi Arabia on the Map of the Arabian Peninsula Scale 1:500000) (Jeddah: Madani Publishing, 1996).

Al-Ayni, Muhsin. *Khamsoun 'Aman Fi Al-Rimal Al-Mutaharikah: Gissati M'a Bina Al-Dawlah Al-Hadithah Fi Al-Yaman* (Fifty Years in Shifting Sands: My Story of the Building of the Modern State of the Yemen) (Beirut: Dal al-Nahaar, 2000).

Al-Enazy, A. H. *The Legal Status of the Saudi Yemeni Treaty of Taif.* Unpublished Ph.D. dissertation, Faculty of International Law, Moscow State Institute of International Relations (MGIMO), Moscow, the Russian Federation, 2001.

Al-Ghamdi, Ahmad Abdullah. *Gadhiyat Al-Hudud Al-Su'Udiyah Al-Yamaniyah* (The Saudi-Yemeni Border Question) (Riyadh: n.p., 1999).

Al-Juhani, Eed Mas'ud. *Al-Hudud Wa 'Al-'Alagaat Al-Su'udiyah-al-Yamaniyah* (Saudi-Yemeni Border relations) (Riyadh: Dar al-Ma'arif al-Su'udiyah, 1994).

Al-Na'im, Mshari A. *Al-Hudud Al-Siyasiyah Al-Su'udiyah: Albahth 'An Al-Istigrar* (Saudi Political Boundaries: In Search of Stability) (London: Al-Saqi Books, 1999).

Al-Shihari, Muhammad Ali. *Al-Matam'i Al-Su'udiyah Al-Tawassu'iyah Fi Al-Yaman* (Saudi Expansionist Designs on Yemen) (Beirut: Dar Ibn Khaldun, 1979).

Al-Thawr, Abdullah Ahmad. *Hathi-Hiya Al-Yaman* (This is Yemen) (Cairo: Almadani Press, 1969).

Boutros-Ghali, Boutros. "The Anglo-Yemini [sic] Dispute." *Revue Egyptienne de Droit International 11* (1955).

Brownlie, Ian. *Principles of Public International Law* (2nd edition) (Oxford: Clarendon Press, 1973).

Central Intelligence Agency. *Arabian Peninsula: Official Standard Names, Approved by the US Board on Geographic Names* (Washington, DC: July 1961).

David, Arie E. *The Strategy of Treaty Termination: Lawful Breaches and Retaliations* (New Haven, CT: Yale University Press, 1975).

El-Rayyes, Riad Najib. Riyah Al-Janoub: Al-Yaman Wa Dawrahu Fi Al-Jazeerah Al-'Arabiyah 1990-1997 (The Winds of the South: the Role of Yemen in Arabian Peninsula: 1990-1997) (Beirut: Riad el-Rayyes Books, 1998).

Gause III, F. Gregory. *Saudi-Yemeni Relations: Domestic Structures and Foreign Influence* (New York, NY: Colombia University Press, 1990).

Haraszti, Gyorgy. *Some Fundamental Problems of the Law of Treaties* (Budapest: Akademiai Kiado, 1973).

Hamza, Fuad. *Galb Jazeerat Al'Arab* (The Heart of Arabia) (Cairo, 1937).

Henkin, Louis, Richard C. Pugh et al. *International Law: Cases and Materials* (St. Paul, MN: West Publishing Co., 1980).

Hussain A. Al-Hubaishi. *Al-Yaman Wa Albahr Alahmar: Almawd'i Wa Almakan* (Yemen and the Red Sea: the Place and Location) (Beirut: n.p. 1992).

Ingrams, Doreen and Leila Ingrams (editors) *Records of Yemen: 1798-1960, vol.8: 1933-1945* (London: Archive Editions, 1993).

Ingrams, Doreen and Leila Ingrams (editors) *Records of Yemen: 1798-1960, vol. 14: 1957-1958* (London: Archive Editions, 1993).

Jacqué, Jean-Paul. "German Unification and the European Community," *European Journal of International Law* vol. 2 no.1 (1991), 1-17, also at http://www.ejil.org/journal/Vol2/No1/index.html.

Kawasaki, Yutaka. "Was the 1910 Annexation Treaty Between Korea and Japan Concluded Legally?" *E Law-Murdoch University Electronic Journal of Law* vol. 3, no. 2 (July 1996), 2-5 at http://www.murdoch.edu.au/elaw/issues/v3n2/kawasaki.html (visited March 17, 2002 and October 10, 1999).

Kern, Nathaniel. "Saudi-Yemeni Border Dispute." *Petroleum Politics* (June 1992), 28-35.

King Abdulaziz Public Library. *Mawsu'at Tarikh Al-Malik 'Abdulaziz Al-Dublumasi* (Encyclopaedia of the Diplomatic History of King Abdulaziz) (Riyadh: 1999).

Leatherdale, Clive. *Britain and Saudi Arabia 1925-1939: The Imperial Oasis* (London: Frank Cass Publishers, 1983).

Lotilla, Raphael P. "Treaties Termination Clausula Rebus sic Stantibus." *Asian Yearbook of International Law* (1991).

Malanczuk, Peter. *Akehurst's Modern Introduction to International Law* (7th edition) (London: Routledge, 1999).

Marhoun, Abduljalil. "Niza'at Al-Hudud Fi Shibh Al-Jazeerah Al-'Arabiyah" (Border Dispute in the Arabian Peninsula), *Shu'un Awsatiyah* no. 47, 47-65.

Meek, James. "UK to open consulate in Mecca for pilgrims," *The Guardian*, November 5, 1999 at www.guardianunlimited.co.uk/Archive/Article/0,4273, 3926088,00.html.

Ministry of Foreign Affairs (Saudi Arabia). *Majmu'at Al-Mu'ahadat, aljuza alawwal: Min 1341 Ila 1370 Hijriyah, Almuwafiq:1922 -1951* (Collection of Treaties, vol. 1: 1922-1951) (Mecca: Government Printing Office, 1375h/ 1955).

Ministry of Higher Education (Saudi Arabia). *Atlas Al-Mamlakah Al-'Arabiyah Al-Sau'diyah* (Atlas of the Kingdom of Saudi Arabia) (Riyadh: Ministry of Higher Education, 1999).

National Information Center. *Al-Kharitah Alsiyasiyah Li'l Al-Jumhuriyah Al-Yamaniyah* ("Political Map of the Yemeni Republic") Office of the President, Sana'a at the NIC's Arabic language website at http://www.nic.gov.ye/SITE/20%CONTAINTS/geography/maps/mm.JPG (last visit March 2, 2002).

National Information Center. *Al-Kharitah Al-Tabi'iyah l'il Al-Jumhuriyah Al-Yamaniyah* (Natural Map of the Yemeni Republic) at the NIC's Arabic language website at http://www.nic.gov.ye/SITE%CONTAINTS/aboutyemen/history/MAPS/M.htm (last visited March 2, 2002).

National Information Center. *Khara'it Tafsiliyah* (Detailed maps) (Map no. E38c1, at the NIC's Arabic language website at http://www.nic.gov.ye/SITE%20CONTAINTS/geography/maps/SADAHMAP1.htm (last visited March 2, 2002).

Nozari, Fariborz. *Unequal Treaties in International Law* (Stockholm: S-Byran Sundt and Co., 1971).

Oppenheim, L.F. (H. Lauterpacht, ed.) (7th edition) *International Law* vol. I (London: Longman, 1953).

Oppenheim, L.F. (H. Lauterpacht, ed.) (8th edition) *International Law* vol. II (London: Longman, 1958).

Philby, H. St. J.B. *Arabian Highlands* (New York, NY: Cornell University Press, 1952).

Philby, H. St. J.B. *Sheba's Daughters: Being a Record of Travel in Southern Arabia* (London: Methuen and Co. Ltd., 1939).

Prescott, J.R.V. *Political Frontiers and Boundaries* (London: Allen and Unwin, 1987).

Reisman, Michael W. "The Government of the State of Eritrea and the Government of the Republic of Yemen: Award on Sovereignty over Disputed Islands in the Red Sea." *American Journal of International Law* vol. 93 (1999), 668-682.

Ress, George. "The Delimitation and Demarcation of Frontiers in International Treaties and Maps," *Thesaurus Acroasium* XIV 395-437 (1985).

Rozakis, Christos L. *The Concept of Jus Cogens in the Law of Treaties* (Oxford: North-Holland Publishing Co., 1976).

Schofield, Richard. "Negotiating the Saudi-Yemeni international boundary." Lecture delivered before a meeting of the British Yemeni Society (March 31, 1999) at http://www.al-bab.com/bys/articles/schofield00.htm.

Schofield, Richard (editor) *Arabian Boundary Disputes: Saudi Arabia-Yemen, 1913-1992 vol. 20* (London: Archive Editions 1993).

Schofield, Richard (editor) *Arabian Boundaries Disputes: Saudi Arabia-Iraq 1922-1991 vol. 6* (London: Archive Editions, 1992).

Schofield, Richard and Gerald Blake (editors) *Arabian Boundaries: Primary Documents 1853-1957: Saudi Arabia-Imamate of Yemen, 1931-1957 vol. 4* (London: Archive Editions, 1988).

Schofield, Richard and Gerald Blake (editors) *Arabian Boundaries: Primary Documents 1853-1960: vol. 29 1958-1960* (London: Archive Editions, 1990).

Shamiyah, Jibran (editor) *Lubnan, Al-Yaman, Ittihad Al-Janoub Al-'Arabi: Sijjil Al-Ara Hawl Al-Wagai'I Al-Siyasiyah fi Al-Bilad Al-Arabiyah* (Lebanon,

Yemen, South Arabian Federation: Records of Opinions on Political Events in the Arab Lands) (Beirut: Dar Albhath wa Alnashr, 1966).

Sharma, Surya Prakash. *Delimitation of Land & Sea Boundaries Between Neighboring Countries* (Lancer's Book, 1989).

Starke, J.G. *Introduction to International Law* (London: Butterworths, 1989).

Stevens, Paul. "Pipelines or Pipe Dreams? Lessons From the History of Arab Transit Pipelines." *Middle East Journal* vol. 54 no. 2 (Winter 2000), 224-42.

Talalyev, A.N. "Unequal Treaties as a mode of prolonging the colonial dependence of the new States of Asia and Africa." *Sovietskii Ezhegodnik Mezhdynardnogo Prava* (1961).

Talalyev, A.N. "Unequal Treaties as a mode of prolonging the colonial dependence of the new States of Asia and Africa." *Sovietskii Ezhegodnik Mezhdynarodnogo Prava* (1961), 169-170.

Toynbee, Arnold J. (ed.) *Survey of International Affairs 1934* (Oxford: Oxford University Press, 1935).

Türk, Danilo. "Annex 1: Declaration on the 'Guidelines on the Recognition of New States in Eastern Europe and in the Soviet Union (16 December 1991)," *European Journal of International Law* (EJIL) vol. 4, no. 1 (1993), 72 at http://www.ejil.org/journal/Vol4/No1/index.html (visited May 12, 2001).

Tuson, Penelope and Emma Quick (editors) *Arabian Treaties 1600-1960, vol. 4* (London: Archive Editions, 1992).

Tuson, Penelope and Anita Burdett (editors) *Records of Saudi Arabia: Primary Documents: 1902-1960, vol. 5: 1932-1935* (London: Archive Editions, 1992).

Tuson, Penelope and Anita Burdett (editors) *Records of Saudi Arabia: Primary documents: 1902-1960, Vol. 6: 1935-37* (London: Archive Editions, 1992).

Tuson, Penelope and Anita Burdett (editors) *Records of Saudi Arabia: Primary documents: 1902-1960, Vol. 7: 1938-1946* (London: Archive Editions, 1992).

US Department of State. "Transcript: Press Conference with Ambassador Edward S. Walker Assistant Secretary of State for Near Eastern Affairs," US Embassy, Sana'a, Yemen, February 14, 2000, Office of International Information Programs, US Department of State at http://www. usinfo.state.gov.

US Department of State. *The Island of Palmas Arbitration Before the Permanent Court of Arbitration of the Hague Under the Special Agreement Concluded Between the United States and the Netherlands, January 23, 1925* (Washington, DC: Department of State, 1928).

US Department of State. *Foreign Relations of the United States, 1964-1968, Volume XXI: Near East Region: Arabian Peninsula* (Washington, DC: US Printing Office).

US Department of State. "Iraq-Saudi Arabia Boundary as agreed at Baghdad on 26 December 1981 in the International Frontier Treaty between the Kingdom of Saudi Arabia and the Republic of Iraq, with supporting documents as deposited with the United Nations by Saudi Arabia on 1 June 1991," Office of the Geographer, *Geographic Notes* vol. 2 no. 2 (Summer 1992), 11-12.

US Defense Mapping Agency. *Saudi Arabia: Official Standard Names, Approved by the US Board on Geographic Names* (Washington, DC: March 1978).

Vagts, Detlev F. "Treaty Interpretation and the New American Ways of Law Reading" *European Journal of International Law* vol. 4 no. 4 (1993), 472-506.

Von Glahn, Gerhard. *Law Among Nations: An Introduction to Public International Law* (5th edition) (New York, NY: Macmillan Publishing Co., Inc. 1986).

Wahba, Hafiz. *Jazeerat Al-Arab Fi Al-Qarn Al-Ishreen* (Arabia in the Twentieth Century) (Cairo: 1936).

Wallace, C. D. (R. Bernhardt, ed.) "Kellogg-Briand Pact." *Encyclopedia of Public International Law* vol. 3 (1982), 235-9.

Waysi, Hussain Ali. *Al-Yaman Al-Kubra: Kitab Jughraphi, Julugi, Tarikhi* (Greater Yemen: Geographical, Geological and Historical Study) vol. I (2nd edition) (Sana'a, Yemen: Al-Irshad Books, 1991).

Whitaker, Brian. "Crisis over the Border," *Middle East International*, January 19, 1995 at www.al-bab.com/yemen/artic/mei10.htm.

Whitaker, Brian. "Crisis over the Border." *Middle East International*, January 29, 1995 at http:// www.al-bab.com/yemen/artic/mei10.htm.

Whitaker, Brian. "Border Deal Nearer." *Middle East International*, September 26, 1997 at http://www.al-bab.com/yemen/artic/mei27.htm (last visited December 2000).

Whitaker, Brian. "Tensions with the Saudis." *Middle East International*, December 19, 1997 at www.al-bab.com/yemen/artic/mei29.htm.

Whitaker, Brian. "Border Row with the Saudis." *Middle East International*, July 31, 1998 at www.al-bab.com/yemen/artic/mei38.htm.

Wilkinson, John Craven. *Arabia's Frontiers: the Story of Britain's Boundary Drawing in the Desert* (New York, NY: I. B. Tauris, 1991).

Newspapers, Magazines and News Agencies

Ain Al-Yaqeen (English weekly, Saudi Arabia)

Agence France-Presse (AFP)

Alahram (Egyptian daily)

Alayyam (Yemeni opposition weekly)

Aleqtisadiah (Saudi daily)

Algumhuryah (Yemeni daily)

Alhawdith (Lebanese weekly magazine)

Aljazeerah (Saudi daily)

Aljazeera TV (Qatar)

Aljumhuriyah (Iraqi daily)

Almajallah (Saudi weekly magazine, London)

Alquds Alarabi (Arabic daily, London)

Alra'y (Yemeni opposition party weekly)

Alriyadh (Saudi newspaper)

Alsahwah (Yemeni opposition party weekly)

Alsharq Alawsat (Saudi daily, London)

Alsiyasah (Kuwaiti daily)

Althawrah (Yemeni daily)

Alwahdawi (Yemeni opposition party weekly)

Alwasat (Saudi Arabic weekly, London)

Alwatan (Saudi daily)

Alyawm Alsabi' (Arabic weekly, Paris)

Assafir (Lebanese daily)

Asshura (Yemeni political party weekly)

BBC Arabic News

The Daily Telegraph (London)

The Guardian (London)

Hawl Al'Alam (defunct Jordanian weekly)

LBC TV (Lebanon)

Middle East Economic Survey (MEES)

Middle East International

Middle East News Agency (MENA, Egypt)

New York Times

Okaz (Saudi daily)

Riyadh Daily

Saudi Press Agency (SPA)

Shihan (Jordanian weekly newspaper)

Sitta-Wa-Ishreen Septambar (Yemeni armed forces weekly)

Um Alqura (Saudi Government official gazette)

Yemeni Press Agency (SABA)

Yemeni Republic Radio (Sana'a)

Yemen Times (weekly newspaper)

About the Author

Askar H. Al-Enazy is a lecturer in International Relations in Riyadh, Saudi Arabia. He obtained a Master's degree in International Relations from Carleton University, Ottawa, Canada in 1983 and a Master's degree in Islamic Law and Middle Eastern Studies from McGill University, Montreal, Canada in 1986. In 2000 he obtained a doctorate in International Law from the Moscow State Institute of International Relations (MGIMO) in the Russian Federation.

INDEX

A

'Aayidh 12
Abdulalaziz Al-Saud, King of Saudi Arabia 11–2
Abdullah, Crown Prince 41
'Abr agreement (1948) 37, 81, 145
acquiescence 66, 96–100
Aden, British Protectorate of
    and 'Abr agreement 81
        Saudi border dispute with 7, 23, 34, 36–7
        Yemeni border dispute with 34, 36–7, 100
        Yemeni claim to 8
Ahmad, Imam 19, 20, 54, 59, 71
Al-'Aayidh 74
Al-'Abadilah 60
Al Abide 10
Al-Akhasheem 7
Al-Iryani, Adbulkarim 63–4, 70
Al Kharkhair 48, 80
Al-Muwassam 49
Al-Rhub' al-Khali *see* Empty Quarter
Al-Wadi'ah 23, 48, 80
Al-Wazir, Abdullah Ahmad 53–4, 59, 67
Al-Zawalima tribe 124
"ancient title" doctrine 76, 77–8
Anglo-Ottoman Convention (1914) 28, 78
animus possidendi 98
Arab Brotherhood, Treaty of 99
Arabian Peninsula 78
Arab League 38, 43–4
Arab Republic of Yemen *see* North Yemen
'Aru Agreement (1931) 149
    and Saudi border claim 10–1
        Yemeni denial of 10
'Aru mountain 10
Asir *see* Idrisi emirate
Asir Surat 10
Asir Tihamat 10

B

Bab Al-Mandab, Strait of 50
Bahrain 81, 98
Bani-Malik 60, 75
border posts 115
boundaries
    1934 boundary
        controversy over 37–9
    see also under Taif, Treaty of (1934)/Articles
    1984 claim boundary 29, 48
    disputed segments 7–8
    permanence of 63, 72, 102–3, 105–6, 131, 136, 145
    see also Como Line; Hamza Line; Riyadh Line; Violet Line
boundary markers 13–14, 29, 34
Britain
    and Hawar islands 98
    and Idrisi emirate 9, 73, 75
British Line (1935) *see* Riyadh Line

C

Clinton, Bill 41
Como agreement (1997) 35–7, 39
    revised border 48–9, 145–6
    and Treaty of Jeddah 35
Como Line 36
Convention Against Torture, and other Cruel, Inhuman or Degrading Treatment or Punishment 138
conventional law 84
Convention Relating to the Status of Refugees 138
corpus possessionis 98
Council of the League of Nations 57–8
Covenant of the League of Nations (1919) 57
    limited membership 58
    and Saudi-Yemeni war 55, 58, 65, 75
    and Treaty of Taif 87
customary law 84, 98

D
Da'an Accord (1911) 79
Dahm-Alhamra tribe 124
demilitarized zones 46–7
Dhu-Hirab 49
Dhu-Yahya tribe 124
dual citizenship 125
Duwaimah island 38, 49
    Saudi-Yemeni hostilities at 39

E
effectivités principle 80–1, 98
effet utile interpretation 92
Egypt 21
Empty Quarter (Al-Rhub' al-Khali) 7, 76
Eritrea 50, 78
Eritrea–Yemen Arbitration Award (1998) 77–82
estoppel, principle of 66, 96–8
European Community 59
executed treaties 104

F
Fahad, King of Saudi Arabia 129–30
Farasan islands 28, 79
Fayfa 10, 60, 75
Faysal, Crown Prince 20
First World War 78

G
General Agreement between the Kingdom of Saudi Arabia and the Kingdom of Yemen Concerning the Settlement of Matters relating to the Subjects of the two Kingdoms (1936) 83, 91–2
    full text [*Appendix*] 176–8, 187–9
    and Yemeni privileges 66–7, 69–70, 113–5
General Agreement on the Settlement of Frontier Questions and Movement of Subjects between the Two Countries (1937) 18, 83, 96
General Treaty on the Renunciation of War (1928) *see* Kellogg–Briand Pact
Geneva talks (1992)
    preparatory meeting 27
    Saudi position 28–30
    Yemeni position 27–8

grazing rights 45, 47
Great Britain *see* Britain
Greater Yemen (*al-yaman al-kubra*)
    Saudi rejection of 28
    Yemeni notion of 27–8, 36, 76–7
Gulf Cooperation Council (GCC) 113, 117

H
Hadhramout 37, 81
Hamza, Fuad 95
Hamza Line
    1935 line 23, 37, 145
    1955 modification 48
    and Saudi 1984 claim 29, 48
    tribal allegiance basis of 81, 145
Hanish islands 80, 143
Hasan al-Idrisi, Imam 8
Hawar islands 81, 98
Hodiedah 11–2, 86–7
human rights 138
Hormuz, Strait of 50

I
Ibn Saud, King of Saudi Arabia
    pre-1934 war negotiations 60–61
    relations with Britain 73
    signs Mecca Treaty 8
    and Treaty of Taif 19, 53, 74, 85–6
Idrisi, Imam 73
Idrisi emirate
    anti-Saudi rebellion 74
    incorporation into Saudi Arabia 8–9, 28, 48, 60, 73–5
    independent status of 9, 75
    relations with Britain 73, 75
    and Treaty of Taif 12–3, 74
    Yemeni claim to 8–9, 21, 73–4, 76, 79
    Yemeni-Saudi agreement 95
Independence Line *see* Riyadh Line
in precario possessionis 98
International Convention on Civil and Political Rights 138
International Convention on Economic, Social and Cultural Rights 138
International Convention on the Protection of the Rights of All Migrant Workers and Members of their Families 138
International Court of Justice (ICJ)
    international agreements defined 33

and League of Nations 57
legal disputes defined 136
legal precedents
   Aegean Sea Continental Shelf Case 93, 103
   Cambodia vs Thailand Case (1962) 136
   Chad vs Libya Case (1994) 32, 63–4, 96, 102–3, 136, 143
   Eastern Greenland Case 97
   Eritrea–Yemen Award (1998) 136, 143–4
   Qatar vs Bahrain Case (1995) 135
   Qatar vs Bahrain Case on Jurisdiction and Admissibility (1994) 33, 93
   Qatar vs Bahrain Case (Merits) (2001) 81, 98
   South West Africa Cases (1962) 135–6
   Temple of Preah Vihar Case (1962) 95, 97, 103
International Law Commission
   definition of "treaty" 92
   effect of *jus cogens* 65
   treaties fixing boundaries 105–6
intertemporal law 56–7, 58, 65
Iraq 25
Iraq–Kuwait boundary (1991) 59
Italy 9, 59, 75

J

Jabal al-Thar 14, 29, 38, 45
Jabal 'Aru 10
Japan 59
Jeddah, Treaty of (2000) 11, 15
   full text [*Appendix*] 182–6
   salient features of 44, 141
   Articles
      1: reaffirmation of Taif/MOU 45
      2: boundary definition 45, 127
         nationality of border villages 46, 122–3, 126
         plebiscite clause 123, 126
      3: demarcation of area/boundary 46–7
      4: demilitarized zones 46–7
   contradictions within 148
   boundary
      and 1934 boundary 44–5, 121–4, 128
      border-dwellers' rejection of 123–5
      and Como Agreement 35
      conflict with Taif Treaty 122
      demarcation of 44–7, 121
      errors in coordinates 148
      exemption from arbitration 136
      likely boundary changes 121, 127–8
      maritime boundary 46–7, 49
      and post-1934 demographic changes 124–6
      Treaty as boundary solution 142
   conflict with Taif Treaty/MOU 148
   duration clause 141
   implementation of 47, 118
   incorporated agreements
      1995 MOU 44, 109–10, 137, 141, 147
      Treaty of Taif 44, 52, 137
         duration clause question 130–31
         inherited defects 141–2, 147–9
         Yemeni approval 108–111
   inherent weakness of 141–2, 147–8
   international law 137–8, 142, 147–8
   interpretation by arbitration 132–6
   nationality problems 126
   ratification of 43, 127, 130
   and Saudi municipal law 129–30
   suggested form of treaty 148–9
   termination possibilities 138–9
   territorial compromise 47–50
   and Yemeni municipal law 127–8, 137–8
   and Yemeni "privileges" 138, 142
      Saudi confirmation 116–7, 118–9
      Yemeni expectations 108, 110, 112–13
   see also under Saudi Arabia; Yemen, Republic of
Jibal Fayfa *see* Fayfa
Jizan 13, 21, 28, 48, 76
Joint Communiqué (1973)
   as international agreement 32–3

and Taif Treaty boundary 63, 87, 90
  as Taif Treaty extension 22, 93–4, 101
  and Taif Treaty validity 22, 87, 90
jus cogens principle 64–6, 138–9

K
Karab tribe 37, 145
Kellogg–Briand Pact
  limitations of 58
  restrictions on war 57
  Saudi membership of 57–8, 65, 75–6
  and Saudi-Yemeni war 58, 65
  and Treaty of Taif 55
Khalid ibn Abdulaziz, Prince 67–8
Kuwait, Iraqi invasion of 25

L
Lake Como Agreement *see* Como Agreement
Land of Yemen (*bilad al-yemen*)
  extent of 76
  and Idrisi emirate 8
  and Treaty of Jeddah 142
  Tribunal's rejection of 78–9
  Yemeni notion of 27, 28, 76–7
Lausanne, Treaty of (1923) 78
law of treaty *see under* Vienna Convention on the Law of Treaty
  legal precedents *see under* International Court of Justice
League of Arab States *see* Arab League
League of Nations 87
Libya 102

M
Manahil tribe 37, 145
Mecca 30
Mecca Treaty (Mecca Agreement) (1926) 8–10, 60
  as "colonial" treaty 73–4
  and Treaty of Taif 73–6
  Yemeni denial of 8–9, 10
Memorandum of Understanding (MOU) (1973) 62, 64
Memorandum of Understanding (MOU) (1995) 30–35, 91–2, 96
  arbitration clauses 132
  full text [*Appendix*] 179–81

and Sana'a Protocol 39
  Saudi commitment to 39
  as a treaty in itself 92
  and Treaty of Jeddah 44, 109–10, 137, 141, 147
  as Treaty of Taif confirmation 30, 62–4, 87, 90
  and Treaty of Taif extension 64, 93–4, 96, 101
  Yemeni view of 33, 39, 62
migration 125
military confrontations
  Duwaima (1998) 39
  see also Saudi-Yemeni war
military installations 47
Mixed Delimitation Commission (1904) 97
Muhammad bin Shaji, Shaykh 125

N
Naef, Prince 110–1, 116–7
Najran 49, 113
  Saudi sovereignty 13, 48
  and Treaty of Taif 12, 28
  Yemeni claim to 10, 21, 76
  Yemeni occupation of 10–1, 60
Najran valley 67
nationality 15, 46, 122–3, 126
NATO 59
nomadic territories 80
North Yemen
  Saudi recognition of 22
  unity with South Yemen 8, 24, 72

O
Oman
  1990 Saudi border treaty 30, 37, 50, 145
  1992 Yemeni border treaty 30, 36, 50, 76–7, 144
Omani-Saudi-Yemeni border 30
Ottoman empire 78–9

P
pacta sunt servanda 84
passports 114
peace and boundary treaties 104–5
People's Democratic Republic of Yemen *see* South Yemen

Permanent Court of International Justice
   see International Court of Justice
Potsdam Declaration 59
prisoners, repatriation of 69

R
Radm al-Amir 14, 29
Ra's al-Mu'waj 14, 38, 45
rebus sic stantibus 70–73, 84, 106
Red Sea islands 77–8
res judicata 98
res nullius territories 80
retroactive laws 55–6, 58–9, 65, 87
"reversion" doctrine 78–9
Riyadh Line
   1935 line 23, 28
   1955 modification 23, 28, 36–7, 145–6
   Yemeni view 35–6

S
Saleh, Ali Abdullah 33, 35, 38, 41
   on arbitration 82
   boundary statement 77
   and special privileges 112–3
   and Treaty of Jeddah 43
Sana'a 118
Sana'a Protocol (1998) 39–40
   as separate "treaty" 92–3
   and Taif interpretation 91, 96
   as Taif reaffirmation 87, 90
Saudi Arabia
   and 1934 boundary 107, 144
   1984 boundary claim 29, 48
   and 'Abr Agreement 37, 81, 145
   arbitration stance 81–2, 133
   and Como agreement 35–7, 145–6
   constitution 129
   as military aggressor 54–5, 58
   relations with Britain 73
   Shura (Consultative) Council 129–30
   Treaty of Jeddah
      arbitration stance 144
      ratification of 130
      and Taif Treaty 110–1
      territorial concessions 48–50, 146
      view of 51
   Treaty of Taif
      1934 boundary support 51
      abrogation threat 20, 71
      accused of coercion 53–5
      authority to conclude 85
      capacity to conclude 84
      commitment to 29, 39, 48, 51
      evacuation of troops 87–8
      socio-political power argument 80
      territorial view of 147
      see also Taif, Treaty of (1934),
   Saudi arguments
      Yemeni "privileges"
         positive Saudi moves 116–19
         repeal of 20, 25–6, 66–70, 111–2
         traditional granting of 115
      Yemeni tribes granted citizenship 125
Saudi Arabia–British Aden border 23
Saudi Arabia–South Yemen Border
   (1968–90) 23–4
Saudi-Idrisi Treaty of Mecca 144
Saudi-Iraqi-Yemeni treaty 99
Saudi-Omani agreement (1990) 30, 37, 50, 145
Saudi-Ottoman agreement (1914) 28
Saudi-Yemeni Coordination Council
   (SYCC) 117–8
Saudi-Yemeni war
   defeat of Yemen 11
   Saudis as aggressors 54–5, 58
   Saudi war declaration 65
   and Treaty of Taif 52, 54–61
   Yemenis as aggressors 60, 75–6
Second World War 59
Sei'ar tribe 37, 145
Sharorah 48, 80
socio-political power 80
South Africa, Republic of 136
South Yemen
   differences with Saudi Arabia 23
   unity with North Yemen 8, 24, 72
   see also Aden, British Protectorate of
Suez Canal 50
Sultan, Prince 35
Surat Asir 8

T
Taif, Treaty of (1934)
   1926 Mecca Agreement 9, 73–6
   1936 general agreement 18, 83, 96, 99
   1937 joint commission report
      boundary approval 104–5
      boundary demarcation 37, 87, 122

unanimous approval 99
1953 renewal agreement 19, 87
  approval of 89, 99
  as interpretation means 91, 96
  as separate "treaty" 92
1973 Joint Communiqué *see* Joint Communiqué
1998 Sana'a Protocol *see* Sana'a Protocol
MOU *see* Memorandum of Understanding (1973)/(1995)
full text of [*Appendix*] 156–68
and 'Aru Agreement (1931) 149
boundary
  description of 7
  and Mecca Agreement 9
  permanence debate 131
  and Treaty of Jeddah 121
  see also under Taif, Treaty of (1934), Articles
Covenant of Arbitration 16–7, 132–3
  attached side letters [*Appendix*] 171–5
  full text [*Appendix*] 169–71
and customary law 84
entry into force 86–7
as general agreement 130–1
as peace and boundary treaty 104–6, 130
ratification of 12, 85–6
recurrent international obligations 104–5
registration of 87
as result of war 54–5, 64–5
scope of 11–5, 84, 104–6
signing of 11–2
validity of 83–7
as VCT predecessor 83–4
Yemeni "privileges" 112–3, 119
  importance to Yemen 33, 51–2, 110, 147
  and Treaty of Jeddah 107–8, 110
see also under Saudi Arabia; Yemen, Republic of
Taif, Treaty of (1934), Articles
1: termination of war 12, 105, 131
2: cessation of territorial claims 12–3, 48, 74, 131

4: Saudi-Yemeni boundary 12, 48, 87, 131
  cross-border privileges 18, 66–77, 69–70, 113
  description of 13–5
  and Idrisi emirate 9
  nationality of border villages 122–3
  Saudi-Yemeni disputes 33–5, 37–9
  side letters
    1: evacuation of troops/prisoners 69
    5: cross-border movements 17, 66–7, 69–70, 88, 113–4
    limited status of 69, 88
5: demilitarized zones 46
7: cross-border movement 7, 9–10, 18, 114
8: bilateral arbitration 16–7, 89–91, 99, 102, 132
12: nationality of border areas 15, 123, 126
21: nullification of preceding instrument 149
22: modification and duration 15, 88–9
  boundary question 106, 131
  effect of linked agreements 93, 101–2
  entry into force 86–7
  intention of parties 95–6
  ratification 85–6
  termination grounds 61–4
  "termination" not in text 89, 101
  and Treaty of Jeddah 130–2
Taif, Treaty of (1934), Saudi arguments
  acquiescence and estoppel 96–100
  authority of side letters 88
  authority to conclude 84–5
  entry into force 86–7
  intention of parties 94–6
  mutual consent 85–6
  as peace and boundary treaty 104–6
  permanence of boundaries 100–3
  registration of Treaty 87
  supporting international agreements 89–94
Taif, Treaty of (1934), Yemeni case against
  1926 Mecca Agreement 73–6

"ancient title and "reversion" 76–7
Eritrea–Yemen Arbitration Award
    77–82
fixed duration provision 61–4, 101
imposed treaty 54–61
invalidity of side letters 88
jus cogens principle 64–6
rebus sic stantibus principle 70–3
Saudi revocation of Yemeni
    exemptions 66–70
signed under duress 52–4
Taiz 52
Tihamat 8, 88
treaties, definitions of 83, 92
tribal privileges 18, 67
troops, withdrawal of 47, 69
Turkey 75, 78

U

Um Alqura 12
United Arab Emirates 50
United Arab Republic 19 20, 71
United Nations 38, 43–4
    Saudi membership 146
United Nations Charter (1945) 58–9
    registration of treaties 87
    and Saudi-Yemeni war 55–6
    and Treaty of Jeddah 134–5
United Nations Yemen Observation
    Mission 100
United States
    conciliation assistance 26
    mediation effort 40–1
UN Security Council 59
U Thant 100
uti possidetis juris 97–8

V

Vienna Convention on the Law of
    Treaties (VCT)
    Articles
        2: definition of "treaty" 83, 92
        4: treaties predating VCT 56, 66,
            83–4
        6: capacity to conclude 84
        7: ratification 86
        24: entry into force 86
        31: "good faith" interpretation 91
            use of subsequent agreements
            91
        45: acquiescence of states 96–7
        51: use of coercion 53–4
        52: use of force 55–7
        53: peremptory norm violation
            (*jus cogens*) 64, 138
        54: termination of treaties 61,
            62–3, 101
        60: material breaches 68–9
        62: fundamental change (*rebus
            sic stantibus*) 70, 72
            "treaties fixing boundaries"
            exception 72, 106
        64: new peremptory norms 64–6,
            138–9
        65: arbitration clause priority
            132, 134
        67: advice of termination 61
        71: continuation of established
            situation 65
Vienna Convention on the Succession of
    States in Respect of Treaties (VCS) 72
Violet Line (1914) 23, 28, 36–7, 77

W

Wa'ilah tribe 11, 14, 18, 67, 113, 124–5
Walker, Edward S. 40–1
watering rights 45, 47
Western Sahara 80–1

Y

Yahya, Imam
    "forced" into war 54
    Idrisi territory claim 8–9, 73
    and Mecca Treaty 8–9
    pre-1934 war negotiations 60–1
    and Saudi sovereignty 95
    Treaty of Taif 53–4, 59, 85–6
Yam tribe 11, 12–3, 14, 124
Yemen Arab Republic *see* North Yemen
Yemeni-Omani agreement (1992) 30, 36,
    50, 76–7, 144
Yemen, Republic of
    1962 revolution 21, 71
    1990 proclamation of 8, 25, 71–2
    arbitration stance 82, 133
    civil war 21–2, 26
    and Como agreement 35–8
    Council of Deputies 127–8
    disputes Mecca Treaty 8–10
    Idrisi escape to 74

joins UAE 20, 71
as military aggressor 60
recognition of Saudi sovereignty 13, 48, 87, 95
Saudi investment in 118, 150
Treaty of Jeddah
   and 1934 line 127–8
   and constitution of 1994 127–8
   and legal precedents 32–3, 143–4
   non-territorial view 147, 150
   parliamentary acceptance 110
   ratification 127
   and Saudi sovereignty 48
   seen as comprehensive 108–9
   and "special exemptions" 142
   territorial gains 48–9, 108, 142–3
   and Treaty of Taif 107–10
   universal support for 107–10
Treaty of Taif
   and 1973 joint communiqué 32–3
   and 1995 MOU 33
   acquiescence to 32–3, 39, 48, 63–4, 98–100
   authority to conclude 85
   capacity to conclude 84
   reluctance to terminate 62–4
   and Saudi sovereignty 13, 87, 95
   Saudi territories recognized 12–3
   seen as voidable 21–2, 28, 51–2, 61, 73, 101
   "special privileges" 26, 33, 51–2, 110, 112–3, 119, 147
   see also Taif, Treaty of (1934), Yemeni case against
Yugoslavia 59

Z

Zakat tax 37, 145
Zugar 80